PHILIP PROWSE

This is London

HEINEMANN

BEGINNER LEVEL

Series Editor: John Milne

The Heinemann Guided Readers provide a choice of enjoyable reading material for learners of English. The Series is published at five levels – Starter, Beginner, Elementary, Intermediate and Upper. At **Beginner Level**, the control of content and language has the following main features:

Information Control
The stories are written in a fluent and pleasing style with straightforward plots and a restricted number of main characters. The cultural background is made explicit through both words and illustrations. Information which is vital to the story is clearly presented and repeated where necessary.

Structure Control
Special care is taken with sentence length. Most sentences contain only one clause, though compound sentences are used occasionally with the clauses joined by the conjunctions 'and', 'but', and 'or'. The use of these compound sentences gives the text balance and rhythm. The use of Past Simple and Past Continuous Tenses is permitted since these are the basic tenses used in narration and students must become familiar with these as they continue to extend and develop their reading ability.

Vocabulary Control
At **Beginner Level** there is a controlled vocabulary of approximately 600 basic words, so that students with a basic knowledge of English will be able to read with understanding and enjoyment. Help is also given in the form of vivid illustrations which are closely related to the text.

For further information on the full selection of Readers at all five levels in the series, please refer to the Heinemann Guided Readers catalogue.

CONTENTS

INTRODUCTION

London is the biggest city in Britain. More than seven million people live and work there.

London is also one of the most important cities in the world. It is a centre for business and for tourism.

In London you can find some of the best theatres and museums in the world. You can find old and new buildings, and many beautiful parks.

This book begins with a little of London's history. Then we look at the London of today. You can see and do many things in London. We will have a look at this great city.

Shoppers, buses and taxis in Oxford Street

1 HISTORY of LONDON

The Romans

Roman London was called Londinium

The Romans came to England in AD 43. They built a town on the River Thames. The name of the town was Londinium.

The Romans chose a good place for the town. It was easy to cross the river there. Soon, they built a bridge over the river.

Londinium got bigger and bigger. Ships came to the town from all over Europe. The Romans built roads from Londinium to other parts of Britain.

Above is a picture of Londinium. By the year 400, there were fifty thousand people in the city.

Soon after 400, the Romans left Britain. We do not know very much about Londinium between the years 400 and 1000.

William the Conqueror

In 1066, William the Conqueror came to England. William came from Normandy in France. He became King of England and lived in London.

But William was afraid of the people of London. He built a big building for himself – the White Tower. Now it is part of the Tower of London.

Many tourists visit the Tower of London every year. The Crown Jewels – the Queen's gold and diamonds – are kept there.

All the Kings and Queens of England lived in London. It was the biggest town in England. By 1600, there were more than two hundred thousand people in London.

The Tower of London

Shakespeare's London

Shakespeare was born in Stratford-on-Avon in 1564. Later, he lived in London. Shakespeare wrote thirty-six plays. They are still read and acted all over the world.

The plays were acted in the Globe Theatre. You can see the Globe in the picture below. The theatre was demolished in 1644.

The Globe Theatre in 1616

The Great Fire

The houses in Shakespeare's London were built very close to one another. They were made of wood. Sometimes there were small fires.

On Saturday 2nd September 1666, there was a big fire.

It started in the house of the King's baker, in Pudding Lane, near London Bridge.

The baker's wife woke up in the middle of the night. The house was burning. Soon the next house started burning. Then the next and the next... The fire burned until Thursday.

Most of London was burnt. A quarter of a million people lost their homes.

People escape from the Great Fire

Dickens' London

People built houses again after the Great Fire. But they built them of stone and brick.

The city grew larger and larger. By 1830, there were more than one and a half million people in London.

The railways came. There were factories all over the city. London became richer and richer.

But there were also other changes. The city became dark and dirty. The air was full of smoke. People lived in very bad houses. Some very poor people did not have houses. They slept in buildings like the one on page 10.

Charles Dickens lived from 1812 to 1870. He lived in London for many years. In his books we read about London at that time.

We read about the rich people in their big houses. And we read about the poor people. Many of the London poor had little to eat.

Most children did not go to school. Some of them worked all day in factories. Other children lived in the streets. Every day children died in the streets of London.

But London is better now. The city is much cleaner. And many Londoners work in offices or shops. But a lot of people still work in factories.

London's poor – beds for homeless people (1859)

London's rich – a summer day in Hyde Park

The River Thames

The River Thames is part of London's history. The Romans built Londinium beside the river. It was a small town then. Now, it is a very large city. But the River Thames is still the centre of London.

Until 1749, there was only one bridge across the river: London Bridge. The old London Bridge looked very strange. There were houses and shops on the bridge.

The water did not flow under the bridge quickly. Often, the river froze in winter. The water became ice. The people walked on the river. There were cafés and restaurants on the ice.

In the nineteenth century, many new bridges were built. Now there are more than twenty bridges over the Thames in London.

There were shops and houses on the old London Bridge

2 PLACES to VISIT

You can visit many interesting places in London. This chapter tells you about some of them. You can find these places on the map on pages 14–15. In London you are never far from the River Thames. It is a very beautiful river. Tourists go on boat trips on the river.

One of the best trips is from Tower Bridge to Westminster. Tower Bridge is near the Tower of London.

Most of the famous old buildings are north of the river. On the South Bank, there are some fine, modern buildings. The *Royal Festival Hall*, the *National Theatre*, the *Museum of the Moving Image* and many art galleries and restaurants are on the South Bank.

The River Thames and Tower Bridge

The Houses of Parliament

Big Ben and The Houses of Parliament

The Houses of Parliament are in Westminster. They are the centre of the British government. Members of Parliament (MPs) come from all over Britain. They meet in the Houses of Parliament.

You can see the large clock in the photograph. It is called *Big Ben*. To the right of Big Ben is *Whitehall*. Many government buildings are in this street. *Downing Street* is off Whitehall. The Prime Minister lives in number ten Downing Street.

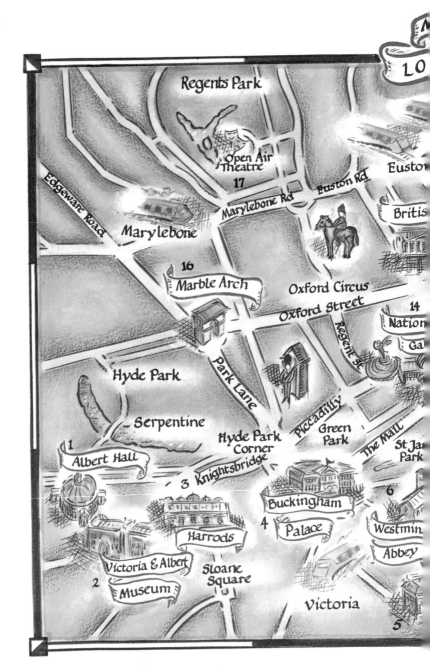

Regents Park

Open Air Theatre

17

Edgeware Road

Marylebone Rd

Euston Rd

Euston

British

Marylebone

16

Marble Arch

Oxford Circus

Oxford Street

14

Nation

Gal

Hyde Park

Park Lane

Regent St

Serpentine

1

Albert Hall

Hyde Park Corner

3 Knightsbridge

Piccadilly

Green Park

The Mall

St Ja
Park

Buckingham

6

4 Palace

Westmin

Abbey

Harrods

Victoria & Albert

2 Museum

Sloane Square

Victoria

5

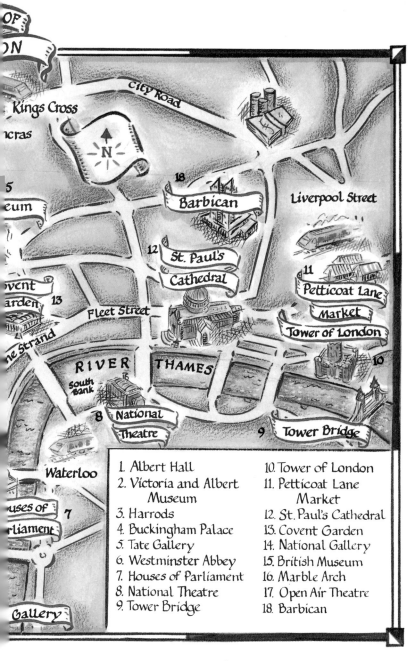

OF
ON

Kings Cross

cras

City Road

N

18

Barbican

Liverpool Street

12 St. Paul's
    Cathedral

eum

5

11

Petticoat Lane

vent
arden 13

Fleet Street

Market

Tower of London

ne Strand

RIVER   THAMES

South
Bank

10

8 National
   Theatre

9 Tower Bridge

Waterloo

uses of 7
rliament

Gallery

1. Albert Hall
2. Victoria and Albert
   Museum
3. Harrods
4. Buckingham Palace
5. Tate Gallery
6. Westminster Abbey
7. Houses of Parliament
8. National Theatre
9. Tower Bridge

10. Tower of London
11. Petticoat Lane
    Market
12. St. Paul's Cathedral
13. Covent Garden
14. National Gallery
15. British Museum
16. Marble Arch
17. Open Air Theatre
18. Barbican

Churches

Westminster Abbey is one of the most famous churches in London. It is very near to the Houses of Parliament.

The Abbey is more than nine hundred years old. William the Conqueror visited the Abbey in 1066. In 1953, Queen Elizabeth II was crowned there. Nearly all English Kings and Queens are crowned in Westminster Abbey.

Another great London church is *St Paul's Cathedral*. The cathedral was built by Sir Christopher Wren after the Great Fire of 1666.

Visitors can climb to the top of the cathedral. From the top, there is a good view of the City of London.

There are many beautiful Wren churches in and around the City.

St Paul's Cathedral at Night

Art Galleries

Trafalgar Square – the National Gallery is on the left

You can find many art galleries in London. The most famous of all is the *National Gallery* in Trafalgar Square. It has many of the best paintings in the world. You can see paintings by Constable, Goya, Van Dyck, Leonardo da Vinci, Michelangelo, Rembrandt, Renoir, Rubens and Titian.

Another of the great London galleries is the Tate. *The Tate Gallery* was built in 1897 – sixty years after the National Gallery. It is on the north bank of the Thames near Lambeth Bridge.

In the Tate, you will find paintings by British artists. The best known are Turner and William Blake. The Tate also has collections of modern paintings by foreign artists – for example, Picasso.

Museums

The British Museum is one of the largest and greatest museums in the world. You can see collections from many different countries. For example, there have been exhibitions about the Vikings from Scandinavia, Tutankhamun from Egypt and the Treasury of San Marco from Venice in Italy.

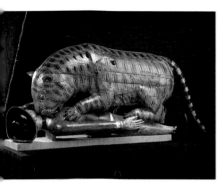

Tipoo's Tiger is in the Victoria and Albert Museum

Another very interesting museum is the *Victoria and Albert Museum* (the V and A). The V and A has many different collections – clothes, furniture, carpets, ceramics, paintings, sculpture, jewellery.

Two other important museums are near the V and A: the *Science Museum* and the *Natural History Museum*.

Inside the Natural History Museum

Palaces

Buckingham Palace is the London home of the Queen. You can walk from Westminster Abbey to the Palace. The walk goes through St James's Park.

Soldiers always guard the Palace. At half past eleven every morning, the soldiers change guard. You can stand outside the front of the Palace. You can watch the changing of the guard.

The *Queen's Gallery* is in Buckingham Palace. Tourists can visit the gallery and see the Queen's collection of paintings. The gallery is open all day Tuesday to Saturday and on Sunday afternoon. It is closed on Monday.

Buckingham Palace is the home of the Queen

Windsor Castle is near London

Another of the Queen's homes is *Windsor Castle*. Windsor is on the River Thames, about forty kilometres from London. The Queen often stays at Windsor at Christmas and at Easter. The castle is eight hundred years old. Inside the castle, there is a lovely old church. It is called St George's Chapel.

Hampton Court is another old palace near London. In the sixteenth century, King Henry VIII of England lived in Hampton Court. Now it is a museum. The Queen does not live there. The gardens around the palace are among the most beautiful in England.

St James's Park

Parks

Every visitor knows some of the parks of London. There are more than eighty of them! The best known parks, near the centre of London, are Hyde Park, Regent's Park and St James's Park.

Hyde Park is a large park of three hundred and forty acres. In the sixteenth century, King Henry VIII hunted wild animals in Hyde Park! Today, people walk in the park or sit on the grass.

The Serpentine is a lake in the middle of Hyde Park. In summer, you can swim in the Serpentine at the Lido or go out in a boat.

Speakers' Corner is also in Hyde Park, near Marble Arch. You can see it in the photograph below. Anyone can make a speech at Speakers' Corner.

Speakers' Corner in Hyde Park

Regent's Park is larger than Hyde Park. The *London Zoo* is in Regent's Park. There are more than six thousand animals and birds in the Zoo. You can visit the Zoo by boat. The boat goes along the Regent's Canal. There is also an open-air theatre in Regent's Park. You can see Shakespeare's plays there in the summer.

St James's Park is the oldest and the smallest of these three parks. It is very near Buckingham Palace. The lake and gardens in St James's Park are very beautiful.

3 TRAVELLING in LONDON

The tube is London's underground railway. A journey by tube is quick and easy. But you do not see very much. The trains run under the streets. You will find a map of the tube at the back of this book.

Some of the tube lines are very old. The Metropolitan line is the oldest in the world. It opened in 1863. A new part of the Piccadilly line opened in 1977. It runs from Heathrow – London's largest airport – to the centre of London. The Jubilee tube line was opened in 1979.

The Docklands Light Railway is the newest railway line in London. The trains have no drivers. The newest part of this line opened in 1991.

Most taxis are black

London's underground railway – the tube

You see much more of London from a bus. From the top of a red London bus, you get a good view of the city.

London Transport has special buses for tourists. A tourist bus takes visitors to some of the famous places in London. The tourist buses leave from Piccadilly Circus, Victoria Station or Marble Arch.

Visit an information centre to find out about special travel tickets to use on the tube and on the buses. You will find details of these information centres at the end of this book.

The buses and the tube are very busy in the morning between eight o'clock and ten o'clock. They are also busy in the evening between five o'clock and half past six. It is better not to travel at these times.

There are lots of taxis in London. Taxi drivers are usually friendly and helpful.

A London bus

4 SHOPPING

Oxford Street is London's main shopping centre. Walk along Oxford Street, from Marble Arch to Oxford Circus. You will pass hundreds of shops.

You can buy clothes, shoes and food in the larger stores: *Selfridges, John Lewis, Debenhams, Marks and Spencer*. Or you can shop in the small boutiques.

People come from all over the world to shop in London. They go to Oxford Street, Bond Street and Covent Garden.

The best-known London store is not in Oxford Street. It is *Harrods* in Knightsbridge. You can buy anything in Harrods – from a pin to an elephant!

Harrods at night

The market in
Portobello Road

A small old-fashioned shop

There are also hundreds of open-air markets in London. They sell all kinds of things: vegetables, clothes, records, furniture. The two best known markets are in Petticoat Lane and in Portobello Road.

Petticoat Lane is on the east side of London, near Liverpool Street station. The market is open on Sundays. You can buy anything there. Some of the things are very cheap. But not many things are both good and cheap!

Portobello Road market is in west London. You can get there by tube. The nearest tube stations are Notting Hill Gate and Ladbroke Grove. The market is very busy on Saturday. You will find old furniture and antiques on many of the stalls in Portobello Road.

5 LONDON at NIGHT

Pubs

There are more than seven thousand pubs in London! Some are now open from 11 o'clock in the morning until 11 o'clock at night.

Every pub sells beer and many other drinks. You can eat in most pubs.

Pubs are friendly places. You can talk to people or play games. Or you can listen to music, like the people in the photograph below.

There are lots of famous pubs in London. Many of the oldest pubs are in the east of the city. One of them is the *Olde Wine Shades* near London Bridge. It is three hundred years old. Then there is *The Grapes* in Marlow Street, beside the River Thames. Charles Dickens often drank in this pub. Another well-known pub, *The Prospect of Whitby*, is not far away.

People listen to music in a pub

26

Theatres and Cinemas

Most theatres and cinemas in London are in the *West End*. The nearest tube stations are Piccadilly Circus and Leicester Square. You can also go to the National Theatre, or the Barbican Centre in The City.

You can see all kinds of plays in London's theatres. You can watch musicals, comedies and plays by modern writers.

Theatres in the West End

The open-air theatre in Regent's Park

There are some unusual theatres in London. In the summer, there is an open-air theatre in Regent's Park. You can watch Shakespearean plays there. New films in Britain are generally shown first in the West End cinemas.

Buy an evening newspaper or an entertainments guide to find out what is on.

Restaurants

Soho is a district in the West End. It is near the theatres and the cinemas. Soho is full of foreign restaurants, cafés, shops and nightclubs. People go to the theatre in the West End. Then they eat in a Soho restaurant.

Look at Gerrard Street in the photograph on page 29. Nearly every building in Gerrard Street is a Chinese restaurant. Chinese food is usually good and quite cheap. French and Italian food is usually more expensive.

You can eat many kinds of food in London's West End. You can go to Caribbean, German, Greek, Turkish, Hungarian, Indian, Japanese, Russian or African restaurants. Many young people enjoy eating at hamburger restaurants.

A café in Soho

Chinese signs in Gerrard Street

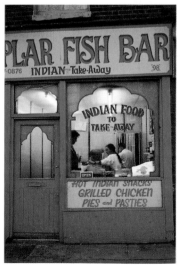

Many kinds of food!

6 INFORMATION and ADVICE

Perhaps you will visit London one day. Here is some advice –

Buy a good map; don't get lost! Ask for help; people are friendly! London is a great city. Have fun!

General Information

Tourist Offices

London Tourist Board
26 Grosvenor Gardens
London SW1W 0DU
071 730 3488

Hotel Accommodation
  Service
(Tourist Information Centre)
Personal Callers only:
outside Victoria Station,
London SW1

British Tourist Authority
Thames Tower
Blacks Road
Hammersmith
London W6 9EL
081 846 9000

Transport Information

London Transport Enquiry
Offices at tube stations:
  Oxford Circus, Piccadilly
  Circus, King's Cross, Liver-
  pool Street and the British
  Rail stations at Euston and
  Victoria.

There are also Enquiry
Offices at Heathrow Airport,
in terminals 1, 2, 3 and 4 and
the tube station.

Useful Phone Numbers

The time 123
Emergency:
  Police, Fire or Ambulance
  999
Leisureline Information about
daily events in and around
London:
  English 0483 8041
  French 071 246 8043
  German 071 246 8045

Magazines/Books

A to Z London Atlas and
  Street Index
Nicholson's Visitor's London
Time Out Magazine

UNDERGROUND

LRT registered user no. 91/1465

31

Heinemann English Language Teaching
A division of Reed Educational and Professional Publishing Limited
Halley Court, Jordan Hill, Oxford OX2 8EJ

OXFORD MADRID FLORENCE ATHENS PRAGUE
SÃO PAULO MEXICO CITY CHICAGO PORTSMOUTH (NH)
TOKYO SINGAPORE KUALA LUMPUR MELBOURNE
AUCKLAND JOHANNESBURG IBADAN GABORONE

ISBN 0 435 27177 6

© Philip Prowse 1977, 1992
First published 1977
Reprinted five times
This edition published 1992

A recorded version of this story is available on cassette.
ISBN 0 435 27285 3

Acknowledgements
The authors and publishers would like to thank the following for permission to
reproduce their photographs and artwork: Bridgeman Art Library/British library p7;
Jane Garner p28; Grand Metropolitan Estates p26; Susan Griggs Agency/Stewart
Galloway p23; Susan Griggs Agency/Adam Woolfitt p6, p29 (br); Robert Harding
Picture Library/A. Evans p29 (bl); Robert Harding Picture Library/Walter Rawlings
p4, p21, p25 (b); The Mansell Collection p8, p10 (t), p11; Museum of London p5,
p10 (b); St John Pope p20 (b); Tony Stone Photo Library/Doug Armand p18 (b);
Tony Stone Photo Library/Janet Gill p22 (br); Tony Stone Photo Library/Hideo
Kuriha p20 (t); Tony Stone Photo Library/Ed Pritchard p12; By courtesy of the
Board of Trustees of the Victoria and Albert Museum p18 (t); Visionbank Library
Ltd, London p19, p27; Visionbank Library Ltd, London/Tony Page p22 (bl); Zefa
p16, p24, p29 (t); Zefa/Damm p13, p25 (t); Zefa/Weir p17.

Typography by Adrian Hodgkins
Cover by Mick Armson and Threefold Design
Map by Phil Devine and Anne Clue
Typeset in 12/16 pt Goudy
by Joshua Associates Ltd, Oxford
Printed and bound in Malta by Interprint Limited

97 98 99 00 10 9 8 7

WALKING IN
THE RAIN

How do you cope when your
worst nightmare comes true?

The second of the Drumbeats Trilogy

Julia Ibbotson

Award-winning acclaimed author of
Drumbeats, the first novel in the Drumbeats trilogy
The Old Rectory: Escape to a Country Kitchen (a memoir with
recipes to feed the soul, from the rectory kitchen)
S.C.A.R.S, a children's medieval fantasy novel
and an easy-reading academic text with current interest about the
place of women in management:
Talking the Walk: should CEOs think more about sex? How gender
impacts management and leadership communication.

Front cover design by www.BerniStevensdesign.com

ISBN: 1508419612
ISBN 13: 9781508419617

PRAISE FOR JULIA'S PREVIOUS WORK

For Drumbeats (the first of the Drumbeats trilogy)
Drumbeats gained Honourable Mention at the Hollywood Book Festival, USA 2014 and New England and London Book Festivals 2014 and was shortlisted for the Readers' Awards at the Festival of Romance Fiction 2014

Media praise for Drumbeats:
"Drumbeats is about confronting challenges and looking beyond what we know" *Janice Ross*
"A truly heart-warming story and one that will stay in my mind" *Hannah Wood*
"Wonderful quality of writing … a brilliantly crafted book … sights, sounds and even smells of the Ghanaian way of life are conjured up vividly … a brilliant read" *Jo Lambert*
"A thought-provoking story" *Kindle review*
"I loved how swoon-worthy Jim was, but also mysterious and possibly dangerous. I'm totally invested in (Jess's) life now!" *Chicklitchickadees*
"One could often feel the searing heat of the country burning right off the pages …a writing style that

for me flowed seamlessly and drew the reader into a fascinating story ...really looking forward to the sequel!" *JB Johnston*

For The Old Rectory: Escape to a Country Kitchen (a memoir)

The Old Rectory won the Biography category in the London Book Festival 2013 and Honourable Mention in three other international Book Festivals 2013

Media praise for The Old Rectory:

"Destined to become a classic ... I adored this book and think you will too ..." *Rebecca Johnson, book reviewer, USA*

"The book is a wonderful blend of personal story (one so many of us can identify with), enchantingly told, with recipes ... It all spreads happiness. Lovely!" *Bel Mooney, UK, author and journalist, Daily Mail*

"What a jewel this book is ... truly a delight ... a great writer ... a delightful read, all the way to the end ... loved it!" *Peggy Fellouris, Massachusetts, USA, author of Dancing in the Rain*

"A most talented writer...a charming story written by a writer with a wonderful voice" *Nancy Mills, California, USA, travel writer and founder of thespiritedwoman.com*

"A beautiful tale ... delightful" *Vicky DeCoster, Nebraska, USA, author of From Diapers to Dorkville*

"An inspirational tale that offers many surprises ..." *Carol Hoenig, USA*

"A delight for those who love to cook and those who love to read about old English villages ... 5 out of 5!" *DizzyC's Little Book Blog review*

"A fascinating and absorbing book ..." *Today I'm Reading review*

"Julia's writing style is so warm and engaging ... I could hardly peel myself away from the pages ... I'm a huge fan of Julia's writing!" *Cosmochicklitan review*

"It is a fascinating and absorbing book ..." *Today I'm Reading*

"It will warm your heart ... Lovely book. To be cherished ... 5 stars!" *Bemiown Book Reviews*

"A very charming book..." *True Book Addict*

For S.C.A.R.S (a children's medieval fantasy story, loved by adults too)

S.C.A.R.S gained Honourable Mention at the London and New England Book Festivals 2014

Media praise for S.C.A.R.S:

"This is a tale of friendship and strength when the world about you is full of evil." *Hannah Ward*

"If you are feeling a little lost and in need of a fantastical escape, this is the book for you, regardless of your age!" *Bestchicklit.com*

"... captures the imagination and awakens a sense of adventure in the reader." *Bestchicklit.com*

"I like Julia's writing style; it is so easy to read and just flows so well you just get caught up in this wonderful fantasy story." *AJ Book Review Club*

"Julia's descriptions just instantly transport you into this world and you can see it all in your mind. You are there with them all." *AJ Book Review Club*

"A magical story that had me turning page after page, dying to know what happens next …" *Cometbabesbooks*

"This book has everything: adventure, magic, heart-stopping moments – a lovely story, beautifully woven." *Jo Lambert*

"I really hope that S.C.A.R.S is going to be the first book in a series as I'd love to see our hero and his friends on more exciting adventures. Highly recommended! Just brilliant!" *JB Johnston Brook Cottage Books*

"This tale is destined to become a classic and to be read and re-read many, many times until it bears its well-thumbed pages like the scars left by the monsters in Unor." *Sterna Kruger*

"A must read … a journey of emotions, laughs and magic that will not easily be forgotten, tickling that spot of belief in magic, tucked into a corner somewhere, that all children harbour, it is true, there is still magic in the world." *Sterna Kruger*

CONTENTS

ACKNOWLEDGEMENTS

For my dear husband, Clive, for all the cups of sustaining coffee, dinners and household tasks while I slave over a hot keyboard – thank you, and all my love x

For my lovely family who provide quiet (sometimes!) support in the background and keep me grounded: Tam, Mel, Neil, Sally, Charlie, Zoe, Grace and Jacob, not forgetting Maria, Rob and David. Thank you for being there x

For my editor, publisher, consultant, beta readers, and all my lovely friends in the Romantic Novelists' Association who are so supportive and generous: you have all made my journey so much easier, more informed, and certainly more entertaining!

For Berni Stevens (www.BerniStevensdesign.com) for her stunning cover (again!), for JB Johnston (www.brookcottage books.blogspot.com) for her unstinting and efficient organisation of book tours and advertising, for Gary Walker (www.look4books.com) for his advertising, ingenious posters and social media expertise.

For the many reviewers, bloggers, facebookers and tweeters who have said so many lovely words about my writing. It means a lot!

1

SILENCE IS GOLDEN

July 20th 1986

That was the date Jess would remember for ever more. It would be embedded in her brain and her soul.

She stood in the newly refurbished kitchen of their large house, leaning on the counter and staring blindly out of the window. Her knuckles white as she gripped the edges of the stylish circular twin stainless steel sinks she had chosen so happily just a few months before, not knowing what was to come.

How odd it was that dates had such resonances across the years: she had told her students that Shakespeare had entered the world and left it on 23rd April, St George's Day, only 52 years apart. That George Orwell had mulled over what to call his futuristic novel

1

and ended up reversing the last two digits of the year he wrote it: 1948 became the famous novel title 1984.

And now, with Jess, 20th July was the date she re-found the love of her life, 20th July 1968 was the day she married him, 20th July 1986 the day she lost him. Reflections and reversals.

The gentle resonances of 10cc's '*The Things we do for Love*' echoed in her ears and she recalled the way the builders had played it over and over as they refitted the kitchen, such a short time ago, and how she had sung along with them as she brought in countless mugs of tea. By the time she heard the refrain "*like walking in the rain* ..." she knew that her tears were coursing silently down her cheeks and soaking her hands like raindrops in a storm.

Her mind travelled back to twenty years before ...

"Surely you are not going back to *Africa*, Jessamy!" said her mother, shaking her head in disbelief, frowning over her spectacles, always disapproving. "But *why*?"

Jess studied her nails. She had polished them with transparent gloss and they looked healthy and shiny. Her usually silent, detached father had grabbed her hand that morning and glared at them intently for some embarrassing minutes, then muttered, "Well, I don't know what your mother will say to *this* – like a painted hussy!"

Good god, it was clear varnish not scarlet or even pink. She didn't even have her make-up on in her parents' home, in deference to her strict conservative Quaker family. Why did they always make her feel somehow dirty? This was exactly why she had fled to Ghana in the first place.

But at nineteen (and a half, nearly twenty!) and having returned from Ghana a few weeks ago after nearly a year of escape from her stifling family home, Jess was not about to be cowed by parental disapproval any more.

"I've some unfinished business, Mother." Jess noted, but no longer reacted to, her mother's familiar disapproving frown and pursed lips. "Now that Simon has ... well, frankly, dumped me, I'll go back to complete what I started."

Her mother stared at Jess's broken foot, still strapped in the support shoe the hospital had given her, and resting propped up on the blue velvet stool. "But you have only just got back home. And you have your university place set for October. You cannot just walk away from everything." Jess surreptitiously smiled at the idea of walking anywhere on her foot, damaged in an accident in Ghana and the reason why she had to return to the UK early.

"Well, Simon did," Jess retorted, recalling the icy scene when he had walked out slamming the door behind him, telling her that he had no intention of continuing where they had left off when she had gone out to Africa for her gap year the summer before. All year in Ghana she had missed him, reading his wonderful loving letters over and over, longing to be back in his arms again. But when she returned home after the accident he had spurned her with no real explanation except that she basically wasn't what he wanted any more.

Then she relented her sharpness and glanced up more softly at her mother again. "But actually, I'm not intending to go until after uni. When I've got my degree I'll be much better placed to do what I want to do. So you needn't worry about that, Mother!"

"Well, thank goodness for that!"

"Mother …" she began, wanting to say that there was no danger in going back to Ghana, to reassure her, but then remembering that it was clearly not the case. She had faced a whole new world out there, in Africa. She had gone with unrealistic idealistic hopes which had been all but shattered. Mentally, she listed them:

Firstly, she had gone expecting to teach as an unqualified class tutor at a poor village school where she could really feel she was doing good, changing the world. Teaching kids to read and write. But she ended up in a privileged church secondary school, teaching the daughters of government officials and professionals, lawyers, doctors, university lecturers.

Secondly, she had gone expecting warmth and sunshine that she could bask in, and found heat so intense that make-up slid off her face, hair became lank and greasy unless she washed it every day and tied it up in a chignon. She found the harmattan oppressive, squalls and tornadoes and tropical storms frightening.

And thirdly, she had gone looking forward to seeing the animals of the African bush, but had found herself covered in flying termites, mosquitoes, giant cockroaches. Bats swooping into her long hair if she wore it loose in the evening.

She had found horrifying ignorance, unbelievable poverty, shocking disease.

Yet she had brought back an experience she would never forget and probably would change her for the rest of her life.

Danger, tragedy, horrors. But also joys, friendship. Love.

No, Jess would never, ever, forget Ghana.

But yet the only person she had told about the reality she had discovered was her best friend, Polly ...

"You did *what?*" Polly's eyes were wide and she had to clutch her coffee mug with both hands to avoid dropping it on Jess's mother's rug. She turned fully towards Jess and her gaze swept her friend's prone body. Jess could feel the probing gaze that quested her figure as she slumped on the sofa, leg and shattered foot supported on cushions and an upholstered stool. The journey home from Accra two days before had exhausted her more than she had anticipated, and she struggled to sit more comfortably. She winced.

"Shshsh!"

"Your parents are out!"

"I know but I don't want anyone coming in and overhearing."

"They don't know?"

"Of course not. They'd go mental."

Polly frowned and shook her head.

"Listen, they didn't want me to go in the first place, did they? So if they knew what it was really like, they'd never let me out of the house again."

"Well, you're nineteen now and about to go to uni, so they couldn't keep you under house arrest."

"No … but I just don't want to worry them, even in retrospect."

"Jess, there you go again. You're too kind for your own good. Always thinking about how other people feel." She leaned over to Jess, her blonde hair swinging forwards. "You could actually manage to be a bit selfish sometimes. I won't say "live a little" because, my god, you sound as though you've already lived a few more lifetimes than the rest of us!"

"I feel that too, I have to confess."

"By the way, your hair looks fabulous, swept up like that." Polly nodded at Jess's chignon.

"Oh, it was the only way I could keep it looking half way decent in temperatures over 90 degrees. Ugh!"

"Maybe I'll grow mine." Polly smoothed her blonde Mary Quant full fringe and straight bob and Jess looked enviously at the way her friend, as always, seemed so casually elegant. So sophisticated. So cool. "But, listen … tell me more about Ghana! *You got shot?*"

"Yes."

"On the *street?*"

Jess sighed. "It was back in February. I didn't tell you at the time. I didn't tell anyone …" She grimaced apologetically.

"No, you hardly even *wrote* to me while you were out there … your supposed best friend!" Polly sipped her coffee, eyebrows raised humorously above the rim of the mug.

"I did! I sent you postcards all the time, well, whenever there was something to tell – well, stuff that I was able to tell, anyway."

"Hmm, I'd hear nothing for months and then they'd come in drifts of three at a time, like Birmingham buses." She stared into her mug. "I really missed our chats."

Jess reached over to Polly, head bent. "Me too. Even though it was only in the holidays when I was back from boarding school. Not like when we were at the local school together."

"I know. We've been friends for so long but actually I even missed you last summer before you went off to god knows where in the middle of the jungle …" Jess snorted. "OK I'm exaggerating. The middle of the bush then. But you were very … er … *involved* with Simon last summer. I hardly saw you!"

"Well, we're going to be hanging out together a lot more now, what with going off to the same uni together. I know you'll be second year but I guess we'll be able to team up."

"And before we get there, Jess, I would really like to hear about what happened – what *really* happened in Ghana …!"

Jess shuffled her bottom on the sofa and grimaced. Memories flooded back into her mind.

"I went up to Accra with Jim …"

"And Jim is …?"

"The peace corps guy. I told you."

"Yes, just checking. Um … the gorgeous piano player? The one who wooed you with Mozart? The swoony American from Washington whose father is a famous surgeon? The hot medic?"

Crisp curly dark hair, chiselled square chin, wide firm mouth.

"All these things are true. But … Anyway ... We went to the Peace Corps HQ in Accra …" Polly frowned. "Accra, Polly. The capital city of Ghana? You ignorant soul who unbelievably is studying geography at uni …"

"Human sciences. That's different. And geology. Dead things. Fossils. And rocks."

Jess huffed. "Anyway, do you want to hear this or not?" Polly nodded, shamefaced, mouthing "sorry!" "We got to the PC House but Jim was called away, some urgent thing, and he told me … he did tell me very clearly … not to venture out. But I was curious. And

I went out into the streets. Everything had been tense for ages. In fact we'd been involved in military stuff in Upper Volta and Mali on our Christmas trek up north to the southern Sahara desert."

Polly nodded slowly. "Yes, I remember."

"I say military stuff – it was civil war in Upper Volta, a coup d'état. Soldiers, young boys, wielding machine guns, AK47s ..."

Her mind drifted back to that day. She remembered it so vividly:

She remembered Chrissie stopping the car at the border checkpoint behind Glenda's Land Rover. Opening the door and getting out, looking around for the border guards to check the four passports she held. Nobody appearing out of the guard hut.

Hearing the loud laughing chatter of the passengers alighting from the bus in front of the Land Rover. Noticing the streets cordoned off. Hearing Glenda shouting in impatience at the hut, storming over to the barrier. To her horror, Glenda yanking at the metal barrier, trying to force it open for them to pass through.

Then the crack of gunfire. Shrieks. Screaming women and children pushing, tumbling over each other in the haste to get clear of the bus. Riot squads in tin helmets pouring out of lorries as they screeched and skidded to a halt in front of the barrier. Armed police. Soldiers shouting, running over to the cars, gesturing them all out of the vehicles, machine guns, pistols, rifles, AK 47s, cocked towards them, fingers twitching on triggers. Very young, terrified fingers. Only boys really. But all the more dangerous.

Scuffling, screams, only a few feet away from her, the glimpse of a man on the ground, boy-soldiers surrounding him, kicking, beating with clubs. Black arms pummelling violently. The man's face, mashed and bloody, white shirt soaked now with red, his arms raised to shield his head.

God, the horror of it all. Then somehow having to struggle through with her schoolgirl French to plead with the commander to let them go, that they were only innocent travellers from England, with no evil intent to the country of Upper Volta in its revolution.

"And the tension had spilled out to Ghana as well. But we rode it out and never thought there would be a problem for us. School term started as usual. A month or so later, Jim suggested I go with him to Accra for a break. He had some business." Jess paused, not sure how to suggest her fears to her friend. "Always a bit mysterious … I don't know … always something there in the background …"

"But you went with him?"

"Yes, of course. We were good friends." Jess glanced at Polly. Polly smirked. "I mean it, that's what we were …" *Were*, thought Jess. *Were.*

"Not a dirty weekend, then?"

"No! What do you think I am?" *No, not then* – well, not ever, not a *dirty weekend*, that was not at all what it was … "I told you, we were close friends. He was so kind. So thoughtful." Jess remembered the mosquito

nets Jim had procured for "her" villages, and, ultimately, the quinine, the anti-malaria tablets. The day she
left to fly home. After … *after* …

"So, OK, then, you went up to Accra with Jim to
the Peace Corps HQ and he was called away, told you
not to go out onto the streets, obviously something was
happening. It was all tense, and what did you do? You
went out. Typical Jess. Walked right into it."

"It was stupid. *I* was stupid. You don't need to tell
me that. I know."

She remembered:

She'd thought: *What was going on? She slipped out
of her room and noticed that there was nobody at the reception desk, so she slipped out on to the street. Independence
Street was oddly empty; there were none of the usual beggars
sprawled on the filthy pavements, none of the usual noise and
bustle, the crowds, the traffic. The office buildings looked de-
serted. Where was everyone? A sudden screech of tyres as a car
swerved and skidded round the corner and sped past her. A
loud crack. A car backfiring? Then screams, shouting, rent
the air. All at once she knew what she was hearing, because
she had heard it before, in Upper Volta: the sound of gunfire.
Again and again. Over and over. Another car, bucking to
a halt, skewed across the road. Someone leapt out and ran
down the street …*

*Shouting, a lot of shouting: instructions, warnings, or-
ders. There were battle fatigues, camouflage outfits, green and
brown helmets, rifles held aloft or clutched menacingly. Jess
cowered back into the hollow of the doorway and scrunched*

herself up as small as she could, gripping her knees to her body, muscles taut.

Bullets must have hit the wall beside her because she felt the impact and saw the concrete dust spurt out.

Near the corner of the street, a bulky uniform lay motionless, felled at an odd angle. Dare she run? Dare she run past him? She was shaking violently. It was her only chance.

She ran, her legs fuzzy beneath her, hardly able to support her weight. She had just reached the body of the felled soldier when she heard a shout and her legs gave way. She stumbled and sprawled on the pavement. Her hands felt blood, sticky on the concrete.

More shots rang out. She saw the dust rise angrily, smelled the acrid cordite, felt her leg jerk and a sharp pain that made her yelp. She heard the scream and realised it was hers. She could feel the coldness of the hard ground and knew that at least that meant she was still alive. But she felt as though she was dying, her life ebbing away on the streets of Accra

Then the young soldier, Kobina, who pulled her to safety and into the Peace Corps HQ, and then disappeared into the hot dusty bullet-ridden streets again.

"And so, that was it. I got shot."

"Cool as that, eh? My god, Jess." Polly gulped the remains of her coffee and Jess thought it must be quite cold by now. "But that wasn't what caused …?" She gestured at Jess's damaged foot.

"Well, it contributed to it. It was already damaged and weakened by the Accra fiasco and then after …*after*…" She drifted. "I fell on the concrete steps and the wound opened up and then there were …" she glanced sideways at Polly, "*maggots…*"

"Good god!"

"They're actually good for cleaning out a wound. So I was told …" She could see Polly's horrified, disgusted expression. "Anyway, that's when I was advised to come home. More sterile environment. And so on."

"I can see why you don't want to tell the parents."

"I haven't told anyone out of Ghana. I couldn't."

Polly looked at her shrewdly. "It's not your fault, Jess. You've got to stop taking everything on your shoulders. Holding it all in. Bearing it on your own."

After Polly had gone home, rather pale and unusually quiet, Jess sat still for a while, remembering. She remembered the things she hadn't told Polly, no, not even Polly, because it was so close to her heart. About Jim. About that night in Accra. About the good things. About desperately trying to cling to Simon through the letters she wrote every week, holding on to the love that Simon had poured over her like a comfort blanket. Polly was lovely, and of course they'd talked about Simon a lot before Jess went to Ghana for her gap year:

"*Hey, good one, babes! Handsome. Rich. Good family. Brought up as a Quaker like you. Lucky gal! Sickening!*"

But Polly didn't really understand how difficult it was when you were thousands of miles apart for a year. That Simon had clearly moved on. Polly had hugged her when she told her that they had split up and murmured "*bastard!*" but Jess knew that it was, for Polly, just like her own short-lived relationships: off with the old, on with the new. Polly rarely grieved over a break-up because she rarely became so engrossed in a guy. Jess had fallen abruptly and hard.

And then there was Jim.

Jim who had touched Jess's heart but from whom she had fled (why was she always fleeing?) – why? Out of loyalty and love, long-time love, for Simon. And now she was alone again, with neither of them. What was she to do?

2

DEDICATED TO THE ONE I LOVE

J ess stared at the metal steamer trunk before her on her bedroom floor. She picked at the labels stuck to its top that declared its arrival at the port of London from Sekondi/Takoradi, Ghana, West Africa.

Involuntarily, she reached for her leg and foot, rubbing the circulation back. In the month since she had returned home, her foot and leg had been healing well but she still got cramps and of course she was still sore. As the damage faded, so did the memories. Now they flooded back into her mind.

The searing heat, the oppressive harmattan blowing in from the north bringing with it the hot dry desert sands on the wind, the sudden torrential monsoon downpours that were such a relief after the sweaty heat. A picture swamped her mind, of herself and Sandra,

her flat mate, sitting on their veranda sipping the ubiquitous lager, gazing out over the African bush at the
mango trees, watching the approach of the tornadoes
whirling violently in from the ocean. So clear and
vivid, that she could see the brilliant sharp colours of
the jewel-bright bougainvillea, the flame-red flamboy-
ant; she could smell the sweet hibiscus, the rich earthy
scents of the bush, the deep aroma of the cooking pots
outside the huts steaming with groundnut stew. She
heard again the drumbeats: the pounding rhythms
of the dondo haunting her dreams as the souls and
spirits of the near-by bush villages of Kakomdo and
Ebubonku called quietly to her as she slept.

    She thought of Chrissie, her colleague at the
Ghanaian school where they both taught, who had become a close friend, and of Betty, her mentor, the assistant headteacher at the school, with her calm quiet
Quaker ways. She glanced at their recent letters, the familiar blue airmail fold-ups on her bedside table, that
she read and re-read, trying to hold on to that amazing, often traumatic, time. She had never written to
Glenda, the aggressive fellow teacher who was always
angry. But she had written to Sandra, with whom she
shared flat 4 on the school compound; she had never
received a reply. Yet she thought of her often. And of
course, of Jim Kennedy. What had happened to him?
If he hadn't so strangely disappeared, would she have
returned to England? Chrissie had no news of him either, no further information had come from the Peace

Corps operation. Clearly, Jess had to close the door on that life, that past.

She turned the key and snapped open the locks on the trunk. The small kpanlogo drum was there, a replica of the one she had lost. The wooden fertility dolls. The paintings she had hung in the flat: canoes and drummers, stylised representations of Ghanaian stories. She rummaged around the bright woven kente cloth, the cotton dresses she had worn for teaching, for forays into the bush villages to take basic first aid to the sick children. The cream linen shift dress that she had worn that last night with Jim … She held it up to her face, inhaling the scent as if to recapture his musky after-shave. But all she could smell was the lingering perfume she had worn; she could smell only herself.

After Simon had left her, she had promised herself that she would return after university and find Jim again, if only to put her mind at rest about what had happened to him. But what if he had indeed become one of the "*disparu*", the political "disappeared ones" after Nkrumah's overthrow? What if the former President's men had captured him … imprisoned him somewhere unknown, untraceable … killed him? The officials at the Peace Corps HQ where he was based had not been able to provide her with any information. Did they indeed know?

Under the linen dress, she found the books and photos that she had kept on her bedside in the flat. She felt something hard and heavy. She pulled out the fat hardback edition of Yeats's poems that Simon's mother had given her to take to Ghana. As she read the flyleaf, Hilary's copperplate inscription, Jess felt the tears blur her vision. How could things have changed so much, so drastically, so abruptly? What had happened with Simon? How could he suddenly not love her any more? How could anyone love someone one minute and then suddenly not love them; she couldn't ever switch on and off like that! And she missed him.

She swiped the tears from her eyes and cheeks, she must be brave and strong; she must turn to her own future. She reached for the papers that the university had sent her in advance of her degree course: the reading list (she really must get focused on that), the information about freshers' week and accommodation in halls of residence, her student grant … It steadied her mind to read about the courses she had chosen to follow, English and Psychology. There was a booklet about taking a teaching qualification concurrently with her degree. That would be good. If she returned to Ghana she would need that as well as her degree.

She heard the telephone downstairs. It would be one of her mother's Quaker friends ringing about some committee or other. She emptied the trunk, piled the clothes, books and artefacts beside her on the floor, and shoved the trunk under her bed, ready to repack for university.

She heard her mother's footsteps stomping heavily up the stairs and then her call, "Jessamy! Phone for you! Do you need me to help you down the stairs?"

Her mother was holding out the telephone receiver towards her as she navigated the staircase taking care not to put weight on her injured leg and foot. She couldn't read her mother's expression.

"Hello, Jess here." She frowned.

There was a pause and Jess heard a slow intake of breath on the other end of the phone. "Jess …"

"*Simon?*" Oh, please, not again, no more cold revelations, I don't want to hear it all again. You've said it, now leave me alone. It breaks my heart – don't you understand?

"Jess, please don't put the phone down on me. Listen to what I have to say …"

"Oh Simon, I don't think there's anything more to be said." She sank onto the upholstered telephone seat in the hall and felt her heart thrumming loud in her ears.

"Jess, I'll understand if you say no, but I need to see you, talk to you." He sounded distraught. She could hear the break in his voice. At once she was alert.

"Oh god, what's the matter, what's happened?"

"I've made such a stupid mess of everything. Just let me explain. Let me come over and pick you up and we can go to the pub and talk. I just need to … you're the only person who understands me …*Please?*"

She settled herself uncomfortably on the padded wooden bench of the Horse and Hound, wriggling her leg and trying to prop her left foot on the cross bar under the table. She glanced over at Simon standing at the bar ordering the drinks. He looked as he always did, fair hair flopping over his brow, keen blue eyes, soft full lips and high cheekbones, tall, suave, attractive. She noticed a couple of girls across the room watching him with greedy eyes.

She knew exactly what Polly would have said and that's why she hadn't told her she was meeting him again. "For god's sake, Jess. You know what's happened – he's broken up with this girl he's been seeing behind your back and now he's wanting you to fit in with him again. Men don't like to be without a girl for long!"

And she knew that she would have responded, "But you don't understand at all, Polly. He's unhappy. I'm worried for him. I still care about him." And Polly would have humphed loudly and stomped off. But she really needed to know what he wanted. She couldn't bear the thought that she could go the rest of her life without knowing. She couldn't turn him away.

Simon placed the glass of dry white wine in front of Jess and his own beer across the table. He sat and stared at her for a while. Jess was not about to speak first; that was up to him. *He'd* wanted to see *her* after all. She waited for him to tell her why. Her heart thudded and her hands felt damp.

"You look great, Jess," he murmured softly, smiling. That familiar sweet smile.

She smoothed her tight blue jeans over her slim thighs and adjusted her fine-knit long loose red sweater, for something to do with her hands. She was aware that Simon was watching her intently. She took a deep breath in and found herself touching her long auburn hair that she'd left loose today and the full fringe that Polly said made her look like Françoise Hardy.

"I like the hair."

"Simon," she sighed. "What do you want?"

He looked across the table at her, an ice-blue gaze so intense and intimate that she felt herself melt. His hand reached out to her, and she found herself taking it.

"Jess, we had … have … so much in common. I realise now that I don't want to lose that."

"Simon, you went off with someone else. You said that I wasn't "*enough*" for you, you wanted *more* than me … what are you saying now?"

Simon squeezed her hand, and stared down at his beer. "I was so wrong! I suppose I thought that the year apart – god, you'd been to Africa, had experiences I would never share, I thought you must have moved on, changed so much that you wouldn't want me any more."

"Oh Simon, that simply wasn't true!"

He stroked her hand with his thumb. "I had to get in first before *you* could dump *me*."

"That's just stupid. Don't you know me better than that?"

"Clearly not. Or at least it was my insecurities that overcame anything else."

"Are you really *that* insecure?" Why hadn't he told her the truth? She would have understood.

"I would really like us to try again."

Try? It sounded like some kind of effort involved. He caught her frown.

"I mean that I'm sorry. I don't know what made me do what I did. Jess, forgive me." He smiled sheepishly and her heart cartwheeled. "I love you. I know you're the best thing that's ever happened to me." He glanced down towards her injured leg. "And I want to look after you." After all she had been through, Jess was undone. She returned his smile with only a moment's hesitation, but she couldn't help but notice the flicker of his eyes as he registered the pause. He frowned into his beer.

Then he winced and rubbed his forehead.

"Are you OK, Simon? Is it one of your migraines again?"

Jess slept badly that night. It reminded her of the still suffocating nights in Ghana when her dreams were suffused with the echoes of drumbeats from the bush villages.

Simon had dropped her off at home the night before and chatted with her mother as though none of the last four weeks had happened. Jess watched him as he talked and laughed with her mother, so easily, so charmingly. He seemed so … so *nice*. As he drove off in his mother's grey mini that he used as if it was his own, and she hobbled back in to the living room, her mother had looked up from her writing, fountain pen poised over the committee minutes, peering expectantly over her spectacles.

"So are you back together again?" Jess sank onto the sofa and raised her leg onto the pouffé with relief, grimacing at the soreness.

"Wait, wait, wait! We're just going out, seeing what happens. Don't start planning a wedding or anything!"

"Jessamy, you are so on and off. It is quite unstable." She bent her head to her work.

But as she tossed and turned that night Simon's words echoed across her mind and melded with images of him slamming the door when she returned from Ghana, her tears, and yet also the sadness and hope in his eyes in the Horse and Hound as he looked over his beer across the table at her, so winningly. It was so easy to fall back again into their relationship, their shared interests in books, films and the theatre, and current events and mutual friends. It wasn't just that he was good-looking; he was attentive, he spoke to her as though she was the only person in the world. He was charming, a good conversationalist, enthusiastic and lively. A breath of fresh air amidst the strictures of her stifling home.

"Let's go up to Scotland!"

Jess, bemused, collected and shuffled her university papers that were spread across the table at the Horse and Hound, and stacked them in a neat pile. She smiled across at Simon. "I'm trying to prepare myself for uni. You may be in your stride going in to your third year but it's all new to me!"

"Oh, come on," he grinned, lowering his newspaper and stretching across to clutch her hand. His eyes were bright and clear, as always when he was suffused with boyish enthusiasm for an impulsive idea. "Just a few days. Next week! Spur of the moment, and all that! We could drive up and stay in B and Bs. I want to explore Edinburgh again and Inverness. Walk in the Cairngorms!" Jess saw that the newspaper in front of him carried a double page spread on the Scottish highlands. "You've never been there, have you?" Jess shook her head. "It's brilliant. You'll love it." He stroked her hand. "I really want to show you the places I love."

"Well, OK. I guess I can get sorted for uni before that. And what I don't do, I'll just have to wing it."

The "few days" turned out to be a week, and Simon announced that he had organised an itinerary and booked bed and breakfast stop-overs in appropriate places en route.

"Oh, right," said Jess, scouring Simon's list. She had an uneasy moment of déjà vue as she remembered

Glenda in Ghana scheduling the Timbuktu trip and the irritation she had felt in not being included in the planning.

"And I'm paying. I've got plenty." How could she be so mean-spirited as to refuse, or to gripe about not sharing in the details?

"I assume that he has booked separate rooms, Jessamy," frowned her mother as she peeled potatoes for dinner. "I am not sure that this is appropriate for a good Quaker girl."

"Oh yes," said Jess, although she hadn't thought to ask. Would it really matter so much? Well, soon she'd be at university and who would know what she did or didn't do? She'd travelled sub-Saharan West Africa and her mother certainly didn't know what had happened there. "But you have to let me make my own decisions, Mother."

"Well." Her mother's hands paused and she turned from the sink to face Jess, lips pursed. "I sincerely hope that you are not about to behave like a common slut, Jessamy. I didn't mould a daughter in my image in order for her to either become with child unwed or indeed develop any of those disgusting diseases."

"Mother, I'm not exactly in your image! I'm my own person. And no, I'm not going to get preggers or VD."

Her mother looked shocked. "Don't bring shame on this family, Jessamy. We have worked very hard to give you an education and a decent home. Please do not repay us with ungodly behaviour." She wiped her hands down the shabby faded apron and Jess thought of all that her mother had sacrificed to give them a good home.

She put her arm round her mother. "Oh, come on. You know I'd never do anything like that." Her mother smiled but shrugged Jess away.

"Let me get on. I have a lot to do."

Her father shuffled in from the garden obediently removing his boots at the door. He placed a trug of beans and apples on the kitchen table.

"All right, Jessie?"

"Do not call her Jessie," snapped her mother sharply. "Her name is Jessamy."

Her mother turned back to her potato peeler. Her father pulled a face behind his wife's back.

"Jessamy is talking about this trip to Scotland with Simon. I have told her they must have separate rooms. She's only nineteen. You agree with me, don't you?" For one moment Jess hoped that for once in his life he would say "no".

"Yes, of course, Mother." Her father glanced up at Jess and winked, waggling his eyebrows. Jess shuddered. Flitting shadows of memories flickered across her mind like old black and white films: her father, the bathroom, naked, standing up from the bath tub, hand sliding down lower and rhythmically rubbing, grinning. Leering oddly. Or creeping up silently behind her, catching her by surprise, hugging but hands in the wrong places …

She turned abruptly away from him. The only person she had confided in about her father was Jim, that last night in Accra. It was a dark secret of her heart, like a maggot in an apple. She had tried to speak to her mother but she had not wanted to listen (why should she want to hear such a ghastly thing, after all?) and she knew that she could never tell Simon because the families knew each other; how could any of them live with that? Anyway, nobody would believe her. She drew in her breath deeply. No, far better to keep silent, bear it on her own, deal with it herself, as she had always done. It was not as if anything actually horrendous had happened. And now she was no longer a bewildered child; she had her future to think about.

The landlady in Edinburgh frowned icily as she opened the two bedroom doors, opposite each other on the first floor landing.

"This one is yours, young lady," she glared and stood in front of Simon as though to block him from following Jess into the bedroom. He had booked two separate rooms after all. "And there's no … hanky panky … in this house. It's a respectable establishment."

"Goodness," gasped Simon with raised eyebrows, "Of course not!" He thrust his hands into his jeans pockets and smiled charmingly into the landlady's stern face. "Although of course we *are* engaged." Jess raised her eyebrows and tilted her head over the landlady's shoulder.

"Oh I'm sorry, my dear, I didn't know. Well, er, congratulations. But even so …" She turned briskly and gestured Simon towards the room opposite.

As her footsteps retreated down the narrow steep staircase back to the kitchen, Jess leaned against the doorway to her bedroom, arms crossed over her chest.

"What on earth …?" she hissed, shaking her head.

Simon leaned casually against his own doorjamb, one foot crossed over the other, and grinned at her across the dark panelled landing. "I couldn't resist it! There was no need for that. I had asked for two rooms anyway."

"Well, next time you decide we're getting married, please have the courtesy to ask me first!" Jess turned away from him into her room and slammed her door. She sank onto the bed with its rose pink eiderdown and rolled her eyes. How dare he, wrong-footing her, showing her up like that! How embarrassing.

There was nobody else in the little dining room for supper at six. Jess felt rather exposed, as the landlady hovered over them with what she called "high tea": ham salad, a heavily flowered china three tiered stand of sandwiches and cakes, and a huge brown pot of strong tea. She pottered at the heavy oak sideboard while they ate and so their conversation was quiet and strained.

"Let's go for a walk," murmured Simon as he gulped the last of the tea. "Not too far, 'cause of your foot."

"It's getting better every day," Jess assured him. "Just a little pain now and then but at least I can walk on it, a reasonable distance. Not ten mile hikes, though!" She could swim again and manage a few machines in the gym, just not the ones that required a great deal of weight-bearing on her left leg. But it was gradually improving.

As they wandered down Queen Street, along Hanover Street and into Prince's Street in the rainy darkness, street lights pooling their golden glow around them on the shiny black pavements, he took her hand. "I'm so sorry, Jess. I didn't mean any harm. She just got my goat. I wouldn't possibly have booked a double room for us, you know that, don't you? I respect you too much for that. She didn't have to be so smutty."

Jess felt mean and guilty. "It's OK. Don't worry about it. Sorry for snapping at you."

He smiled down at her, blue eyes tender and crinkling at the edges. "I hope that it's not totally out of the question, though?"

Jess's reply was lost in the sudden magnificent view of Castle Rock rising grimly above the town streets, the harsh stone walls of the castle towering above the sheer drop of the black basalt cliffs. It was floodlit and both beautiful and eerily ghostly.

They wandered along the road, snuggling under the shared umbrella. Simon draped his arm around her shoulders. She shivered. "Cold?"

"No, not really. But I've been a little chilly ever since I got back from Africa."

"Understandable, I guess. Change of climate and all that. Let's try this bar, it looks cosy enough. We can get warm and dry."

Simon found a seat near the huge open fire and they drank hot toddy and watched the flames. Simon stretched his arms along the back of the bench and spread his legs. It reminded Jess of Jim, although Simon was fair and handsome in a more boyish-looking way, where Jim had been dark, tall, experienced … and dangerous. And for all she knew, now captive, or even dead. So far away. A different life. Her face must have shown a glimmer of confusion because Simon leaned in to her and touched the end of her nose tenderly.

"Your face is still damp," he grinned. "Here, let me …" He reached for a clean paper napkin from the table and gently patted her cheeks and forehead. She felt warm, cared for, loved, and her heart suffused with love in return. "You know what I like most about being with you?"

"No, what?"

"I can be myself. I don't have to amuse someone. We don't even have to talk. We're comfortable. We can even sit in silence without it being embarrassing. But if I want, I can talk to you about anything. Things I'd never tell anyone else. That's really important to me."

Jess felt herself blushing. "Well, I'm glad."

"I mean it. You're so easy to talk to. About anything."

Jess was aware that he shifted in his seat and was drumming his glass with his fingernail. "Is there a problem?"

"Just the parents." Simon stared down into his glass and frowned. "There's a lot of pressure. My father has high expectations. Because he went to Cambridge, he expects me to do as well as him. He was very disappointed I didn't get in to Oxbridge, but he's more or less got over that now, and he's turned his attention to my degree. Well, when I say attention, I mean that when he's not absorbed with his job, or away somewhere, he grills me about how much work I'm doing."

"And your mother?"

"Oh, they are totally united. Jess, when I was a kid, they used to go away together on business trips and I was left with my grandmother and aunt. And we were always moving house just when I'd got settled at a new school, then another, and another. I felt … excluded from their relationship. They were together. I was outside."

"Oh dear, poor thing. And you've had such a hard time keeping moving for his job promotions, moving schools … It can't have been easy."

"No, it's been very disruptive, made me unsettled, insecure. I know people think I'm confident and out-going, but underneath … well, it's not like that. You get practised at it. Always having to make new friends. But underneath …"

"But at boarding school, things were better?"

"Hated it! Pretentious. Some real bullies. Nasty types. Always felt I had to fit into being someone I wasn't."

"I thought you enjoyed it there. You always seemed to fit in?"

"No, I hated York." He took a gulp of his beer and for a moment looked quite angry. She was surprised at his venom; she remembered how he'd high-fived his friends at the Strawberry Dance after he'd been un-kind to her, a time she desperately wanted to forget. Simon was so different now; *they* were so different now. "Still, it's more settled now at uni. I've got my group of friends. I feel more … included." He smiled at her. "And, of course, … now there's you …"

"Yes," she took his hand, "there's me."

The rain stopped the next day and they were able to walk in the fresh air. Although damp and misty, the hills were verdant green and the trees hazy blue.

"If this is anything to go by, Scotland is beautiful!" declared Jess as she strode along in her sturdy hiking boots, which well supported her foot and ankle, Simon holding her hand, the smell of the fresh rain-washed leaves arcing above them. "The castle looks magnificent from here."

"Yep. St Margaret's Chapel dates from the twelfth century, you know. Imagine, eleven hundred and something. The time of the Knights Templar, the Crusades, Thomas Becket …"

"Oh gosh, yes, Murder in the Cathedral and all that! King Henry."

"Well, yes, there were the first two Henrys then Richard Lionheart …"

"Medieval stone castles and clanking armour, great strong horses galloping around and people in long dirty robes. The first Miracle Play and Middle English developing from Old English. Did they have the travelling players then? Goodness, just imagine this landscape at that time."

"Probably scrubby fields and wooden houses in the town that burned down when …"

Jess laughed. "But noble knights, and ladies in heavy velvet gowns and fur trims."

"Anyway, as I was saying," Simon frowned, "the castle here was built by David 1st, crowned King of the Scots. He founded the royal burg of the city, so that's when it all took off as an important centre." Was she being lectured at? "Then the Great Hall was added in the sixteenth century by James 1V and then it became a British army barracks and prison as well as a royal residence. I think prisoners of war were housed here in the eighteenth and nineteenth centuries when it all became very bloody."

"Goodness. Those walls have certainly seen some harrowing events since the twelfth century."

Jess was reminded of Elmina Castle in Ghana where Jim had told her of its history, of the slaves, the ghastly trade that haunted it. But then it had not seemed like a lecture but a commentary of her weird feelings there. How oddly affected she had been ... her strange visions ...

"And in sub-Saharan Africa, kente cloth started to be woven by the first Akan Ashanti weavers for the Chiefs," added Jess contemplatively.

"*What?*"

"Oh, nothing!" Jess bit her lip.

Simon moved his hand from hers and to her shoulders; he hugged her to his side. Jess looked up at the wide sky and the clouds and felt warm and comfortable again. Suddenly she thought how wonderful it was to be young and free and adventurous, with so much ahead of her, so much to learn.

Afterwards, the rain enveloped the land again and Jess couldn't remember much about where they'd been to on the rest of their tour; after Edinburgh, journeying to the north, one small grey Highland town merged with the next in her mind. The rows of identical houses all seemed to be built of the same dull featureless concrete and the hills were windy and cold. It rained incessantly. Wet mists obliterated the views and enveloped the roads as they drove.

It was on the drive back home. Simon played his car cassette loudly and sang along, raw jazz, tapping the steering wheel with the palm of his hand. Jess watched the mesmerising windscreen wipers as they flicked away the rain.

He stopped the car in a layby on the A6. He turned down the music and stared straight ahead out of the windscreen at the rain. Jess turned to him and smiled at his profile. He was ridiculously handsome, fair hair short but curled round the nape of his neck, a stray lock flopping over his forehead. Eyes deep blue and crinkled at the edges when he smiled. Strong nose and chin. Full lips …

"Jess, I do love you. I really do. I think … I think you're the love of my life."

Polly paused momentarily mid-action, then fought the pink sweater into folded submission and thrust it into Jess's university trunk. Only then did she swivel towards Jess, narrow-eyed and tight-lipped. "And what did you say?" she demanded.

"Oh Poll, don't let's fall out about this." Jess reached out to touch her friend's arm. "Don't be cross. I'm not running away to marry him."

Polly stood there, hands on hips, red-faced. "Hang on. You don't tell me you're going out with him again. You don't tell me you're going away with him. Then suddenly you tell me he's asked you to marry him! What do you think I'm going to feel? I thought we were supposed to be best friends!"

Jess sank onto her bed and pulled Polly down beside her. "Poll, I told him I wasn't about to get married – not to *anyone*! I'm going to university. I'm getting my degree. I'm doing all the things I planned. Nothing's changed."

"Humph," snorted Polly and brushed a tear away from her cheek. She sighed. "Maybe I'm just jealous. Nobody's ever proposed to me. But, you see, with Simon …" she patted Jess's knee, "I'm afraid that I'm not sure … I don't know, there's just something …"

"I know you're a super friend and you only have my interests at heart, but, really, honestly, Poll, he's just maybe a bit insecure in himself."

"Insecure? He's the most confident, assured bloke I know!"

"No, he's not really, Poll. Not when you get to know him."

Polly chewed at her lip for a moment, pondering. "I think … I wonder if he just wants to get you into bed and – no, don't protest! – he can't Do It without marrying you, because of his puritan background, and …What are you laughing about?"

Jess shook her head and stood up to resume her packing. "That is just the daftest thing I ever heard. Simon is the sort to do just what he wants to do."

"Hmmm, exactly. So, you just went away with him on a totally chaste holiday to Scotland. What's wrong with him? Doesn't he want to sleep with you?"

3

DREAM A LITTLE DREAM OF ME

"**S**o he's coming up *again* this weekend?" asked Polly as she sprawled on her bed in the shared campus room. It wasn't usual for a second year to share with a first year but they had pleaded with the chap in the accommodations office that Polly was Jess's student-mentor and that, although they didn't share classes, they were both in Drama Club and choir together. In the end he had capitulated.

Polly even looked elegant and "cool" as she sprawled, her knees raised to prop up her geology text book and her biro between her fingers like the French gauloise cigarettes she often smoked. Her sleek fair hair fell forward silkily as she reached over to turn the volume down on the dancette record player; the LP of Mozart's clarinet concerto in A was soothing as they studied.

"Yes, and don't say 'again' like that; he only comes up every two or three weeks." Jess barely looked up from her book ledged on the desk as she frantically scribbled her notes on BF Skinner for the psychology seminar that afternoon.

"And just how did I say 'again'?" Polly smiled down into the open ring-binder folder that lay on the bed beside her.

"With a huff and a puff," grinned Jess. She stopped and stretched her arms towards the artexed ceiling. Through the window she could see the rich autumn colours of the copper beech trees, burnished red maples, verdant green conifers, and blue spruce, the purple and yellowing shrubs in the parkland outside the college residence block. How she wished she was out in the fresh air, walking in the soft golden sunshine rather than indoors studying. But at the weekend, in just two days' time, she would be, strolling hand in hand with Simon, kicking up the russet leaves, hearing about his looming finals. They would wander past the great crenelated turreted hall that formed the focal point of the campus, after the modern square block of the union building, and they would walk slowly round the lake, admiring the graceful royal swans that glided elegantly over the water and through the overhanging willow boughs. And they would both be reflecting on how very *English* it all was. Which Jess found comforting and calm, and, yes, *stable*, after Ghana.

She turned away from the window and her dreams, and back to her lever arch file.

"God, this psych is hard this week," she groaned. "All these experiments on behaviourism. Pavlov's dogs, auto-reactive responses. Phew. English is so much easier. Or maybe I should have done law with English for my double honours, or biology, or something, anything. Maybe I would then have had time to write stories and poems, like I used to in Ghana … But talking about biology, how is your marine biologist Arthur?"

"Art. Art, like Art Garfunkle," corrected Polly with a pseudo-severe pout. "As in Simon and Garfunkle. As in *I am a Rock*." Jess swivelled in her desk chair to face Polly and they broke into a harmonious version of the song, the chorus rising to a crescendo until there was a furious knocking on the wall from next door. They collapsed in giggles.

"And I thought our harmonies were improving!" laughed Jess, bent double. She took a deep breath to compose herself and turned back to Skinner. "So are you ensconced with your marine biologist student Art Garfunkle, in his bed in the Nissens, all this weekend *again*?"

"Touché."

Jess smiled, but she puzzled as to why Simon didn't want to go that extra step with her. Puzzled, and perhaps a little flattered, actually, as he kept saying that he 'respected her as a woman' and wouldn't ever 'violate her', she was 'his best friend'. She liked the way that made her feel the glow of being special; he wasn't seeing her as just a convenient lay but as a person, a best friend. It made him seem sensitive and caring.

But she also remembered the way, in the heat of passionate snogging, he stopped her hand as she touched him. "No!" he had shuddered and then he had smiled at her and stroked her head, "We don't want to risk anything ... And you know I can't resist you." She had shrugged but felt embarrassed.

There was a sharp knock on the door of the college room and Jess and Polly both called out "Come in!" together. Bernadette poked her head round the door and said in her soft Dublin brogue, "Phone call, Jess ... it's your mother!"

Jess glanced at Polly and grimaced. "OK, thanks!" She swung out of the room and ran down the stairs to the communal hallway. Picking up the black plastic receiver which dangled on its curled flex from the set on the wall, she took a deep breath. "Hi, mum!"

She heard the sharp intake of breath the other end of the line. Quickly she corrected herself. "Hello, Mother. Is everything alright?"

"Jessamy. I hear from Hilary that Simon is coming up to stay with you again this weekend ..." She left the implication hanging.

"Yes."

"He's coming up a great deal to spend weekends with you."

"Yes."

"Why does he come the whole weekend? Why not just a day, then he can go back to university for the night."

"Mother, it's a long way from Wales to Staffordshire, even in the car. It'd hardly be worth it for just a day." Jess waited for the next comment and she knew what it would be.

"Jessamy. You know that I love Simon. Our families are friends. He is one of your brother David's best friends. He has come to many get-togethers at our house over the years. But …" Jess held her breath for the inevitable. "Where does he sleep? I need to know. I only have your best interests at heart. I am your mother, after all, and I know what's best for you." Jess's right eye developed a nervous twitch and she pressed her finger against its throbbing.

"Mother, I have a good friend Chris who goes home most weekends to Manchester to see his girlfriend, so he lets Simon have his room."

"And is that in your student block?"

"No, Mother. I have told you before, the halls of residence are segregated. Ours is all women. Chris's block is all men. It's the other side of the campus and it's in the old army Nissen huts … I have told you all this before."

"And are they single beds?"

"Yes."

"Right, Jessamy. Well, I just have to get it straight for Hilary. It is *her son*, after all. She was quite concerned."

I doubt it, thought Jess. "So, is everything going well with your studies? What are your grades like? How are you managing on your own? I hope you are not taking any alcohol and I hope that you are attending Quaker Meeting every Sunday."

Finally, Jess was able to extract herself from her mother's Rulebook memos and return to her room. Polly took one look at Jess's face and leaned back against her wooden headboard, looking up at Jess with a sympathetic half-smile. "Hey, babes, there's a live band at the Union bar tonight. Let's go – just the two of us, a few lagers, a bit of a bop … a girlie night out?"

In the event, their evening turned out somewhat differently than they had expected. The live band was playing the Stones's "*I can't get no Satisfaction*" and Jess and Polly were dancing wildly, even in their vertiginous high heels, stomping unselfconsciously after a couple of lagers. The Union bar was heaving, hot, loud with laughter, and gloriously dark, shadowy and decadent.

"This is mad!" shouted Polly. "I'm dripping!"

"Gonna have to get some black coffee!" yelled Jess to Polly, as the room whirled about her and sweaty bodies drunkenly collided. "My head's splitting!"

"I'll take your mind off that," leered a ginger-haired bloke with beery breath she'd never seen before. "Come to my room and I'll make you forget your headache, gorgeous!" He mimed a crude hip thrust towards her.

"I bet! In your dreams!" laughed Jess, pushing her way off the crowded dance floor behind Polly.

"Are you OK?" came a melting-chocolate voice from in front of the bar. Jess, who had had Polly in her sights through the crowd, swung round and saw a tall, broad, dark-haired vision of masculinity leaning on the bar, tankard of beer in his hand. "I don't think he'll bother you; a bit of a chancer but harmless!"

"It's fine," Jess said, noticing the warm confident grin, laughing dark eyes and loose well-made body, close fitting blue denim jeans and blue striped rugby shirt, with the university logo on the chest.

He held out his hand. "I'm Matt. Actually I'm in Drama Club with you and Polly but I guess you didn't notice me!"

"Oh, I … er … sorry," Jess stuttered, thankful for the noise of the music covering a little of her embarrassment. She quickly wiped her hands down her monochrome mini dress and shook his outstretched hand; a firm handshake, cool palm. "There are so many new faces …" How could she possibly have missed him? He was strikingly good-looking.

Matt smiled slowly, lazily. "I'm teasing. I've only called in on the first session briefly and stayed at the back, while you were doing your warm-ups. I was in it last year but I've had a lot of court experience this term so the timing's not fitted in. I'm doing law."

"I see. So how did you know it was me?"

"I made enquiries," he smiled enigmatically. "Can I get you a drink – Jess, isn't it?"

"Thanks, but I think Polly's just getting us both a back coffee over there," Jess nodded towards her friend at the coffee bar. "But do come over and join us."

Polly turned with two coffee mugs in her hands. "Oh hi, Matt!" she fluttered.

Somehow Matt, beer in hand, managed to find a free table and they all sat down. Polly kicked off her shoes. "Phew, that's better! I need a foot massage. Where's Art when you need him? Or maybe you could take the job, Matt?"

Matt raised his hand self-deprecatingly. "So where *is* Art?" The corners of Matt's eyes crinkled with amusement.

"Oh, some silly marine biology field course, or whatever they call them." Polly stretched her legs. "He's always off somewhere."

Jess caught Matt's glance and smiled conspiratorially. How much longer would Art last, she wondered. Clearly Matt, too, knew Polly well enough to know that her affairs were short and sweet. Matt held her gaze.

"So, Jess," Matt swivelled round in his chair and gave her all his attention. His deep eyes were bright, interested and probing. "Tell me about yourself. I need to know everything."

Jess was just telling him about Simon when suddenly the music ground to a halt, the heavy bass rumbling away into nothing. Jess, startled, turned back to the band. Hywel, the student union president, bounced on to the stage, grabbed the mic off the startled singer, and raised his hands. "Folks, sorry to interrupt, but just heard some terrible news from south Wales where I come from. Some of you might want to carry on bopping but I guess there are some who'll feel bad in the morning if they do. Up to you."

Polly, Jess and Matt looked at each other briefly and, as one, scraped their chairs back. Jess gulped the last of her coffee and Matt, tankard in one hand, guided her with the other, gently easing her through the crowd, Polly leading the way.

They hurried with most of the others across to the television room at the back of Horwood and piled in to the dim wood-panelled room where the black and white images flickered in the corner. Matt cleared a space for Polly and Jess to sit down and stood behind them. The pictures showed a huge coal slag heap rising above the mining village of Aberfan. It had collapsed and the landslide had engulfed a primary school earlier that day. Film footage showed that, even as darkness fell, rescuers and emergency services were still trying desperately to claw at the coal to reach the children trapped underneath. Jess watched with horror the devastation. Sobbing parents who had left their small children at school that morning, believing them safe, were now huddled together in disbelief. 144 missing, believed dead, including 116 children. Some families had lost all their children.

"How could you cope with that?" whispered Jess to Polly, tears coursing down her cheeks.

"Terrible. Oh god …" Polly's voice broke. The room was eerily quiet. Students who had only moments before been jiving and drinking furiously in noisy abandon, fell into shocked silence.

After a while they trooped out but didn't head back to the Students' Union. How could they, now?

"Can I walk you two ladies back to your hall?" asked Matt quietly.

"Yes, thank you," whispered Jess. Polly, unusually, was unable to speak. At the front door of the hall, they all hugged each other in silence, a shared moment of horror. Then Matt said a low, "See you at Drama Club. Goodnight. Take care". His hand brushed her shoulder and then he was gone into the darkness.

Jess was lying quietly in Simon's arms in Chris's room in the Nissen hut. They had settled into companiable silence. She was reading the play "Who's Afraid of Virginia Woolf" for her English contemporary drama class, the book propped against Simon's chest. She was only half concentrating on the text; the other half of her mind was thinking about her birthday in March, only three weeks ahead.

"I'm considering having a party for my twentieth," she pondered. "I thought I might ask some folks I haven't seen for a bit, Si. I don't like losing touch with old friends."

Simon lowered his politics text book. He had decided, after meetings with his tutors, to repeat the year and take his finals the following summer instead of this one. Jess was glad he seemed more relaxed now. "Like who?"

"Oh, a couple of friends from school. And Andy." Jess felt Simon's chest tense.

"Andy?"

"Yes, we used to be great friends. When … when I wasn't seeing you. When …" she dug him in the ribs, "When you were "off" with me!"

Andy had been one of Simon's close friends but after the Strawberry Dance fiasco, he had comforted Jess and often been there for her. She looked forward to spending time with Andy; they shared a quirky sense of humour and he was sweetly affectionate towards her. Her mind drifted back to those days.

They often spent hours sitting side by side on her mother's sofa laughing about – well, goodness knows what, she couldn't even remember now. He always seemed to sense if she was "down" and he cheered her up so much.

"Hey, come on, Jess, let's see that gorgeous smile!" he would say and hug her. She felt as though she had known him for centuries. His smile, in his eyes as well as his mouth, was heart-melting. When he looked at her, in that way, she felt good, and good about herself. He made her feel attractive, appealing, interesting.

During her last year at school, Jess gradually became aware that Simon seemed, at a number of their parties, to place himself between Andy and herself, to join them in their joking, kindly teasing sessions. At first it had annoyed her that he butted in, but then she realised that she felt flattered that Simon, as well as Andy, seemed to want her attention after all, to spend time with her, to talk alone with her.

Gradually she saw that Andy had started to slip quietly away when Simon approached her, making some excuse to leave them together.

"He fancied you," said Simon flatly. His tone made Jess turn to look up at him. He was frowning, irritated.

"It was a long time ago, Si."

Simon said nothing for a while and Jess continued her reading as Simon stared up at the ceiling. "I've been thinking. Jess, I want us to get officially engaged."

Jess sat up abruptly and looked down at Simon. "Why?"

"I want to feel you're really mine, all mine. I want us to get married after I've finished my finals next year." He reached up and stroked her hair. "And then we can really be together. Properly. I want to know that we'll be together forever."

"But I'll only be half way through my degree. I'll still have two more years. I don't know. Anything could happen."

"I won't ever change my mind." He smiled tenderly. "I'll wear you down if I have to, Jessamy Phillips. You know I will." He pulled her down onto his chest.

"I love you, Jess." He kissed the top of her head. "I want to live with you. Be with you all the time, not just the odd weekend. I'm not going to stop you finishing your degree or starting your career. I'll support you. We'll support each other."

The birthday party didn't happen. Instead it was an engagement party. Simon looked gorgeous in his dark suit as he circulated the guests with a natural ease. Jess watched him, hot with pride and love. The hotel ballroom was discreetly decorated with gold ribbons twisted round the white pillars and each table festooned with gold and white flowers.

"Simon's parents," explained Jess to Polly as they stood at the side of the room, balancing wine flutes and smoked salmon canapés in their hands, their eyes sweeping the room. "They were determined to give us a party."

"O - kaaay ..." nodded Polly. "I still think you should be playing the field. You're too young to be tied down. There are plenty of men to be had. I mean Matt seems keen enough. And I'm sure there are others ..."

Jess hesitated. "Poll, a strange thing happened yesterday."

"Oh yes?"

"Andy's mother had come to see Mother about something."

Polly raised her eyebrows. "Ah, the lovely Andy."

"The thing is, when she left I showed her to the door and she turned to me and said congratulations on your engagement, hope you'll be happy, and all that. Blah blah. But then she leaned in to me and whispered, we'd hoped it would be us being your in-laws."

"Good god!"

"I know. I mean, I've hardly seen him since the summer when I got back from Ghana. And before that, well, not much since I've been with Simon."

"Hmmm, interesting. Maybe he still holds a candle for you. Well, he's much … easier … than Simon. More fun. Like Matt. And, actually like most other guys! You can always get out of the engagement. While there's time!"

Jess laughed. "Oh for god's sake, Poll!"

"What?"

"You know full well I made a decision and I'd never go back on it. It's a promise."

"Is he here? Andy?"

"No. Simon was a bit vague. I thought he was going to be Simon's best man. But I'm not sure that he actually asked him – or invited him here."

Polly drew in a deep breath but she didn't speak.

"Next July! Are you joking?"

"No, Poll, and please keep your voice down." They were stretched out on the comfortable armchairs in the television room, watching Wimbledon on the new TV the university Students' Union had bought, the first they'd seen in colour. A roar went up in the room as John Newcombe aced his serve again.

"You're actually getting married next July, bang in the middle of your degree course?" whispered Polly marginally less loudly.

"Yes, we've decided to do it as soon as Simon finishes his finals."

"You haven't even got an engagement ring yet."

"Well, no, because as I told you Simon wanted to buy his new car and it's very expensive getting it on the road and anyway the car's for both of us."

"The ring's for both of you, isn't it?"

"Not really, and I don't mind. It's just a conventional affectation anyway. I get the benefit of the car. It's our first purchase together."

"Ah, a 'conventional affectation' is it? Sounds like something Simon would say."

"Well, I mean it's not anything *useful,* is it? Whereas a car is. We can't *splash* money around. And I've never been used to much anyway."

"Oh, *Jess* …!"

"No, I mean it. It really doesn't matter."

"But he's not short of a bob or two – at least his family isn't, and they give him whatever he wants."

"I wouldn't want his family buying me an engagement ring, for goodness sake. And we've got to be economical. Simon's decided to do a postgrad teaching diploma and teach for a while, and hope to get into politics later. We've got to rent a flat, so that won't be cheap. I don't want to be living off his parents."

"So, wait a minute. Where are you going to live?" She bit her lip then steepled her fingers, tapping her mouth. "I hear there are some apartments on campus for married students as well as staff. Hmmm, that'd be OK."

"Oooh, yes, I wouldn't have far to go to lectures and I'd still be in the thick of things here. I wouldn't miss out on the Union Saturday night hops or drama club or choir or the coffee evenings with our friends. Good thinking."

"No, I don't think so," said Simon. "We want to make a new start. And I don't think we can afford the rent for those apartments on campus anyway. They're quite expensive. I'll see how much a flat in town might be." Seeing Jess's downcast face, he added, "We've got to be sensible. And I can easily drop you off at the campus when I go to work in the mornings. No problem."

"But the petrol, or maybe bus fare if I have to get to lectures in that way, will be an added expense. If we're on campus, I can walk."

"Jess, I'll be in my PG year then my first teaching job. I won't be earning much, not enough to afford expensive swanky campus apartments."

"Then maybe we ought to wait."

Simon glanced at her. "I don't want to do that."

JULIA IBBOTSON

It was in May, a couple of months before the wedding when Simon came bounding up the stairs to Jess's college room waving a type-written sheet of paper. Jess had worked half the night to finish her Anglo-Saxon translation of *Beowulf* for her Monday assignment so that she could have a free weekend with him, and was waiting for him on the landing to divert him from her room where Polly was enjoying a relaxed afternoon with Mike, her latest. Art had long since fallen off the list.

She wanted to tell him all about the work she and her two friends, fellow second year students, were undertaking in the new world-class language laboratory that had been installed for the medieval studies she was specialising in that year. She was so excited about learning the Anglo-Saxon runes and replicating the wonderful sounds the letters made, reading the old precious manuscripts.

"I've found us a flat!" Simon yelled as he leapt up the steps two at a time. He whisked Jess off her feet and ran her down the stairs and out into the hot summer's day. "Cheap rent that we can afford. In town. Central. Ideal!"

His enthusiasm and energy, as always, made Jess laugh and melt. "OK. Where?"

"Between the Michelin tyre factory and the football ground!"

"Right. Hmmm. Sounds very attractive ... not."

"It's above and behind a hairdresser's. And there's a garage too, round the back! And it's such a good rent, we'll actually be able to eat as well!"

"Wow!" she laughed. "Well, that's always a bonus!"

"There's a living room and bedroom upstairs, and a kitchen and loo downstairs at the back. And there's a back yard to hang out the washing." Simon hugged her to him as they wandered across to the Union in the warm heart-embracing sunshine, under the arching English oaks, and round the huge clipped holly bushes. The air smelled of tranquil new-mown lawns. "It'll be our little paradise! We can shut the door and it'll be us against the world outside!"

Jess saw the student protest sit-in before Simon noticed. It was more a sit-out than in, as the students were sprawled on the grassy rise in front of the Union building. Some of the men were waving placards. They were wearing shorts but no tops, baring their chests to the sun. A couple of girls were sitting on the grass, completely naked, leaning back on their hands, little hard-nippled breasts raised to the sky, legs spread apart, their pubes, and more, clearly on show.

"What on earth ...?" gasped Jess, shocked. "Oh, god, that's disgusting!"

"Oh!" breathed Simon, staring.

"What the hell is this show about?"

"Freedom!" shrieked one of the girls, raising her left fist to the sky, breast wobbling.

"We're protesting against the university restrictions on our freedom," explained one of the men, holding a pile of leaflets. "In solidarity with our Parisian brothers at the Sorbonne." One of the men thrust a flier into Jess's hand. Then misreading her expression, he added, "And sisters, of course."

"You're ogling me!" shouted one of the naked girls, not closing her spread thighs.

"Perhaps you should put some clothes on then," called Simon, gracing her with a charming smile. The girl smirked back and wriggled her bottom on the grass. Jess, red-faced and breathing hard, grabbed his hand and pulled him away into the Union coffee bar. He kept looking back.

"God, you could see everything," breathed Jess as she slumped into a plastic chair and grabbed the menu to hide her blushing face. "And I do mean, *everything*! How horribly embarrassing!"

There was a buzz in the coffee bar as people looked through the plate glass windows at the protest. One or two of the male onlookers gawped. Jess moved her chair so that the back was to the window. Simon glanced at her and did the same.

"Well, that's a bit much," said Jess. "Not sure that all that was necessary. Can't think how that helps their cause. Horrible sight."

"Oh, don't be such a prude, Jess. And that one was pretty hot, though," murmured Simon, smiling. Jess flushed. He tilted his head to the side. "But not as great as you, of course." That was not really the problem, but she let it go.

He brought a couple of coffees over to their table, medium white for Jess, strong black for himself. The Mamas and the Papas were warbling softly "*Dream a little Dream of Me*" in the background through the speakers.

"There's so much unrest at the moment, protests and riots," mused Jess. "Race riots. CND. Civil Rights marches. Martin Luther King assassinated. Dear god. When will it all end?"

"It's the only way people can be heard." Simon emptied three spoonfuls of sugar into his thick syrupy coffee and then stirred it thoughtfully. "We're living through a time of political change, Jess. In ten years' time the world will be a very different place. In twenty, probably unrecognisable."

"Well, you're the one doing politics."

"The problem is that I think there'll be a backlash before it all settles down. The right wing are scared. Look at Enoch Powell's Rivers of Blood speech. It only gets the fascists going. Not helpful."

"Surely there aren't so many people supporting that. He was surely not speaking for the majority?"

"He was speaking for the powerful right wing. There are sadly a lot of them. But we've got to get the left activated."

"I hope you're not becoming an activist, Simon." Jess gulped her coffee. It was still very hot and she felt her tongue burn.

"I guess I'm more of the socialist intellectual thinker than the marching activist," he smiled ruefully.

"Well, thank god for that! I don't really want to be married to someone in prison. Or on a hunger strike."

Simon shrugged.

As Simon drove through the back streets to show her the flat, Jess's heart sank. The dingy red-brick terrace houses crammed together on both sides of the street four feet behind low walls and scruffy patches of scrub. A whole crowded area of dusty red brick. Pavements littered with old cans and crumpled cigarette packets. Neglected, abandoned, unloved. Simon pulled up outside a house with a battered sign over the front window that read simply "Hair Style".

Not much imagination there, then, thought Jess, biting at the inside of her mouth. An elderly woman with a blue rinse and leaning heavily on her walking stick slowly ambled out of the front door and the few paces to the wrought iron door. She glared as she passed them. A plump woman in her thirties, Jess guessed, stood in the doorway and beckoned them in.

"Simon, isn' it, duck? I'm Sue, the owner and landlady," She patted her beehive hairdo which seemed to be fixed, immobile, on top of her head, like a helmet, and ushered them through the narrow crowded hallway. As they squeezed in, Jess smelled the pervading scent of cheap hairspray and acrid perm solution. "Yer can use the phone in the salon when we're closed," she gestured at a frosted glass door through which Jess could hear hair driers shrieking and the strains of Radio Luxemburg playing *Hi-Ho Silver Lining*, a young girl's voice singing along, out of tune. "That's Sharon, my assistant … er …stylist."

She led them into the small kitchen at the back, with its basic cooker and sink, a grubby window that stared despondently out at a solid forbidding brick wall, a fridge under the formica counter, and a fold-out table with two plastic chairs. Beyond that was a cramped hallway, a bathroom that just managed to squeeze in a bath, toilet and washbasin. Outside the back door was a little overgrown crumbling paved yard with a bottle green peeling door of an outhouse.

"There's a washin' machine in there," said Sue. "Yer can use it when the salon's closed, duck."

Up the steep narrow staircase that led between pink wallpapered walls to the main part of the flat, Jess was a little more heartened. She looked around the living room with its panelled walls, furnished with brown dralon sofa and armchairs, thick cream rug and empty bookshelves filling the alcoves either side of the cast iron Victorian fireplace. Jess guessed that the small oak table with its carved pedestal and the matching ladder-back chairs were also Victorian antiques. Jess peered round the door to the one bedroom and took in its pink flowered flock wallpaper and Victorian fireplace, a replica of the one in the living room. She turned to Simon and shrugged. Stepping inside, she saw that there was a double bed rather oddly squashed into an alcove, a tall sash window and a huge wardrobe beside the fireplace.

"So are yer interested, duck?" Sue called from behind. Jess glanced at Simon and grimaced.

"It's all we can afford, Jess," he whispered. She hated the area, she hated the idea of living above a grotty hairdresser's with that awful smell of cheapness and poverty. She thought of the campus married students' apartments with their airy well-equipped kitchens and clean bright bathrooms, and light fresh emulsion, spacious rooms and independent front doors.

But Simon was smiling at her and stroking her hair. "And I love it!" he murmured. "A bit of history. Period Victorian features. Much more interesting than those bland flats on campus! And we'll be on our own, away from everyone else." He kissed the top of her head. "What do you say?"

How could she refuse? If he was happy, then she was too.

The wedding was arranged for July 20th, giving Jess a little time after the end of term to organise the little she needed to do. Her mother had decided on a simple Quaker ceremony and a small buffet reception in the Meeting House's back room, pots of tea, no wine allowed, although Jess did manage to veer her away from ham sandwiches and on to mini beef wellingtons. Jess would rather have had a simple registry office and local pub "do", or, preferably a small church wedding, but neither her family nor Simon's would countenance such a thing. By working her vacations and finding second hand text books, Jess had saved up some of her university grant money to help pay for the wedding buffet and to buy the dress, long, white, slim and unadorned, Edwardian style. She wouldn't be wearing a veil, just white ribbons threaded through her hair that she would wind up on top of her head.

"Hmm," said her mother. "I am not sure about a wedding dress. It looks a bit Church of England. Why do you not get a nice plain white skirt suit, or a trouser suit, then you can wear it again."

"I'd like it to be something special," said Jess. "Not something I can wear again."

"But that is not very economical." Her mother frowned. "Oh, and I have invited the Friends from Bull Street Meeting. And Muriel, my old friend from school, and my other friend, Mavis. And Harold …"

"Harold?"

"Yes, Jessamy, our very nice milkman."

"The milkman? You've invited the milkman to my wedding?"

"Of course. He is a poor old thing. His wife died last year. He looks as if he needs a good meal."

"Mother, I wasn't aware that it was a charity do. I thought it was my wedding. And you told me we could only have fifty guests between us because of the cost of the buffet."

"So what is the point you are making, Jessamy?"

"I'm saying that we had to limit *our* guests, friends we would have really liked to come! Friends we've had for a long time, who are meaningful in our lives. We'd have liked them to share the day and be with us. Not any old bod we don't know!"

"Jessamy! That is not a very Christian thought."

"Friends, I take this, my friend, Jessamy, to be my wife, promising, with God's help, to be unto her a loving and faithful husband, for as long as we both on earth shall live."

Simon's voice rang out loud and clear in the simple unadorned Meeting House room, with its wooden chairs arranged in a square and the single row where they stood facing the congregation, flanked by four Elders of the church. He smiled at her as he gently slid the plain gold ring onto the third finger of her left hand. As Jess lifted her eyes she saw Andy, who Simon had finally asked to be his 'best man', looking uncomfortably at her with a sad, yearning smile. She smiled back, a little uneasy.

"All mine now," Simon whispered, as Jess felt the room drift and shimmer, and somewhere in the back of her mind she heard the low insistent ghostly echo of kpanlogo drumbeats and the whispering of spirits and lost souls reverberating in her head.

4

A WHITER SHADE OF PALE

"Can't do it," grunted Simon. He shifted his weight off her, flaccid, pushing her hands away from their pressure on his lower back, disentangling their hot sweaty bodies, pushing her enfolding legs away from him. He flopped down heavily beside her in the bed in the alcove, making Jess bounce roughly on the mattress. She moved over and stared up at the ceiling, biting her lip, deflated and trying to take deep breaths to calm her racing heart and still her passions at such an abrupt halting.

Only a moment before, she had been losing herself in him, pressing him to her, threading her fingers in his hair, grasping his back, his hips. What on earth was wrong with him? They'd waited so long to be alone together, to spend the night together, to be married in all ways. Even though there was no honeymoon. She took a deep breath.

"It's OK. It doesn't matter," she lied. "It often happens. I read it somewhere. The excitement of the wedding and everything." She reached over and stroked his arm. He shrugged it away. Yet she wondered whether it was connected to the obvious disfigurement that had made her startle a little while before. He'd never let her see him naked before the wedding night. His right testicle was misshapen, withered. She wondered whether that was why he had not wanted to sleep with her before they were safely married. But it didn't disgust her; she felt for him, how difficult it must have been, in the showers with other boys at boarding school, always anticipating a future reaction from a lover.

"Yes, it *does* matter," he said sharply. "Of course it matters." He brushed away the sweat from his forehead. Jess could feel the heat that was now emanating from his body. And she knew that it was not the heat of passion, but of anger. He was shaking. "It's you."

"*What?* What do you mean?" A feeling of dread washed over her.

"It must be your fault."

"No … no, Simon. It's nobody's *fault*. It just happens to men sometimes." Why was *she* saying that to *him?* He twisted around to stare at her.

"You're obviously not attractive enough for me. It's never happened before to me. It doesn't happen to me with other girls." What other girls? What did he mean?

He pushed himself up and whipped the bedcovers aside so that he could free himself of their bed. Jess pulled the covers back over herself, shivering. He stomped out of the bedroom and she heard him bound down the stairs to the kitchen.

She lay there, listening to the rain beating on the casement window, one moment the backdrop to their love and the next to confusion and dread threatening to spill out from her staring eyes. She heard the opening and closing of the fridge door, the clank of the bottle and glass on the counter top. Now her whole body was tense, where only a few moments before she had been relaxed, soft and accommodating, heat and sweat suffusing her blissfully. It only took a moment for everything to change.

What to make of that? What did it mean? He had been a little tense during the wedding reception yesterday. She had noticed that he shifted his weight from one foot to the other, that he seemed agitated as he spoke to guests, where normally he was so easy and charming. He must be anxious about something. Performing in bed? How she would react? He shouldn't have been nervous. Surely he knew that they could talk about it together, maybe even laugh secretly and intimately about it. It didn't matter that much. It happened …

She needed to be understanding and calm. She needed to be the one who stroked it all away. She needed to give him some of her strength and confidence. He couldn't help it. He was insecure. She needed to assure him that it really didn't matter. It would be fine. They would work it out. Together.

She heard him climbing back up the steep stairs, breathing heavily. She reached for her crumpled discarded nightdress and pulled it back over her head, smoothing it down over her clammy body, so that he wouldn't feel that she needed anything else from him, so that he wouldn't feel under any pressure from her expectations.

He sank down on the end of the bed. "I'm sorry," he murmured, raking his hands through his hair.

"Don't worry. It's OK. Come back to bed."

He looked up at her, anguished. "I don't …"

"No, it's all right. Let's just cuddle up and go to sleep. It's been a hard day."

He crawled back in to bed alongside her, but he made no move to take her in his arms, and after a few minutes he rolled over and pulled the bedclothes over his head. In time, she heard his breathing slowing and deepening into slumber. But she stared up at the ceiling and sleep eluded her. Her mind transported her back to Ghana and to Jim, that night in Accra … *He* had said she was beautiful and sexy and he wanted her …

His lips searched for hers and as he found them he groaned between deepening kisses. "Oh, Jess, my beautiful, good, sweet Jess," he murmured. "I want to show you how I feel."

She knew what would happen but she couldn't resist. She saw and felt and held his strong hard body, and her heart, her legs, her soul melted under his touch. And all she knew was that it was beautiful and wonderful. Somehow he led her into his room, and gently laid her on the bed. He was gentle and slow and tentative, giving her time and space to draw back, but she found that she didn't want to.

So, what was it with Simon? What was wrong with him? It didn't make any sense. Was he sick? She had no experience of anything like this, of odd behaviour, so she had no idea what to think, where to even start with her thoughts. She scoured her brain for her psychology text books. She had a sudden image of Glenda in Ghana and her feeling, after reading and talking to Jim, that her difficult behaviour was a manifestation of something called manic depression. Was that what Simon had? Was it a sickness he couldn't help? That plunged him into despair? But yet he was so vivacious and charming most of the time … so enthusiastic, it was infectious, and she loved having that in her life.

When she finally dropped off to sleep, as dawn lightened the sky through the curtains, she slept heavily and woke feeling drugged, a headache pounding. It took a moment for her to recall the events of the night before, and for her heart to sink once again. Simon was not in the bed beside her. She took a deep breath and pushed herself upright.

And then she heard it.

Racking sobs were coming from the living room. Cautiously she swung out of bed and tiptoed into the other room. Simon was sprawled on the sofa, his body heaving.

"Oh my god," she breathed, sinking down beside him and sweeping him into her arms. She hugged him tightly. "What on earth is it?"

He steadied his breathing and crept his arms around her, stroking her back. "God, Jess. I don't know what happened. I don't know why I said those things. I'm so sorry." He shuddered. "Sometimes I feel … odd … Things go through my head. I don't want to lose you."

"Maybe you should see the doctor." Jess wound her fingertips through his ruffled hair. "Don't worry. We'll sort it out. Together." She kept on murmuring, "it's OK. It'll all be OK." But over his head, she frowned. She had no idea how to deal with it.

They stayed clinging on to each other for a long time. As she held him, she could feel that his body relaxed and he became calm. It felt like comforting a distressed child. "Don't tell anyone, will you? I don't want to worry the parents," he whispered into her hair.

Presently, he drew away from her and smiled, "Hey, why don't we go for a drive, and have a walk in the gardens at Trentham?" She heard the usual enthusiasm growing in his voice and breathed a sigh of relief.

That night was so very different that it sunk the memory of the first night together into obscurity in the deep recesses of her mind. Her legs were wrapped around him, drawing him into her, his name moaned on her lips, her fingers raking urgently through his hair.

"Oh my god! You're … it's … fantastic!" he breathed into her ear, as they moved together and the world spun. "Don't ever leave me, will you?"

She laughed softly and ruffled his hair. "Of course not. You need me. Why on earth should I leave?"

He kissed her again. Then raised himself up from her, and lay on his side close beside her, left hand tracing the curves of her body. "Hey, have you heard about Andy?"

"Andy? No. Why?"

"Your mother rang earlier …"

"Oh? You didn't tell me."

"Sorry. Anyway, apparently he telephoned her and seemed upset, she said. But she hadn't really been able to speak to him, so she put him off. Now she feels guilty because he sounded somewhat distraught and said he needed to talk to her, but he hasn't got back to her again. She wanted to know if I'd heard anything from him."

"Why would he …?"

Simon shrugged. "I think she said she'd tried his parents but they hadn't seen him since the wedding."

Even some time later, Simon still hadn't heard from Andy and neither had Jess's mother. He seemed to have disappeared. Simon didn't mention him again.

She heard him laugh, low and intimate, as she came in from the back yard. He was sitting at the

JULIA IBBOTSON

kitchen table, legs akimbo, facing away from her to-wards Sharon, the hairdresser's teenage Saturday girl. She was leaning provocatively against the peeling pink painted door jamb, one knee raised, bright bubble-gum pink mini skirt barely covering her crotch, low cut tight sweater revealing the deep cleavage of her puppy-fat breasts; hair fixed up in a messy beehive, face thickly painted with make-up. She was fifteen for goodness sake. Jess stared at her and even as she caught her eye, the girl smiled knowingly at Simon, and Jess felt, rather than saw, him smile back. The intimacy of the moment between them took away Jess's breath, and she just stood there, in the doorway, washing basket and pegs in her arms.

The girl's eyes flicked back up to Jess and Simon suddenly seemed to sense her presence and turned to follow Sharon's gaze. "Ah, there you are, Jess," he smiled, his eyes cold blue. "Washing done?" He flicked the newspaper that lay open in front of him on the table.

Jess stared coolly at the girl until she decided to stir herself from the doorjamb and with a shrug ambled back into the salon. Jess imagined her middle-aged, matronly and used-looking. "What was that about?" she demanded of Simon, dropping the basket heavily onto the flagstone floor, and turning away from him to the colander of potatoes and carrots on the draining board. She started to peel and cut the vegetables with a savagery she didn't know she possessed. She stared at

70

the two shillings and sixpence worth of minced beef, cut-price tinned steak and kidney pie, lamb's hearts and liver, that was the only meat within her week's budget, and threw the offal and the can into the fridge. God, she was trying so bloody hard to make a decent home life for them both, eeking out the pennies to make ends meet. And this is what she got? "What do you think you were doing?"

"What are you suggesting, Jess?" Simon's voice sounded hurt. "For god's sake! I was just being friendly and neighbourly. Isn't that what you want?" She heard him rise from the table, scrape his chair back and then felt his arms reach gently around her, his hands cupping her breasts. He kissed the nape of her neck.

She sighed. Perhaps she was over-reacting. Perhaps she was still aware, in the recesses of her mind, of that first night, weeks ago. But somehow, it wasn't the behaviour she expected when they were married, and for such a short time. Or ever, really. Did husbands do that; flirt with other girls so openly like that? And girls of fifteen, at that? What if she hadn't come in at that moment? What might have happened?

Or was she seeing too much into something perfectly innocent and simply friendly?

The phone rang out shrilly downstairs in the salon, echoing in its Sunday emptiness. Jess hated going in there. It still smelled of cheap hair lacquer and strong scent. It always reminded her of women trying to cover up body odour. But she was expecting a call from Polly about the end of term exam arrangements, and Simon was out in the car, so she dropped her text book and study file onto the sofa beside her and ran down the stairs to catch it before it stopped.

She was a little breathless as she picked up the sticky avocado green receiver. "Hello? Poll?"

"Er …" came a male voice. Youngish man, heavy local accent, not an educated voice. Jess wondered how she could tell so much from one short word? "Er … 'ow much?"

"Pardon?"

"'ow much fer a sex-u-al intercoo-orse?" Flashes in Jess's brain: my god, this is a punter, the salon's a prostitute's den, or whatever they're called, he thinks I'm one of the whores! She leaned against the salon wall and gently slid down to the floor, gasping. My god, I've been mistaken for a prostitute – or a pimp! What do I do? What do I say?

"Um, I'm sorry," she stuttered, "but I think you've got the wrong number." She slammed the receiver down on the handset, almost throwing it away from her. God, she was so polite! What on earth was she supposed to say? Then she thought, oh my god, the hairdresser, their landlady, Sue, and her assistant Sharon, were tarts – I mean, really tarts, as in 'prostitutes'! Oh my god, we're living above a whorehouse!

And she started to laugh at the absurdity. She giggled until tears ran down her cheeks and she felt hysterical. Oh, just wait till she told Polly!

When Simon returned home later that day, Jess said, "Si, I'm sorry, but I can't go on living here." She had gone through the laughing stage and begun to feel decidedly queasy. What if some hulking unhappy punter turned up on their doorstep or some violent drunk? Her vivid imagination revved up into over drive.

She told him what had happened and he turned his shocked pale face to her. She felt his brain ticking over the situation. Ticking over Sharon. "Good god! Phew!" He sat down abruptly beside her on the sofa. "Well, we'll have to think what to do. I'll have a chat to the parents; see what they think."

Jess refrained from commenting that the campus apartment would have been a wiser bet in the first place, for various reasons. "I really don't feel right here, Si."

The house was a smart brand new semi-detached on a small recent development in the village down the road from the university. There was a bus stop round the corner and a bus could take her right to campus; ten minutes.

But she was struggling.

"Oh, Poll," she said, slowly sipping her coffee when they met up in the student union coffee bar after their respective seminars. "It's a lovely little house, but he's got his parents to buy it for us."

Polly looked up from her hot chocolate and frowned. "And the problem is …?"

"The problem, Poll, is that it's four and a half thousand pounds. It's an unbelievable amount of money. There's no way we could afford it ourselves, not with just my student grant and his first year teaching job. Well, we could have, just about, but with very little left each month for everything else. And he said he couldn't scrimp and save to pay a mortgage. So they told him they'd buy it for us."

"And …?"

"I just don't like it. I feel obligated to them now. It's not right."

"Hey, look, don't knock it, babes!" Polly opened her hands in a wide gesture and shrugged. "Maybe they feel guilty about giving him such a difficult childhood with them always moving around and him having to keep starting new schools in new areas. About you living in such a dump in Stoke for months. About not giving it to you for a wedding present."

"Well, my parents couldn't give us anything like that. And I wouldn't expect it. They don't even own their own house, just rent."

"Well, there you go then," said Polly, shaking her sleek blonde bob. Jess noticed how it swung as if moulded, so beautifully. "Be grateful that someone can help. Take what's offered!"

"It's not as easy as that."

"Why? Do they begrudge it?"

"Oh no, they would do anything for Simon. He just asks and they give. They say four thousand's nothing to them. They want to help out."

"Well, you're a very lucky girl. Just enjoy it."

"I guess."

"They think you're wonderful, and good for their son, so I think they're grateful to you for settling him down. They're just happy about it. And if they can afford it – well, why not?"

"I don't know. It's just like – things will come home to roost one day … I don't like being beholden. I feel bad about it. We could have rented an apartment on campus."

Polly pfuffed. "So when do I get to see this house, then?"

Jess knew that for some reason Simon was wary of Polly and had made his feelings clear that he wasn't keen on her presence. "Well, we move in during the Easter hols, so when you're back from vacation and term starts again, we'll pop down on the bus after classes and have a cup of tea and a piece of homemade Victoria cake."

Polly smiled. "That sounds amazingly domesticated, babes."

"Oh, you'd be surprised how domesticated I've got," smiled Jess, thinking of all the cooking and cleaning she did whenever she was at home and Simon was at work. He hated her doing chores while he was in. He said it made him feel guilty at not helping. Jess knew the retort to that and how illogical it was, but she didn't want to spark off another tantrum. "Simon wants central heating put in and a brick garage built beside it, and I worked out that would cost a further four hundred, but his parents have said they'll add those … I sound ungrateful, don't I?"

Polly reached across the formica table and squeezed Jess's hand. "No," she said quietly. "I know how it is. You're a sweetie. I miss you here on campus."

"It's lovely," breathed Polly, sweeping her eyes over the through living room. "Oh so much nicer than Water Street. Clean, new, fresh. And… er …green. Very green!"

Jess laughed. "Yes, I know that now. I got to choose the paint and flooring and stuff before we moved in as it was brand new. But I didn't realise that I'd chosen everything in various shades of green! I guess it was an unconscious reaction to the grimness of redbrick Water Street, just brick walls and concrete and pavements, no trees or grass or plants. And that flat over the ghastly hairdresser's whorehouse! I could never believe it if I saw a blade of grass or a leaf. A rare sight."

"I'm teasing, it's beautiful. I bet you're thrilled." Polly spun round, arms out wide. "I just love the cushions and curtains. And everything!"

"I made them myself. Mother bought me a second hand sewing machine for Christmas."

"God, Jess! How do you find the time? In the middle of studying too. You're a marvel!"

"I suppose I don't do much partying or going to the pub. I don't even write any more. I study, keep house and do the home-making stuff. We kind of like to chill out at home. Simon doesn't much like going out. His work's hard. He likes to relax at home evenings and weekends."

"And does he help? I mean with household stuff?"

"He gets tired at work."

"I thought the agreement was that he would share the chores at least while you were studying for your degree?"

"He did." Jess turned away and concentrated on straightening the books on the shelf. "But his work's getting harder now. So I'd rather just get on with it when I get home from uni on a Friday afternoon before he gets home from work." She turned back to Polly. "It's easier that way."

"I think, if I may say so, you tiptoe on eggshells around that Simon of yours."

Jess had not told Polly about the scenes she had diffused, Simon's early impotence, his sudden rages and equally sudden shame and contrite hugs, gentle kisses and passionate nights. It had all become easier to handle, now that she knew what to expect and could anticipate crisis points. Yet she felt her shoulders sag.

"Look," said Polly, slipping her arm around Jess and hugging her. "Stay behind at uni tomorrow night after classes. We'll get something to eat at the Union and have an evening with all our friends in my room, drinking coffee and putting the world to rights, just like we used to do. I'm sure Matt, you know, the law student from Drama Club, the one who fancies you, won't mind running you home afterwards; he goes that direction anyway. And maybe I'll get my latest, Jack, to bring a bottle or three of cheapo wine. Yes? It's been ages since we've done that. We miss you."

Jess smiled into Polly's shoulder. "Yes, that'd be great." She pulled away and looked her friend straight in the eye. "You know, I maybe haven't been as sociable as before, when I was living on campus, but there's been a lot on my mind. I don't think I can pull all-nighters like we used to, and I really want to focus on my studies. I'm determined to get a good degree. It's about proving I can do it."

"I know, and you do work hard, you've got that protestant work ethic. But I don't know who you have to prove it to – we all know you're very bright, probably the cleverest of all our crowd, apart from Matt! You two are the ones that'll get the Firsts!

"Oh, I don't know about that! But it's about proving it to myself, to my family. My brother's always been the clever one. I know that's what they think. I'm a bit of an 'also ran', running fast behind him to try to catch up. It's like the red queen running so fast to stay on the same square!"

"But that's nonsense," snorted Polly. "David is serious and studious but he's no cleverer than you, in reality."

"Well, I guess it's what I feel inside. The younger sister, always the second, having to prove herself. I'd like them to be proud of me."

"That sounds like your psychology class."

"Yes, actually the stats show that the second child …"

"OK, OK! Pour that pot of tea before it stews and I'll tell you the saga of me and my latest flame, Jack."

Although they found themselves giggling at Polly's disasters with her boyfriends, her always short-lived relationships with fellow students, Jess couldn't help a glow of comfort that she had the security of Simon, his parents, her own parents, the safety net beneath them that was the support of family. She wasn't smug about it because it wasn't always easy with Simon and his swerving emotions, but she knew that she wouldn't want to go back to the uneasy incomprehension of relationships in normal student life. Her life was a settled backdrop to her ambitions. Or it would be, if only Simon … no, she mustn't go down that road …

Jess spent a satisfying afternoon in the grandly panelled university library. She sighed happily and gathered up her text books, her copy of *Ancrene Wisse* now covered in pencil notes, and her Baugh, Shepherd and Tolkien, and tucked them under her arm and her ringbinder file into her big hobo bag that she swung onto her shoulder. How brilliant, she thought, to be able translate the strange-looking language of the early thirteenth century Middle English, puzzling it together like a murder mystery to solve. Thinking about how the learned scholars spoke and read in the AB dialect of the West Midlands. The debates about its origin. Thinking about that anchoress meditating and writing in her tiny stone cell hewn into the walls of the church, her simple ascetic life of prayer and meditation. Or … ooorr …, she pondered, was it written by a man, an anchorite, as a guide book for the sister anchoresses entering the contemplative life. A man laying down the rules for the women. Hmmm, that figured.

She couldn't wait to discuss it with Simon that evening. He had also taken medieval literature at uni in his first year, although he'd moved across to politics, and he still enthused about the same things she did. He understood her passions. Apart from Polly, he was her best friend.

She smiled to herself and straightened her red sloppy joe and slim denim jeans, flipped her red, black and gold college scarf round her neck. Waving the library porter as she headed for the barriers, she basked in the memory of the professor's letter she had received that day in her uni pigeon hole, telling her that she was in line for a first class honours degree if she played her cards right in the summer exams.

She ran down the steep curved flight of steps out of the library that curved into two elegant widening flights branching out from the huge panelled wooden doors with their great shield crest above. She was aware of the group of chaps at the bottom of the steps, watching her with greedy eyes following her as she ran across the grass to the union building.

Having been ensconced in the library for three hours she breathed in deeply the warm fresh air of the summer's teatime, savouring the sweet smell of new mown grass and the abundant May blossom on the trees that surrounded the lawns. Light golden sunshine dappled the grass through the leaves of the oak and chestnut. The promise of the rest of the day filled her heart with delight. Simon was more settled now and she always looked forward to going home in the evenings to their pretty little house, to seeing Simon again after his working day, to sitting with him on the wooden bench in their small garden, chatting over a glass of wine about their days, catching up with news, learning about each other again, each other's lives, separate yet bound together. He would be pleased, she was sure, that she had received such an encouraging letter from the prof this morning!

But in fact he looked at the letter for several moments before saying, "Right, well, don't get your hopes up. There'll be a lot of work to do and many a slip, etc, etc …" before turning back to his copy of The Guardian.

"So you're up for it, then?" said Polly as she wound her arm through Jess's the following evening, as they wandered back from the Union to Polly's room. "Endless coffee and laughs with the crowd?"

"Yes, sure," Jess smiled. "Simon's got some marking and prep to do tonight so he'll probably be glad of the peace and quiet in the house! And Matt's offered to drive me home late – so, yeah, I'm looking forward to it. Makes a change."

Polly hugged her. "We're all thinking about exams soon, so it'll be good to take a break from studying for one night!"

Polly had decorated her room, a single now that Jess lived off campus and she didn't want to share with anyone else, sociable as she was, and there were candles set in coloured glass bowls on every surface that wasn't littered with text books and files. She had even strung bunting across the window that spelled out "Good luck with exams" in red, gold and black, the uni colours.

"Aaahh, that's so sweet!" smiled Jess.

"It's the little feminine touches," said Polly wrinkling her nose deprecatingly. She gestured towards three bottles on the desk. "See, I got hold of some contraband plonk."

Jess inspected them. "Mmm, not bad for plonk." She picked up a bottle and turned it around to read the label. "A rich little burgundy from the bourgogne region of the Rhône," she intoned in a deep voice, miming opening the cork and inhaling the aroma. "I would say, that it's the mâ on grape from a tiny village in the valley I know well called St Jean-de-Rouges…"

Polly screeched. "He doesn't say that!"

Jess put back the bottle on the desk. "Ah, but you knew exactly who it was supposed to be!"

"Matt is a lovely guy," said Polly firmly as she slipped an LP from its cover and placed it carefully on the dancette. She swung the arm across and the deep sounds of the Stones rang out. "Tall, dark, handsome …"

"So why isn't he in your list of conquests?"

"I guess I'm not his type. Sadly," said Polly ruefully. "Not for want of trying."

"Rugby player. Drama Club, plays the romantic lead. Good Cheshire family. Going to make a brilliant lawyer. A man of the world. Knows about wine."

"Yeah, yeah, OK. Don't rub it in." Polly frowned. "His eyes are elsewhere."

There was a knock on the door and friends from their various courses and clubs started to arrive, settling themselves in a huddle on the floor. Jess was standing near the door as Matt arrived, bearing a wine bottle. Big and broad, he filled the doorway, dark curly chest hair showing through his open-necked rugby shirt. He waved the bottle in the air towards Jess and caught her grin across the room to Polly.

"OK, OK, you two!" He smiled at Jess conspiratorially. "Just a little something dad brought up last weekend. Thought we'd share it!"

"And what region is it from, Matt? What grape is it?" called Polly over the chatting, nodding heads crushed in the room.

Matt grinned. "Not a clue." He turned to Jess and whispered. "I think it's a case of mistaken identity. She thinks I'm some rich-living swank." He manoeuvred her to the small sofa opposite Polly's bed, swooping up two plastic cups on the way. "So how's married life, then, Jess? Don't see you at Drama Club any more. You used to come every week the first two years." He passed the cups to Jess and deftly opened the bottle of red wine. He filled the cups, then placed the bottle on the floor at his feet and took one cup back from Jess. "Cheers!"

"Cheers, Matt! Well, no, it's a bit difficult."

"He doesn't keep you locked up, does he?"

Jess laughed. "God, no! But I have … responsibilities now. I have a house to keep and a husband to …"

"Pleasure …?"

"Keep happy. Look after … whatever."

Matt slid his hand on to hers. It wasn't uncomfortable. It was the gesture of a friend. "I care. Look after yourself." He patted her hand for a moment then withdrew his.

"Of course," puzzled Jess, sipping her wine. It tasted aromatic and smooth; she could tell, even with her limited knowledge, that is was a good one. "So what are you doing at Drama Club these days, then?"

"Becket. Endgame."

"Odd choice."

"Yes. The other choice was The Tragic Tale of Maria Martin, a Victorian melodrama. I could have been the murderer."

"Wasn't that Maria herself?"

"Oh, was it? Anyway, it might have been more fun, especially after a day in the mock courtroom. More wine?"

"Just the one, then I'm on the coffee. I've got an early tutorial with Dr Joan."

"And I must be sober to drive you home. Or I'll get into trouble with your other half. And I've got to go over my prosecution summing-up with the prof tomorrow at nine. Clear head, and all that."

"Jess!" called a voice from the mêlée of students on the floor. "Have you done your *Ancrene Wisse* yet? I need to pick your brains."

"Yes, I did it yesterday …fascinating."

"How can some nun in a stone cell be interesting? What kind of a life did she have that she could write about?"

"Well, another theory is that it was written by an anchorite, a sort of monk, telling the girls what to do. That raises all sorts of interesting notions to debate. But maybe we could have a coffee in the Union bar on Wednesday and talk about it?"

"Hey, what about me? I need your help with my psych project, Jess," came another. "I'm getting muddled with the socio-cultural versus evolutionary perspectives in the nature-nuture debate we've got to do for Thursday."

Matt smiled sideways at her. "Your brain's very popular tonight." He rose and poured them both a coffee.

"Well, I don't know much about it," chimed in Polly, "but I can't believe in the behaviourist bit. That we're all born with a blank slate and that it's filled with experience or social conditioning …"

"*Tabula rasa* …" murmured someone on the floor. "The blank slate. But what about cognitive psychology, Polly … I mean, we are surely born with certain innate mental structures, like schema that may be inherited, just like physical attributes like the colour of hair and eyes, genetic stuff."

"But cognitive psychology also looks at the way those innate structures are changed and adapted by the environment, so that's nurture, surely?"

"Yeah," agreed one of their friends on the English programme. "In Eng Lang we're doing Chomsky and his new stuff on language learning, that innate LAD." Polly frowned. "Language Acquisition Device. But I think that the LAD may be developed and adapted in time by environmental influences."

"OK. But," argued Jess, warming to the theme, and calling above the noise of chatter and asides. "But what about Vygotsky? He argued that language is learned from socialisation, talking to others, children imitating their parents. Don't you think that we learn through talking to each other? Don't we formulate our own thoughts and ideas by talking them through? I'm sure I do."

"And remember Jenson and Galton," added Matt. "What was it? The idea that 80% of intelligence is inherited? That sort of thinking led very directly to the idea that race determines intelligence. As a lawyer that concerns me. There are chilling implications. That one race is superior to another, innately. We all know where that led in the second world war. Nazi concentration camps." Goodness, thought Jess, Matt was very erudite; he seemed to know so much about other subjects, not only the law. She admired that.

"Mmm," murmured Jess. "Simon would say that the genetic debate is a right wing agenda. I wonder what genetics in future research might say? I wonder if they'll ever try to find some strands or cells or something that might be determining variables for, I don't know, criminality or sexuality? God, I hope not."

"Well, if they did, it might make forensics easier," said Matt.

"Talkin' about sexuality," came a Geordie voice from the top of Polly's bed. Everyone laughed. It was Geoff, a well-built rugby player on Polly's geology course.

"Yeah, you would!" shouted another. "One track mind, you!"

"No, seriously. I'm thinking about Freud …"

"Yeah. Right!"

"Freud," Geoff continued unabated. "Freud's psychoanalysis stuff is interesting. And you philistines should know that he actually answers the nature-nurture debate straight off the plate. Innate sex drives … that's yer nature bit …and add social upbringing during childhood … that's yer nurture bit. Mix together and what do yer get? Confusion. Buggered-up adults."

The room erupted into laughter and loud argument.

Matt turned to Jess on the sofa. "And what do you think about that?" he smiled, as if he was blocking out the rest of the room.

Jess cupped her hands around her mug of coffee. She let the conversation of the others wash over her, thankful to just talk to one person rather than fighting to make her voice heard over the hubbub of voices and pop music. "I think … I think that there's an awful lot of responsibility on parents to avoid trying to force their kids to believe the same as them. Sex, politics, religion, whatever. Everyone has to find their own way in life. I guess it must be awfully difficult for a parent to see their kids taking a different path from the one they did, but … sometimes you're marked for life …" she tailed off and stared down at her coffee, at its muddy brown depths, at the powdered milk that hadn't quite been absorbed into the liquid.

"Yes," Matt said. "You and me both." After a moment, he added, "Look, whenever you're ready, let me know and I'll get you home safe and sound."

As he pulled up outside her house, Matt turned to her and whispered. "I hope you're happy. That he's making you happy."

"Oh, I think you make your own happiness, nobody else can *make* you happy, you know, only yourself."

Matt considered for a moment. "But the people you're with can make you or break you. I care that you're happy. You're lovely, Jess … I …" then, catching her expression, he stopped abruptly. Then he leaned across her and opened her door. His hand brushed hers and lingered a little too long. She moved her hand firmly.

"Goodnight, Matt, and thanks for the lift," she said as she swung out.

He sighed. "Goodnight, Jess."

5

WATERLOO SUNSET

J ess sank onto the sofa and dropped her head into
her hands. She felt ill, tired all the time. What
had happened to all the energy she used to have?
She knew: it had gone in to all the studying for finals,
boosted up by the prof's faith in her last year she had
worked even harder, determined to get that First he
believed she could achieve, staying up late and working most of the weekend. Fitting in housework and
laundry, cooking and clearing up. No time for writing
stories or poems any more. And, the last straw, today
her only pair of decent shoes no longer were. The sole
had torn partly off and tripped her up. She'd have to
try to stick it up again with some strong contact adhe-
sive; she couldn't afford a new pair.

She was worried about Simon's state of mind again.
Although he seemed settled in his teaching job, he

relied on her to talk through his lessons, help him with his marking. How could she refuse when he seemed, at times, quite fragile? She'd had to drop out of the concurrent teaching diploma that she had started alongside her degree programme. It was just all too much. She planned to take the diploma after her degree, even though it was an extra year of study. The psychology course now fascinated Jess, although it was hard, but her real love was the English, and especially the medieval studies.

Her tutors wanted her to enrol for a doctorate immediately after her first degree and part of her wanted so much to extend her study of medieval language and literature, become a specialist in the field, maybe be an academic like her tutors. Write papers and publish them in real academic journals, present at conferences, maybe overseas! She'd love that. She even imagined travelling back to Ghana and presenting a paper at the University of Legon!

But then her sensible, feet-on-the-ground self kicked in and a voice growled: how do you think you could do that when you struggle to cope with all this, here, now? Simon often appeared incapable of helping her out. His moods were difficult to catch hold of. But when he was well, he was so gorgeous. She had promised before God to love and cherish him, to look after him whatever befell, through sickness and health, and all that. And that is precisely what she would do.

Her dreams? Well, maybe some time, some day … when the time was right …

Her head was spinning but she knew that Simon was her top priority. Today he had gone to meet his parents in the city; unusual for a Saturday, he normally saw them in school holidays. She struggled in her bare feet to the kitchen drawer and rummaged in it to find the paracetamol, throwing the pills to the back of her throat and gulping down a glass of water. Then she made her unsteady way back in to the living room to lie down for a few moments on the sofa. The room was flickering across her eyes. She must make an appointment to see the doctor. What was it her mother used to say … needing a tonic … something to boost her up … something to keep her going … when she was under the weather … A great weariness swept over her like a pre-op anaesthetic as though her whole body was gradually becoming numb from the feet upwards.

Simon's voice awakened her. She loved to hear his voice and always felt better, glowing when she knew he was home. But today she pushed herself up on the sofa, unable to stand upright, let alone throw her arms around him as usual when he returned home. And his voice sounded so loud, she winced.

He dropped a large plastic carrier bag onto the floor beside the sofa. "What have you got there?" she smiled. Perhaps he had bought her a present to cheer her up. She had been very lethargic when she got up that morning and he had hugged her gently and told her to rest.

"Oh, the parents insisted on buying me some new smart clothes for work. Not that there's anything wrong with my existing ones, frankly. But you know what they're like." Jess looked down at the bag. "The rest of the stuff's in the car. I'll go and get it in. Oh, there's something in there for you." He delved into the carrier bag and pulled out a small packet. She carefully eased aside the wrapping paper, hoping to be able to recycle it, and found a brown silk scarf. She looked up at Simon questioningly. "The parents bought it for you."

"Well, please thank them when you next speak to them on the phone," whispered Jess, hardly daring to raise her voice to normal level, her head felt so raw.

He rushed out to fetch other bags from his car, and Jess peered into the carrier bag beside her. Two pairs of men's shoes, identical except that one was black and the other tan.

It was Polly who finally persuaded Jess to "pull her finger out and go and see the doc."

She sat uncomfortably in the waiting room at the village surgery. An old withered man sat snorting into a handkerchief and grunting, two pregnant women chatted desultorily and a toddler crawled around everyone's feet. The mother, flicking through a magazine ignored him. It was a Monday morning and Jess had phoned in her apologies for her absence at her psychology seminar; she had found it hard enough to move her legs enough to walk round the corner from the house to the surgery which stood by the village pond.

They had to call her name twice before she registered it and stood to follow the doctor into his surgery.

"Now ... What seems to be the matter?" asked the doctor kindly, peering over his half-moon specs at her.

"It's probably nothing at all. But I feel so weary all the time. Sometimes I feel almost paralysed. And sometimes I can hardly face walking through to the next room. I almost feel as though I've got flu but no temperature and I'm eating OK."

"OK, tell me what you do and what might be responsible for this exhaustion."

Jess quickly ran through her normal schedule, the pressures of finals, of studying so hard, of keeping house ... She considered mentioning her worries about Simon's health, but decided against it; that would only complicate matters even further – no need.

Dr Jones asked her questions about the nature of her tiredness, the symptoms she manifested. Did she have muscle or joint pain? Did she have severe headaches? Did she have sensitivity to light and sound? Did her concentration seem impaired, did she fall asleep at odd times?

He swivelled his desk chair round and reached over to her, carefully feeling the sides of her neck. "Hmm, lymph nodes a little swollen." He scribbled a few notes, and then looked up at her. "And what about relaxation, rest? What do you do in your free time?"

Jess almost laughed. "Free time? Well, I don't get much but I do have occasional get-togethers with friends at uni. And I walk round the village when I can."

"Any other exercise?"

"I swim in the university pool every week or so. I do some training in the gym there when I can, between lectures."

The doctor scribbled again. "Other interests? Hobbies?" Goodness, thought Jess, this sounds like an interview or life-style assessment.

"Um … reading. Er … I listen to music."

The doctor looked up, pleased. Maybe something she said had ticked one of his boxes. "Good. Good. Do you sing?"

Jess frowned, startled. "Well, I used to. Choral singing." She thought about Ghana and the choir she sang in there, the wonderful concerts, uplifting rehearsals, Jim. The choir at university she gave up last year. "I used to sing in a choir."

The doctor nodded. "Good. Perhaps you could consider joining a choir again. Maybe there's one at the university? Find time for it. It's relaxing and current medical research also indicates that it has a great effect on the nervous system, serotonin levels in the brain, so it can re-energise." He smiled. "I've just been reading a paper in The Lancet about it. I'm so glad I have a patient who presents suitable symptoms." He sat back in his swivel chair and propped his elbows on the padded arms, templing his fingers together. "I think that you are manifesting the features of a post-viral fatigue syndrome. Have you had influenza recently?"

"Well, yes, I did back in the winter and actually it took a long time to feel right again. But I dosed myself up – it was going round the campus like mad – and then I was OK again for a while until I started feeling increasingly tired. Then I suddenly started feeling absolutely exhausted these last few weeks. Actually, I feel like I've got flu all over again."

The doctor was nodding enthusiastically again, like those tacky little plastic dogs strung up in the backs of cars. "Mmmm … My diagnosis, my theory rather, is that you may have something that's just being investigated, myalgic encephalomyelitis. ME. It's more than TATT – tired all the time. It's about as different as migraine from a headache. There are different names for the condition: chronic fatigue syndrome, post-viral fatigue syndrome."

"O-kaaay, but is it treatable? Because I've got my Finals coming up soon."

"We're going to run a few tests, including a battery of bloods, to rule out anything else. There's no test for ME. It's a question of eliminating everything else as far as we can and assessing the symptoms."

"So what are the things you have to rule out?" Jess grimaced, wondering what other conditions it could be.

"Various, including type II diabetes mellitus, MS, heart, renal and pulmonary diseases, and so on. But don't worry about all that, because you present with the usual reported symptoms so I am 99% sure this is what it is."

"But if it is this … ME, what happens now, what's the treatment?"

"I'm going to advise you to get as much rest as you can. I know you've got Finals coming up but try to ration your time working. The key is energy management – conservation and wise use of energy levels. Eat well, fresh foods. Plenty of iron. You're a little anaemic. My guess is that you haven't been eating as well as you should in the immediate past." She thought of the small amount of money she had to spend on food, although slightly more now than when they lived at the flat. "And you need as much gentle exercise as you can, but nothing too demanding. Get your husband to take some of those chores off your shoulders." Jess felt her heart plummet. "I'm going to give you something to help raise the serotonin levels and we'll take it from there."

As she opened the door to leave, Dr Jones called out to her. "And don't forget to pick up that choir singing again. I do think it will help!"

But she couldn't even think of choir for weeks; she felt so tired and ill. Some days she could hardly move. Some days she felt completely washed out and then another day she'd think she was recovering, only to relapse the following day.

She tried to look up myalgic encephalomyelitis one day when she cadged a lift with Simon into the campus library but there was little to find. A paper or two and some debate on causation but not enough to enlighten her further. She was thankful that her GP happened to be interested enough to have read a paper on it recently. It all seemed a very new discovery.

She did a little studying for her Finals as she lay on the sofa but she knew it was not enough. Polly came over and helped her to revise, but she found herself quite tearful and worried about her exams.

Her mother came up to visit them for the weekend and brought fresh fruit and vegetables from their garden, and a casserole she had made. She insisted on cooking all the meals during their visit and left a home-made shepherd's pie and chicken flan in their fridge. It was such a relief to have someone looking after *her*. Her mother seemed so much more cheerful these days.

"It's nice to be needed," said her mother, as she bustled about the kitchen.

Simon came home from work to a clean and tidy house, hot meal on the table, and constantly told Jess's mother how wonderful she was. "I couldn't manage

without you," he would say as he hugged her, and Jess
felt a mixture of pleasure that he was content but a
certain irritation that he seemed to want someone at
home to manage it all for him. She felt guilty that she
was so often rushing back from classes, hurrying to
make a meal, juggling with washing, ironing, trying
to predict which shirt he wanted for the next day, and
feeling somewhat disorganised. And yet whenever she
asked him to share chores, he would get annoyed and
storm out or depressed and moody. It was easier to just
get on with it. And then he was happy and loving; he
would take her in his arms, stroke her hair and kiss her
face, her neck ... and the nights would be passionate
and glorious.

By the time Finals began, serotonin levels higher,
Jess was feeling well enough to take the exams but anxious that she had missed so many classes that term.
Everyone else seemed to have had a life running on
without her. Polly, now taking a one-year Masters, sat
over coffee in the bar with her, smoking her gauloise,
going over and over the main issues of the literature
critiques. Matt, having gained his First, now doing his
postgrad legal practice year, sprawled on the lawn with
her in the sunshine, behind the old hall, on a tartan
car rug he kept in his room, propped up on his elbow,
slightly on his side with one long leg bent at the knee,
and tested her on her psychology.

"I hope this is helping," commented Matt, pouring out another strong coffee for each of them from

the thermos flask he had brought with him. "I have no idea what this psychology is about, so I'm not sure how much it's supporting you, Jess …"

"Oh, it's very helpful, just refreshing my memory." Actually he seemed to know an awful lot about psychology. She knew he was very bright; he was consistently at the top of his PG course.

He grinned at her and from time to time raked his hand through his dark crisply curling hair, in a way that reminded her of Jim back in Ghana. "Any time, Jess. Glad to help." Much as she loved Simon, she couldn't pretend that she hadn't noticed Matt, his body. His jeans were well fitting over his muscular rugby-player's thighs and his white tee-shirt was closely hugging his chest. He looked distractingly strong and attractive. Jess couldn't see his eyes, hidden behind his sunglasses, but as she looked away from him she had the distinct feeling that they were smiling.

All her other friends were engrossed in their own concerns about the looming Finals and either shut themselves up in their rooms or lay on the grass in the sunshine outside the halls of residence, under the summer trees, heads buried in their text books and their file notes.

All too soon, in the silence of the examination room, Jess was aware of the other students around her, biros flowing across the pages, the soft sound of sheets being flipped over and shuffled, the clock ticking. Outside the trees rustled in the gentle warm breeze. A car murmured past. She made herself focus, but afterwards she knew that she hadn't done herself justice.

"We still want you to register for a doctorate," said her professor. "Even though you didn't get the First we expected. We know that you were unwell and we know what you can do normally. So we're willing to offer you a place if you'd still like to do it."

They were in the prof's study, sitting on soft squashy easy chairs that Jess felt herself sink into. She thought that she might fall asleep in the drowsy, bee-murmuring afternoon, and fought to keep her eyes open and alert. Professor Franklin leaned forward, elbows propped on his bony knees, brown wrinkled hands clasped in front of him. Jess noticed that his nails were manicured neatly, just as his grey hair was well cut and tidy, his toothbrush moustache trimmed immaculately. "It would be good to have you stay with us. Your work up to this term has been exemplary. I am aware that your illness has resulted in a most uncharacteristic falling off of standards. But, given your successes up to now – your work on *Pearl*, and of course, *Tristan and Iseult*, was nothing short of impressive, though I say it myself, as a specialist in epic poems of the Germanic tradition - I do believe that your performance in Finals was an aberration. Yes, I know that we cannot alter the degree award, but I feel that we must provide you with another chance, given your history."

Professor Franklin leaned back in his leather swivel chair, antique-brown and deeply buttoned, looked across with eyebrows raised, and waited for her answer.

"Thank you, professor. It's really kind of you to have faith in my ability despite the disasters of Finals. But I need to think about it. Whether I can manage it. I'm a bit knocked down about what's happened."

"Jessamy, when you have a doctorate, the first degree will hardly count, it will be superceded."

"Yes, I know. And thank you for all you're doing for me, professor. I do appreciate it … I need to think it over … and talk to my husband too. I'd love to be able to say yes right now. But there are various considerations, I'm afraid. Finance, delaying my teaching diploma, and getting a job."

"You could do some paid work here, as a tutor and research assistant. I'd be happy for you to work alongside me. Although obviously it wouldn't pay as much as a teaching post in a school."

"That's really kind."

If she didn't have a husband, if it was just up to her, she'd take up the offer, and make do. But she was married and it wasn't just up to her. She descended the grand staircase of the great hall, sweeping her hand over the polished oak balustrade, feeling the plush carpet beneath her feet. How wonderful it would be to work there. But …

"Well, that's a great offer," said Simon, as he switched on the television and sank down onto the easy chair. "But I can't see how we could do it. I mean you're talking at least a couple of years full time and you've still got a diploma to take before you can teach – and that's another year." He put his arm around her, as she knelt beside him, and nuzzled her neck. "You can't be studying for the rest of your life! I want my wife back!"

Jess sighed. What a dilemma she found herself in. Polly had taken her concurrent teaching diploma and started teaching humanities at a secondary school. It was a grammar school that had recently become a comprehensive under the new legislation.

She knew in her heart that she couldn't go on earning nothing and leaving it all to Simon. She knew that he wasn't happy about that. He had hinted many times that it would be so much better for them both if she had a job. And he didn't seem very keen on her taking a doctorate at all.

"OK," she agreed reluctantly, yet knowing it made sense. "I'll register for the postgrad teaching diploma, and get a job."

"Hey, babes, guess what?" Polly hugged Jess and swung her round even as she stepped through the doorway. It was a year later and Jess had gained a distinction in her teaching diploma. She felt better and ready for a job. "There's a vacancy at my school for an English teacher next term! Not permanent at the moment. But it's a maternity leave to cover Maggie and there's always the possibility that she might decide not to return!"

"Really! That would be fantastic!" Jess ushered her friend into the living room.

"Say you'll apply!"

"Well, it'd be great to be on the staff at the same school."

"And we could share lifts!"

"We could if I had a car."

"I mean, I could pick you up, now that I've moved to the village."

Polly had finally decided to take the plunge and rent a flat in the converted manor house the other side of Jess's village. She taught at a school in the city, twenty minutes away.

"Wait, wait a minute! I may not be appointed!"

"I'll help you with the application. We'll make a fantastic job of it. And you got a distinction in your teaching diploma. Um …" Polly looked a little sheepish. "Actually, I've already mentioned you to the Head and he seemed quite keen."

"Oh, really? And what have you said about me to him? I hope you haven't bigged me up so I have to lie!"

"Would I do that? Oh, come on, Jess, I don't have to big you up. So clever, so competent, so organised, so …"

"I haven't been feeling too much of any of those things the last stretch," confessed Jess, twisting her legs up beneath her on the soft armchair. "But I managed my diploma and I guess I feel a bit better now. I think the serotonin helps."

Polly drew up her knees and hugged her arms around them. "Um …" she peered sideways at Jess.

"Oh god, I know that look. What have you done now?"

"I bumped in to Matt … from uni …"

"Yes, yes, I know who Matt is. Tell me the dirt …"

"In town. And we had a coffee and then a beer. And then the next night we had dinner. And – oh, Jess, we're going out!" Then she launched into an exaggerated version of "*Steppin' out, with my baby* …" And Jess joined in, with jazz hands. She had never gone back to joining a choir; she really didn't have the time. But maybe there'd be one during lunchtime at a school where she ended up teaching.

"Polly! That's great! I know you liked him at uni."

"Yes, I did, but I always thought he was more than a little taken with you …"

"Polly! I'm married, and I was married then!"

"Even so …"

Jess remembered Matt giving her lifts home, sprawling on the lawns at the old hall helping her to revise for Finals. She knew he was keen. But she'd given him no encouragement. She wouldn't ever do that to Simon. She believed in faithfulness. When you were married, it was for ever, and exclusive. Through sickness and health. Wealth and poverty. Good times and bad. Otherwise what was the meaning of it all? She reached over to Polly and touched her arm gently.

"I'm thrilled to bits for you. I hope it works out fine. I have a feeling this is a keeper."

Jess could hardly believe her good fortune when she heard that Polly's school, as she liked to think of it, had agreed to appoint her to cover for a colleague's maternity leave. Initially it was just two terms but the likelihood was that it would be the whole first year allowing her to complete her NQT and be awarded fully qualified teacher status. She was covering the classes for the Head of Department who was about to give birth to her first child but Jess was not expected to deal with the HoD role: the second was going to be Acting HoD. However, the classes were mainly exam classes, O and A level and university entrance, although the second in the department, a vivacious lady called Sally, would be sharing those with her and they would work closely together. Jess was relieved to have a mentor for her first year of real teaching.

"You'll be fine, dear," Sally assured her kindly, pouring her a mug of coffee in the staff room. "We'll have a meeting next week when I've been able to go through your timetable, and I'll get hold of copies of all the texts for you so that you can prepare over the summer hols. We'll look at how we're going to organise the classes and lessons between us."

"Gosh, I feel a bit thrown into the deep end!" Jess sat down on the lumpy armchair by the window that Sally indicated.

"I hear that you are highly thought of at the university, for both your degree and your teaching diploma," smiled Sally, settling her plump frame into the chair next to Jess's and cupping her mug. "And of course you've taught before."

"Well, yes but only as an unqualified teacher in Ghana. It's not the same."

"I'm sure the basics are all the same anywhere, my dear." Sally patted her arm reassuringly. "And I'm looking forward to having a breath of fresh air in this department." She leaned towards Jess and lowered her voice to a whisper. "There are some real stick-in-the-mud types on this staff. Set in their ways. Don't like anything new."

"Oh, I'm very receptive to creative teaching. I had to be in Ghana. And on my postgrad diploma course we looked at some innovative ways of teaching grammar and set exam texts."

"Great! I liked what you said in the interview about teaching Shakespeare to the first years. Loved the idea of "interviews" with Shakespeare himself and getting the kids to plan the questions to him. And the newspaper headlines in the "Stratford Daily Times" about the first performance of Macbeth, and the fire at The Globe! Haha! Love it!" Sally laughed and her whole body seemed to shake with laughter too. "And I hear you like choral singing! We have a staff choir on Wednesday lunchtimes so I hope you'll come along. I think we're going to get along very well."

The evening that Jess and Simon were having Polly and Matt over to dinner started off somewhat tensely as Simon returned home from work, slamming his bag onto the hall floor, pulling off his jacket, flinging it across the sofa, and loosening his tie with abrupt clumsy hands. Jess recognised the symptoms.

"Oh dear, bad day?" She had not been home long but was already scurrying about the kitchen preparing the meal. "Well, glad it's Friday. No work tomorrow. Would you like a glass of wine? Coffee? I've just put some on."

"God, I can't believe those kids!" She heard him fling himself onto the armchair in the living room. She really didn't want to ask him what was wrong and open the floodgates she knew would ensue.

"Oh well," she called, "it's the weekend now." She heard him switch the television on to watch the news. Better to think of good things ahead than dwell over difficulties you can't now do anything about. She hated his post-mortems. He analysed everything so closely, and it seemed to only make things even worse.

"Coffee will be fine if you've already got it on," called Simon in return. "Tell me if you want anything done." But she knew better than to take him up on that offer, which she knew from experience was not actually an invitation to respond. Laying the table would be his job. She could manage the rest; it had become automatic by now.

At least she was glad that over the last year or two she seemed to have felt stronger and ready to face the world. The medications were helping and she had taken the doctor's advice about gentle exercise, plenty of rest and eating healthily. She had researched foods and recipes that used good fresh cheap ingredients: plenty of fish, chicken, fresh vegetables and fruit. Her mother had been kind enough to buy her a slow-cooker for her birthday and she now tried to prepare a casserole of cheap cuts of stewing beef or rabbit, onions, potatoes and carrots, in the mornings before she went to work. Then all she had to do was steam some fresh cabbage or broccoli when she got home. Then fruit for her and a sweet pie that she'd baked at the weekend for Simon, who wasn't keen on fresh fruit, and that lasted until mid-week.

But tonight was going to be a special meal that she had planned carefully. She loved the occasional dinner party: it was sociable, relaxing and she enjoyed cooking and having a chat and a laugh over a shared meal.

She sloshed the red wine into the coq au vin and added the chopped celery and carrots from the wooden board on the counter top. The cast iron casserole was popped into the oven and she finished off the earthenware dish of potatoes dauphinoise with more grated cheese on the top with a good sprinkling of ground sea salt and black pepper. The pudding was already made the night before, a black forest gateau and some cream ready in a jug.

Jess loved to plan menus for dinner parties – not that they held many. But she tried to find recipes that were easy for her to do and which she could leave in the oven to make themselves while she chatted to guests. Simon wasn't proactively keen on dinner parties but he took them in fairly good heart whenever Jess suggested inviting friends or family over, and played his part as host well. He was a good conversationalist and could always be relied on to keep the wine and talk flowing entertainingly. As long as nobody touched a raw nerve.

She took two coffees in to the living room and sank down on the sofa next to Simon's jacket. He himself had taken to sitting on the tweed covered armchair that had come from his bedsitting room at his parents' house. He called it 'my chair' so there was no doubt about its ownership and provenance, and the last time someone else had tried to sit on it, he had asked them to move. He wouldn't sit on the sofa next to her, even for a cuddle; he said it was uncomfortable.

Jess was looking forward to chatting with Polly again; they hadn't seen much of each other that week as Jess was taking some extra exam prep classes at lunchtime and after school. And she hadn't seen Matt for an age. He was now apparently working at a law firm in the city, loving it, and according to Polly was something of a rising star.

When the doorbell rang, Jess jumped up and ran to open the door.

"Hi! Polly!" She flung her arms round her friend, crushing her scarlet silk shift dress.

"As if you haven't been together all day at work!" Jess turned but Matt was grinning indulgently.

"Matt! Lovely to see you again," Jess reached up to his handsome six-foot-something frame and kissed him on the cheek. He caught her in a bear hug.

"Mmmm," he whispered in her ear. "You smell delicious!" She slapped him playfully on the back.

"So how are you enjoying life at the sheriff's office? Lots of bandits for you to lock up?"

Matt laughed, as Jess ushered them into the living room where Simon was starting to pour drinks. "Sadly not that kind of law enforcement! And, Jess, you're obviously watching too many cowboy films. No, I'm in corporate law." He glanced at Jess opening her mouth to interrogate him. "You don't want to know, Jess. But it's interesting to me and I love it!"

"That's all that matters," Jess began as Simon cut across her.

"What's that, assisting the bigwigs of industry to evade taxes, or find offshore havens, make even more money?" He handed Matt the glass of red he'd indicated. "You're one of the hotshots making a lot of money out of the rest of us, then?"

There was an embarrassed pause. Trust Simon. Typical. It couldn't have been more than a nanosecond but to Jess it seemed like an age as she desperately struggled for something to say that would show her guests that she didn't approve of her husband's sentiments without putting him down in front of them. But Matt beat her to it.

"Yeah, I guess that's about it!" was all he said but there was no chance for Simon to come back on it or develop an argument. "Hey, I like this wine, Simon. What is it?" Jess could have hugged him. And, fortunately, Simon smiled.

They sat round the table making flattering comments about Jess's cooking, and the wine and conversation were both flowing well. But Jess was feeling a little uneasy as she noticed Simon's face becoming increasingly red and damp. His foot was tapping on the floor and his fingers beating a rhythm on the table. Jess wondered what he was agitated about.

"… well, we wouldn't be able to do that if these strikes carry on …" Matt was saying.

"That's ridiculous," Simon cut in, banging his fist on the table. "The miners have every reason to strike for their rights. Ted Heath is completely intractable. Do you even know what a miner earns? And the conditions they have to endure down the mines?"

There was a pause, then Matt said, "Actually, the miners earn a good wage. Yes, the conditions in the mines are grim – I wouldn't want to go down the pits. But they have chosen that job …"

"No they haven't *chosen the job.* They don't have any *choice.* They're born into the mining community, it's where their fathers worked and where they were raised …"

"OK, perhaps those were the wrong words to use," Matt conceded, nodding and still smiling. "But at least they have a job. Look at the unemployment in this country. The miners may find that they don't have a job soon if they …"

"*Rubbish*!" shouted Simon. "We rely on coal. It's the major power source in this country! They have a lousy job in lousy conditions. Would you do it? That's the point, that's why they deserve more!"

"Well, no I wouldn't go down the pits. But then I wasn't brought up in a mining community where that's the way of life. And I have the qualifications for a profession."

Jess couldn't resist turning to Simon and asking, "So would you do it?"

"That's not the point!"

"No," sighed Jess. "I don't know why you get so het up about socialist politics, the miners, the dockers and all that, Simon! I mean, look at you. You come from a titled family, pretty wealthy compared with most, professional people, some prominent people in the House of Lords. And yet you talk as though you have some kind of vested interest in the labouring workers …"

"Jess, I am not proud of my heritage. Actually it embarrasses me. I feel guilty that I have had more than others."

"Well, that's fair enough," said Matt. "It's not what you were born into, it's where you go from there. If you have a privileged family background, yet you …"

"No, I didn't have *a privileged background*!"

"OK, OK." Jess held up her hands in a protest, stop gesture. "I shouldn't have brought that up. Sorry. Let me just get the pudding. Simon, would you top up the glasses, please?" Jess scraped back her chair from the table and caught Polly's eye and grimaced. But as she and Polly started to take the plates through to the kitchen, she heard Simon start arguing again. Polly flashed a wry down-turned mouth at her, and Jess shook her head in apology.

As she lifted the black forest gateau out of the fridge, Matt came through carrying the empty casserole dishes. He ran some hot water into them and left them to soak on the counter top.

"Phew," he frowned and stroked Jess's back sympathetically. "Let's keep off politics. And religion. And wealth. And the law. And … anything else, Jess?" He pulled such a funny exaggerated expression that Jess giggled, as she handed him the jug of cream to take into the dining area.

Polly hugged her briefly before they returned to the table.

"Well," said Polly with what Jess could detect as slightly false jollity. "Some great news to share with you!"

"Oh, what, what?" asked Jess as she cut the gateau. Polly turned to Matt and smiled intimately at him.

"I'm moving in with Matt," she said, slightly sheepishly, yet with clear delight.

"Oh, that's wonderful news that you two are really getting together!" exclaimed Jess, reaching across the table to squeeze Polly's hand, then Matt's. But she was aware of the stillness of Simon beside her, and she turned to him. His expression was horrified, his face red again.

"Living together before you're married?" he asked, appalled.

Later as they lay in bed, Jess, feeling a little sad that Simon clearly didn't share her affection for her friends, barely listened to his tirade about how disgusting it was that anyone could live together "in THAT way" without being blessed by the sanctity of marriage.

"They love each other. They're good together. I love them both," whispered Jess. "What does a piece of paper at a ceremony matter?"

"What indeed?" said Simon sarcastically.

"I can't imagine that either of them would betray the other now they've clearly made that commitment. So isn't that what it's all about?"

"Well, I'm just glad that we're married and settled, properly, in the eyes of God. I love you, Jess, and I want us to be a family." Simon reached for her and stroked her face, her neck, her breasts.

But even as they made love, Jess couldn't obliterate from her mind the look of disgust that Simon had thrown her friends at dinner. They were good, kind people. She knew that however much either of them flirted lightly with anyone else, they would never be unfaithful. They were a unit now. An unbreakable item. That was what mattered, surely?

"Maggie isn't coming back to work," whispered Sally to Jess in the staff room, pinching a piece of the Easter cake Jess had brought in and was attempting to cut into slices whilst flicking away the impatient hands that were creeping with dangerous eagerness around her knife. Sally shushed the colleagues away and leaned in towards Jess. "She's decided to make the maternity leave permanent, doesn't want to leave the little one."

"I can well understand that," nodded Jess.

"So the point *is* …" said Sally slowly as though explaining something to an intransigent first year pupil. "There is now a permanent vacancy for a Head of Department."

"I think you'll be great at it," smiled Jess.

"No, no, Jess, I don't want the role. Too much organisation, all that leadership and management stuff. The responsibility. I'm not even a graduate, only got a teaching diploma from training college. No, I'm happy as a second."

Jess turned to face her, gradually realising what she was suggesting. "Oh, no, Sally. I'm so new here. I've hardly found my feet. And I wouldn't want to put people's backs up, going for a promotion over other folks' heads. It wouldn't be right. And I don't know that I could do it anyway."

"Of course you could. Look what you've done this year. And you should have had a lighter timetable being a pre-NQT. But you've attacked it all. I think you'd be brilliant. Have a chat with the Head. I know he's receptive …" She grinned slyly. "I had a little conversation with him over lunch."

"Oh, Sally!"

As it happened the Head asked to see her after school. He offered her the role, as long as the governing board approved, and said it would help him as he wouldn't have to advertise the post and "fiddle around with all those wretched interviews".

"Would you give me some time to think about it, please?"

"Of course. But don't take too long; I need to get the leadership structure in place."

6

KILLING ME SOFTLY

Simon was not happy about Jess taking the Head of Department job, or even staying on at the school on a permanent fulltime basis, despite wanting her to earn an income. Maybe he wanted her to be like his mother who stayed at home but had a private income and paid for cleaners, housekeepers and gardeners.

"We'll talk about it later," he said as he bounded up and down the stairs, looking for items to stuff into his backpack. "I've got to catch the 10.30 train. You're still OK to drive me to the station? You can drop me off at the entrance, no need to park."

"Yes, that's fine." Jess was glad to be able to drive the car, which she rarely got to do, as Simon hated being in the passenger seat. They were supposed to share it but it was really Simon's, after all; it was the mini

WALKING IN THE RAIN

that his parents had bought for him when they were engaged, and Jess never felt that it was hers to lay claim to. She'd passed her driving test quite easily when she returned from Ghana, having been taught over there by Chrissie and Jim. "When will you be back?"

"It'll be late. The march won't be finished until about teatime I guess, so by the time I've got back to the station …"

"Are you sure you'll be OK?" asked Jess as she re-folded his waterproof jacket and fitted it into his bag for him. "I mean, a demonstration … I keep thinking of Bloody Sunday when the troops fired on the dem-onstrators …"

"Jess, that was Northern Ireland for a start, there was civil unrest, it was a whole different scenario politi-cally …"

"But fourteen people were killed …"

"This is nothing like Derry, Jess, this is CND, a properly organised march. There will be important political and public figures there."

"Yes, but it's at the nuclear base at Aldermaston. It's a very sensitive location. I feel really uneasy about it."

"Hey," said Simon, taking her in his arms and kiss-ing her head, then turning her face up towards him to kiss her fully on the lips. "Don't worry about me. But I like that you do."

"We'll need to talk tomorrow, though."

"What?" Simon held her away from him, looking puzzled.

"The HoD post," sighed Jess. "They need to know on Monday."

"OK, OK, but we need to go now. I wish you were coming."

"You know I can't. I've got a whole load of marking to do. But you also know I wouldn't come anyway. It's just not my scene. But you be careful."

Jess spent the rest of the day working on her marking and preparation for the following week at school. She was finding it difficult to concentrate. She rubbed her stomach. She had felt bloated, sore and tired for a few weeks. Her period threatened but didn't come. She sighed; she hated this uncertainty but she'd become used to the irregularity of her system: often missing a period or suffering it heavy and extremely painful. One month she'd had to call a taxi to take her home in the middle of the day; she was almost bent double in agony and feeling weak and dizzy. She just wanted to be home in safety and comfort, but Simon was cross that she'd spent money on a taxi. She fetched a mug of hot sweet tea, took another aspirin and picked up her red pen again.

In the late afternoon, Simon rang to say that he'd got a lift from the station back home by someone he'd met on the march, so she didn't have to turn out to meet him. Later when she began to feel drowsy and her eyes heavy, she decided to call it a day and have a hot aromatherapy bath before taking a book to bed.

In fact she soaked in the warmth of the water and read the next chapter of Harper Lee's 'To Kill a Mockingbird'. She loved that book. She was teaching it as an O level text to her fourth form and rereading it was an opportunity to summon up more inspiration for activities she wanted to design to help the pupils grasp what it must have felt like to live in the racially segregated deep south of America in the 1930s. And with a father who was defending a black man against the accusation of the rape of a white girl. She must show them the classic film with Gregory Peck, so wonderful as Atticus Finch. Yes, she had lots of ideas.

Much later, she fell asleep over the book, her head lolling off the pillow, and was startled awake only by the noise of the front door slamming shut. Simon bounded up the stairs two at a time and swept into their bedroom.

"God, that was a fantastic day!" He threw his backpack onto the bed. His voice penetrated her drowsiness and she struggled to raise herself up in the bed, pulling the duvet up around her against the chill of the night air that had swept up the stairs in his wake.

"Oh, good," she managed to say, blinking her brain awake. "So who brought you back?"

"Er … Alison."

"Alison?"

"A girl I met on the march. Walked along with her actually. And came back on the train with her. She'd parked her car at the station. *Very* attractive." Jess was aware of a strain in his voice, and the unease in the air, but was far too tired to think any further about it. "She's really in to jazz, especially jazz piano." He had pulled off his clothes and slipped under the duvet. He stretched his arms above his head and clasped his hands under his head so that it was tilted forward. "I've been thinking of buying a piano. I hate not having one."

"They must be rather expensive?" she murmured, letting herself fall gently back into sleep.

"Oh, the parents will buy me one, I'm sure. They know I need it." As he snuggled down under the duvet, he murmured meditatively, "Alison said I could go over and play hers whenever I wanted to practise." There was something about the way he said it.

Mmm, I bet she did, thought Jess. But Simon reached over and pulled her to him.

Jess stared at her pills in their foil strip, each labelled with the day of the week. She may as well throw them down the loo. She hadn't taken any for a long time. Simon didn't know that she still had some in her drawer. Just in case. She didn't know what the 'case' may be, especially as he had made it absolutely clear that he didn't want her to stay at her job next academic year, with any commitments. He was determined that she should just take up some supply teaching on the assumption that she would get pregnant very soon. But that hadn't happened. Now that they were trying, she felt herself obsessed with becoming pregnant.

He was desperate to have children. He told every-one he wanted four daughters. As an only child him-self he was determined that wouldn't happen to his own children; they would have companions, playmates surrounding them. He was so enthusiastic about their future family life which would be so different from his own, with parents spending time with their children as his own had not done, that she felt pleased and relieved that he seemed so settled now, after a stormy start. The early days of their marriage she suppressed, marking it down as the uncertainties of a young man facing the realities of a different grown-up life. Even though he had wanted it so much, she knew that it must have up-rooted him somehow. She could understand that.

Jess looked in the bathroom mirror. The face that stared at her was pale, her eyes wide and dark, her lips drained of colour. She had woken up that morning with harsh cramps in her stomach and a wetness in her groin. She ran to the bathroom and sat on the loo, bending double with the pain in her abdomen. She felt the blood gush out of her and the room swim. Another month, then.

She heard Simon playing jazz downstairs on his new piano, singing loudly … '*my mojo working*' … She was suddenly transported to an African school hall in stifling heat, aware of the sweat running rivulets down her back as she listened to a wild rendition of Great Balls of Fire that somehow, amazingly, almost seamlessly, mutated into a gentle Chopin nocturne. Jim.

Suddenly she was gripped again with a violent pain in her lower stomach. Blood. A large clot that slipped into the toilet bowl. This was not what she usually had each month, although she had missed one, but sometimes that happened. She felt dreadful: nauseous and dizzy, the room juddering. When the attack subsided she crawled back to bed and called for Simon. It was a while before he heard her above the piano, but when he paused she yelled again. "Please, please come!"

Simon touched her forehead. "God, you're burning up. I'd better call the doctor." He looked frightened.

"Would you ring my mother as well? I don't think this is going to be a quick thing – I can't even stand up!"

Her mother arrived before the doctor. She bustled up the stairs to Jess's bedroom and in one sweep of her eyes took in Jess's face and, on the bedside table, the container filled with the sample the doctor had asked to be ready for his visit.

"Oh, Jessamy!" Her mother sank onto the end of Jess's bed. "It's a miscarriage?"

Jess felt a bolt of electricity jar through her body as she lay propped up on pillows. "No, no. It's just a bad period. I get them sometimes."

Her mother shook her head. "I don't think so."

When the doctor confirmed the diagnosis, Simon sobbed and her mother hugged him. Jess stared up at the ceiling. All this time and then … *this*. For so long she had watched, enviously, mothers with their babies, had seen them chatting together as they strolled in to the village clinic pushing their prams, had wondered, prayed. Polly had married Matt and quickly found herself pregnant, rather more quickly than she had anticipated, but thrilled at her new status. Jess had watched her gently stroking her small bump, smiling so Madonna-like, a secret soft smile, Matt grinning in delighted wonder.

Dr Jones perched on the end of Jess's hospital bed and said, "I'm so sorry. It was a boy."

He held Jess's hand but she knew she wouldn't cry; she felt numb – apart from the awful soreness from the process and the D and C. She felt as though someone had scraped all her insides out with a sharp spoon. God, would she ever be OK again? Would she ever be able to stand up again? Even though it was early days, and she wasn't even aware that she was pregnant, she felt grief; she'd lost a baby, a potential real person. Tears spilled down her cheeks. What might have been.

"What you have to remember is that these things often happen precisely because the foetus is not viable." She looked blankly at him with his kindly face. "In other words, it is more than likely that the foetus had some serious malfunctioning. A disability. Or a chronic weakness." Her heart sank. "It doesn't mean that it would inevitably happen again, the next time, but it would be sensible to get checked out when you're recovered. And your husband too."

Jess wondered dizzily if Simon's withered testicle was a cause, of both the inability to conceive and this miscarriage. She supposed that it was possible they were connected.

"Thank you, doctor, for getting me here so quickly."

"It's my job." Dr Jones shrugged and smiled.

"But coming back and checking out the details for me was over and above. I'm grateful. I don't want to – I can't – go through this again." She wriggled up on her pillow, so that she was half-sitting upright. She hated being in bed. She hated being ill, 'indisposed', or whatever it was that had happened to her. She had things to do.

"No, of course not. Listen, Jess, let's just get you checked out. But I think it would be best to have your husband's status investigated first, before we do anything else. It's a great deal easier to deal with that than the procedure for the woman, which is much more complex. It's a question of ruling out other possibilities first, starting with the easiest, most straightforward procedures."

"So, what are you thinking, doctor?"

"If there is a problem with low fertility on your husband's part, low sperm count or a malformation, then if we can identify that we wouldn't have to put you through a much more unpleasant procedure."

"And could that be a cause of miscarriage?"

"It is possible. And if so, we may be able to remedy it, depending on the situation and prognosis. Let's try to rule out the easiest obstacles first."

"So, are you saying that it may not be possible to remedy it?"

Dr Jones looked Jess in the eye. "That is a possibility. But let's not jump the gun." He patted her arm. "Get some rest. Is your husband coming to see you?"

"Yes. He'll come after work."

Dr Jones's expression was unfathomable as he turned away. "Well, they'll take good care of you here. You'll be back home in no time. Look after yourself, Jess."

Jess begged Simon to have the test. He stubbornly shook his head. "It's not *me*," he claimed.

"Please, Simon. If it is your low sperm count we can look at what could be done. The doctor explained that it's easier to rule that out, though, before I submit to a much more unpleasant procedure. It's just providing a sample; it's not an operation as it will be for me."

"God, but it's embarrassing! I can't go to a clinic and … and do it … into a jar … for God's sake, am I supposed to leer over pornography, or something?"

"I have no idea. But lots of chaps have to have it done. It's just a sample. I'm sure it's all very discreet. I mean, you don't have to go to some iffy clinic, just the fertility section at the hospital."

"*You've* probably got some hereditary impairment. It's probably in the genes."

"Simon, your parents are the ones who only had one child, so that would be just as likely to apply to your family as mine. Anyway, it really doesn't matter. The point is we need to get to the bottom of this. If we deal with it now, we still have the chance of having a family. I thought that was what you wanted?"

"Yes, I do. More than anything. Let me think about it. I have to get used to the idea."

Jess wondered what was the big deal but held her tongue; he clearly had a problem with the idea that there could be something wrong with his sperm count, with him. It really didn't matter to her. If all was OK his end then she would deal with the consequences of an operation to investigate herself and then hopefully an op to rectify matters. She felt very matter-of-fact about it all, somehow; all her sharp emotions had deadened with the aftermath of the miscarriage. She had been horribly weepy when she first came home from hospital but now just wanted to get on with life, with the practicalities of whatever they needed to do in order to have the family they longed for.

A few days later Simon said, "OK. I'll see the doc about the test." He wrapped his arms around her and stroked her head. "We'll do what we have to do." He kissed her gently. "I don't want you to have an operation, so let's hope it doesn't come to that."

It didn't, because the results arrived within a week: his count was 8.4 million. The letter explained that a lower than normal diagnosis would be anything under 15 million per millilitre so it was well below. It said that although it wasn't a case of "azoospermia", which was the complete absence of sperm, it certainly was "oligospermia". The letter also advised an operation to investigate and treat the "varicocele (varicosed testicle)" as this was considered a possible cause.

"So it says you need to go for a minor op, as a day patient. Ooof! Well, it's moving things along."

"Oh, god! What does that entail?" Simon sat with his elbows on his knees and his face in his hands, the letter hanging limply from his fingers. "So a young nurse has to shave me … there and … well … handle me. God, Jess, what if I get … a reaction? How embarrassing!"

Jess couldn't help laughing. "Do you know, I bet they've seen it all before. It'll all be very clinical and officious. I don't think the atmosphere will exactly encourage excitement!"

"I don't know." Simon looked up and grinned sheepishly. "I've always found nurses rather sexy in their uniforms."

Jess reached behind her for a cushion and threw it across the room, laughing, at Simon. "Oh, for god's sake!"

Simon's operation was booked in an unusually short time scale. Jess took him in to the outpatients' department and wandered around town until it was time to collect him again. He was sitting waiting for her in the waiting room of the ward.

"How did it go?"

"Oh, OK," he grimaced. "Just a local anaesthetic. I've got to come back in a couple of weeks' time to have another test so that they can see if it's made a difference. But the surgeon said he thought it would, so I guess it's hopeful."

Jess sat down beside him and slipped her arm around him. "I'm sure it'll be fine."

"Well, we'll see."

"And how about the nurses?"

"Frankly I was so nervous about what was going to happen in the op, I think I already lost all sensation. Or maybe the pre-op stuff they gave me deadened me. Anyway, nothing untoward … at least I don't think so. I was in happy land for most of the time."

Jess smiled. "What I meant was, were they gentle and kind? Did they look after you well?"

Simon stared at the letter from the hospital without speaking. Jess poured him a glass of wine, but with a heavy heart. Her hands trembled and she watched the red stain spreading on the counter top.

"Well, that's that, then," he said, throwing the letter onto the counter. He took his glass into the sitting room and Jess followed him.

"OK, so the operation didn't make a difference to the count."

"It didn't make a bloody bit of difference."

"It's reduced the varicosity to minimal. So you must feel better about that, surely?"

"But I still can't father children, Jess, that's the point!"

Jess bit her lip and knelt down at his feet, stroking his leg. "We'll just have to investigate adoption. It'll be fine. I'm really OK about that. What do you think?"

"I think we don't have much bloody choice!"

"Well," said Jess, reaching up and gently kissing his cheek. "Let's think about it for a bit. No need to make any decisions yet."

"We're going to adopt. We really want kids, to be a family. We've had an appointment with the adoption society and they've accepted us." Jess explained the process to Polly and Matt. She hadn't seen them for some weeks now, what with supply work and Polly having decided to take maternity leave early. They had come over to visit her while Simon was out, which seemed the best thing to do these days. He was not handling it all very well, and certainly seemed to find Polly's condition a reason for being bad tempered, if not actually rude.

Polly smoothed her hand over her expanding belly and looked up at Jess. "I'm so sorry." Tears were in her eyes and she didn't even bother to brush them away.

"About the miscarriage. About Simon's infertility. About having to adopt ..."

"No, don't think of it as 'having to'." Jess patted Polly's knee. "It'll be fine. I've got used to the idea now. We'll be giving a baby, who's already been brought into the world, a home, a loving home. Another chance."

"But there's me having this one," she rubbed her tummy, "without even planning it. It just seems so unfair for you."

"Please don't think like that. Honestly, these things happen. Life happens."

"Oh, dear Jess. You're so calm and focused about all this. I don't know how you do it."

"We just have to wait now for an appropriate baby they think will suit us and start making us a family. They'll contact us when that happens and then we have to go down to London to meet the little one and hopefully say yes."

Polly looked over at Matt who was daringly sitting in 'Simon's chair' as Jess had shrugged and told them he wouldn't be back until later. She nodded to him and gestured with her hand 'go ahead'. Jess followed the look and gesture with interest; what was that about?

"Matt has something he wants to say to you."

"Okaaay ..." frowned Jess, as Matt leaned forward, resting his forearms on his knees. He looked at Jess and she couldn't read his expression.

"Polly and I have talked about this for a while now. And we are in total agreement."

"Goodness, what's this? I'm intrigued."

"We are all old friends and we want to do something to help you. I'm willing … I'm happy … to provide the wherewithal for you to have a child of your own." Matt raked his hand through his hair and ruffled it. Jess stared with her mouth agape. It took her a few minutes to take in what he had just said and to find a voice.

"Oh god, you two. I just … I don't know what to say … I …How …?"

Polly swung her arm around Jess's shoulders. "We really have talked about it extensively, looking at all the issues and problems. And the legal stuff. We are well aware of what it means. But we want … I want … you to have the wonderful feeling that I have now, bearing a child …" she rubbed her abdomen and smiled. "It's not, obviously, about making a baby together with Matt, in that sense, it's not about sex, god forbid. Matt just provides a sample; he's just a donor, like an organ donor. There's no involvement, no come-back, no parental claims …" She started talking about practicalities of turkey basters and how many people do it, and several people she knew who had done it successfully. And all the time, Jess felt that the words floated over her head. All she could think about was how kind and generous and loving the offer was.

She stood and moved in a dream over to Matt, slipping her arms around him and hugging him tightly. "You have no idea what this means to me," she said, tears spilling from her eyes. "But I couldn't possibly …"

"Wait," pleaded Polly, easing herself off the sofa and joining the group hug. "We want you to think about it. It is a big decision, we know that, but don't dismiss it straight away. Think it through. The offer's there."

"But what on earth would I say to Simon? How could I discuss it with him? He'd be mortified."

"Sometimes these things happen. One in a million chance. There's no need for him to know, surely? And who would know which one was the actual donor anyway? None of us would know!"

"Oh, goodness, I don't think I could possibly … I can't decide that on my own … what if …?"

"Jess, I don't think you could tell him. I know it's a moral dilemma, but the end result would be worth the silence. How could you share that with him? He's so … well, frankly … fragile, mentally, emotionally. But you're strong enough for two. I think you're going to have to make whatever decision you think is best for the two of you."

In February, Simon took a phone call. Jess heard him say, "yes, yes! Of course! Thank you." He came into the kitchen where Jess was preparing the evening meal. Jess turned to see Simon raise his fist in the air in triumph. "Yes!" he shouted.

"What's happened?" Jess leaned against the counter. She had been feeling a little odd for a few weeks and was trying to fend off the bout of flu she knew was creeping up on her.

"That was the adoption agency. They want us to go down to London a week on Saturday to meet a baby. They think they've got one that would be suitable for us." He opened his arms and hugged Jess tightly. She felt herself suffuse with excitement as they laughed delightedly together.

"It's really happening! I can't believe it! Wow!"

"We'll be a family at last! It's wonderful! You'll have to get those Mothercare brochures out again and see what's needed."

She had found so many sweet little clothes and lovely equipment that she would like for her baby. She'd turned down the corners of so many pages in the brochure to mark possible purchases. She'd imagined cuddling her baby in a pretty little pink dress or pale blue romper.

"Did she say anything about the baby? Age? Sex?"

"A little girl, six weeks old."

"Oh goodness, and do we take her home with us if everything is OK?"

"It appears so."

"Oh, we'll have to buy stuff – a cot, a pram, clothes, nappies – oh goodness we'd better get started."

Jess's mind started to rev into overdrive. She had saved up some money for equipment and essentials.

Her mother had said that they would buy the cot and Simon's parents had offered a pram … she felt dizzy with the amount she needed to plan and do so quickly. All that time of hoping and now it had happened so abruptly, it felt like hurtling towards a cliff edge at speed. It was all so thrilling the room seemed to shudder around her and her brain whirl away. She gasped for breath as her body felt suddenly weightless and as fragile as air.

She slithered down the kitchen unit to the floor. Then, blank …

"Jess! Jess!"

She heard his voice softly as on the wind, calling to her, and she struggled to open her eyes. Simon was kneeling down on the kitchen floor beside her. She felt like a crumpled paper thrown onto the tiles. She felt her head and rubbed her brow.

"You fainted," said Simon, gently stroking her cheek. "Let me help you up and into the living room. You need to lie down. Goodness, whatever happened then? Lean on me, that's it."

She struggled to her feet and Simon half-carried her in to the other room, to the safety of the sofa. "Oh dear, that was odd. I think it's flu."

She dosed herself up but still felt ill two days later and struggled to the doctor. She must be well enough to travel to London a week on Saturday.

"Is there anything I can take for this flu?" she asked Dr Jones after he had quizzed her about her symptoms.

He had requested that she take a sample ahead of the appointment and he stared at the container and the lab report on his desk.

"Well, young lady, I don't think flu remedies will fix it," he said gravely. "You appear to be pregnant."

"What!" Jess shook her head in disbelief.

"I do find it a great surprise, I must admit," the doctor frowned. "Your husband's test results were pretty conclusive."

Jess's hand fluttered to her mouth. She felt dizzy and sick, hot with sweat that trickled down her back inside her sweater. She didn't know what to think. Did this mean …? Who …? She fought to breathe normally. "So – how …? When?" she stammered.

Dr Jones peered at her over his half-moon glasses. "The 'how' I don't think I need to discuss with you. As for when … it looks like around eight weeks, so …" he tapped his calendar. "…end of August, beginning of September." He looked up at Jess and smiled. "Plenty of time to make arrangements."

"Oh, good heavens. We're due to go to London next week to meet a baby up for adoption."

"I don't recommend that, not just at the moment!" Dr Jones smiled again. "Well done. Congratulations. Against all the odds." He inclined his head quizzically. Jess just shook her head in wonder.

"God works in a mysterious way, and all that," she said, smoothing her skirt over her knees. "Well, what exciting news! So what happens now?"

"Brilliant!" shouted Simon as he swung her round the living room. "Fantastic news! Our own child! I can hardly believe it."

Jess laughed. "For god's sake, Simon, let me go, I'm getting dizzy!"

He gently lowered her onto the sofa and sat beside her, his arm around her neck. "And what timing!"

"I know. I rang the adoption agency to explain and they said it sometimes happens like that. Odd. But they were very understanding and kind."

Jess felt as though she were in a dream for the next few weeks. She found herself relishing signs of her pregnancy, even the morning sickness, the inability to eat anything but dry bread for breakfast, the avoidance of cooking anything remotely spicy that made her feel so nauseous. It was all worth it because it meant she was carrying a new little life within her.

She gently stroked her abdomen and chatted to her baby as she went about her activities, and as time moved on, when she rested she played music on the stereo, Mozart and Vivaldi, which she had read were soothing and comforting for the child growing and developing in the warmth and security of her womb. She shopped for equipment and went to the prenatal clinic in the village and had coffee and baby-chats with the other expectant mothers she met there. She ignored Simon's odd comments about her being obsessive about the baby. Of course she was! So were all the others.

Her mother had given her a book with amazing photographs of a developing foetus and she poured over it to see what stage her baby would be at as the weeks passed.

"Just look at this!" she held the book out to Simon one evening. "This is what the baby is like now. Look! You can see the arms and legs and the facial features! Isn't that amazing?"

Simon glanced briefly at the book and said, "Jess, the parents are buying me a boat for my birthday and …"

"A boat?" Jess looked up from the book and laid it down on her lap. "What kind of boat? Why?"

"Because I need something to take my mind off … all this."

"All what?" She registered the look in his eye. "You mean the baby? Our baby?"

"Well, you're buying all this equipment and stuff for the baby so I think I can get something for myself," he said and Jess heard the defensive tone with alarm.

"I am buying the baby's things myself from the money I saved from working," countered Jess. "It's not even our joint money. And our parents have bought the cot and pram."

"You're getting very absorbed with all this baby stuff," Simon grumbled. He rose from the sofa beside Jess and began to pace the room. A bad sign that made Jess's heart pound in her chest. "I mean, it's not exactly unique. Everyone has babies – even when they don't want one." He stopped in the middle of the room and stared at Jess. "What about me? I need attention too."

Jess tried to still her trembling. "So what attention do you want that I'm not giving you at the moment? I thought I was …what about the marking I helped you with the other day? And the lesson prep I actually did for you? I try to cook you meals you like, try to be with you when you get back from work, talk about your day …"

"That's not what I'm talking about!"

"So what are you talking about then? We don't go out together any more. You said you don't like me, quote, 'lumping around', or being seen with a 'beached whale'. Well, this 'beached whale' 'lumps' around trying to be attractive and sexy for you, trying to stir you in bed at night. What on earth more do you want?"

"If you don't know …" Simon turned away and towards the door.

"No, I don't! Tell me! What do you want of me?"

Simon glared at her for a moment and then walked out, slamming the door. For a moment she felt a sinking sensation of déja vu … *a door slamming, Simon leaving, herself prostrate in her parents' sitting room, injured foot propped up on the upholstered stool, thin blue Ghanaian airmail letter in her hand … drumbeats echoing on the still frightened air …*

She wished to god she knew what he wanted, why he swerved so violently from elation to despair, why he seemed to take it out on her. She sank her head onto her hands and cried, bitter tears stinging her eyes.

Yet she knew that when he finally returned he would, as usual, beg her forgiveness. And of course she would soothe him, like a mother kissing her hurt child better.

"It's a good day for sailing!" called Simon. "What about you come with me?"

"Sailing your dinghy? I've never sailed before. And in my condition? Will it be OK?"

"Of course!" Simon gathered her up into his arms. "Come with me! We never go out these days! You never come sailing with me!"

"If I wasn't nearly five months pregnant I would, like a shot. But I don't want the boom swinging over and knocking me into the water. I'd never be able to heave myself out!" she laughed. "And I can't jump quickly across the boat to turn about, you know."

Simon put her down and smiled. "Honestly, it'll be fine. I'm an expert sailor now, you know!"

"Hmm," Jess teased, pummelling him on the chest. "That's not what I hear!" He grimaced. "Come on, Simon, I'm just kidding!"

The day started bright and clear, although cold, a lovely spring morning, the water of the lake glinting in the sunlight, the trees around the boathouse of the sailing club verdant with newly budding leaves. There were a couple of men in the boathouse but it was quiet and calm on the water, only one other dinghy out under sail. Jess was a little wobbly with her new centre of gravity but she found she could manage the boat well under Simon's instructions. She watched Simon, intense and commanding at the rudder, staring ahead.

But after a while, she noticed his hands shaking as the sun disappeared behind a dark cloud and the light began to dim.

"Turn about, I said!" shouted Simon. She started and refocused. They tacked successfully and set a straight course towards the boathouse. Jess shivered. It was becoming bitterly cold and her hands were numb. The wind on the water was chilling.

She looked up to the sky and shuddered with apprehension. It seemed grey, and full. Rain? Hail? Or snow?

"Watch out!" yelled Simon as he appeared to fumble with the rudder and the sail boom swung violently towards her.

Before she could realise what was happening, Simon had lost control and the boat was tipping in slow but inexorable motion. Jess slipped and felt herself thrown out of the dinghy, into icy cold water. As she fell, she felt snowflakes scattering upon her helpless body. She heard herself scream but lost her breath as she went under. Rising again to the surface, but shoved and tossed by the choppy water, she gasped for breath and her only thought was, where was Simon. Her safety jacket helped her to bob up and grasp hold of the dinghy hull. She knew that it had capsized, and was completely upturned, but floating. To her relief, she heard Simon calling her from the far side of the hull.

"I'm here! I'm OK!" she gasped. Simon trod water around the boat to her, one hand on the hull, and looked desperately around for help. "There's a boat over there!" She nodded towards the west, and Simon swung round.

"Hey! Hey!" he shouted. "Over here! Help!"

The chap in the other dinghy had clearly seen their plight already and was on his way, expertly navigating his boat across the water towards them.

"What the hell were you doing?" he said to Simon as he approached. "There's hardly any wind. How did you manage to capsize?"

"Just get my wife aboard," said Simon. "For god's sake, she's pregnant."

The rescuer stared at Simon for a moment, then shook his head and reached his hand out towards Jess. "Can you manage?" he asked kindly. "Grab my hand and I'll pull you aboard. I'm sorry, it may hurt." He settled Jess in his boat. "You hang on," he growled at Simon. "I'll be back for you; we're only yards from the jetty. It'll only take a couple of minutes to get your wife safe on shore. She's the priority, I think."

A couple of chaps, members of the boat club, Jess thought, were on the jetty ready to help her onto dry land and wrap her in a thick blanket. "Here you go, love. What *was* he thinking of? Taking a pregnant woman out on the water in this changeable weather. Didn't he look at the forecast?" They had hustled her into the boathouse and handed her a mug of steaming hot sweet tea by the time Simon walked in, dripping. Jess felt as though she had never tasted anything so good as that tea.

"Have you got a change of clothes in the car?" asked one of the men.

"Er, no," confessed Jess. "Oh dear, I'm sorry. I'm not really a sailor."

"I can tell that. But he ought to know better." He glared at Simon.

"Right. We'll be off home," said Simon abruptly and stalked out of the boathouse. Jess shrugged an apology at the men and said a quick but sincere thank you to them as she followed him out. At the car, Simon turned to her. "I don't think I can manage to drive home." He was shivering violently.

"It's OK, I'll drive." One of them had to, but she wondered how she would manage; she was soaking wet and so cold she felt numb. Her brain felt dead as well.

She tried to concentrate hard and for the first half of the journey she managed well, while Simon sat beside her, clutching himself and staring ahead, motionless. It was as they drove out of the next village to theirs that she lost focus for a moment and found herself drifting to the wrong side of the road.

"What the hell are you doing?" shouted Simon with sudden alert anger.

"Oh, god, sorry," Jess gasped and corrected her position. How had that happened? Had she blacked out? She drove the rest of the way with such caution, she felt that they were crawling along at ten miles an hour. Simon seemed to be stuck in complaint mode. She tried to ignore him, but was aware of her suppressed irritation and hurt.

Once home, her determined practicality took over and after she had taken a warm soothing aromatherapy bath and changed into dry clothes, she filled the kettle and made mugs of tea and hot scones. Simon shrugged off the hot bath but had a quick shower and pulled on clean clothes, then switched on the television and sat down on his armchair with a sigh.

"I always mess things up, don't I?" He looked up at her as she handed him a mug of tea.

She smiled. "Oh well, not to worry. We're both OK and back home safe and sound. And I felt the baby kick when I was in the bath! Perhaps he'll be a sailor. Or a swimmer!"

"At least the dinghy's OK. We managed to tow it back and haul it up on the bank."

7

RUBBER BULLETS

J ess spent the final trimester of her pregnancy as calmly as she could, aware that a safe gentle environment was the best for the baby. With no paid work to do, she spent her days making the home comfortable for Simon, helping him with the school work he seemed to find so arduous, and preparing for the coming baby. Housework, washing and ironing she tried to tackle while he was at work, since he didn't like her doing such things when he was around at weekends, but everything seemed to take twice as long as her bulk increased and she became tired more easily. At least, she had not had a repetition of her ME thankfully, so she paced herself and managed to rest in the afternoons, reading, listening to her beloved choral music, or watching Van der Valk on television.

That summer was hot and Jess's energy dissipated more as July came. She looked forward to Simon being on school holiday so that he could at last be with her, and perhaps help her a little more. He had been so engrossed in organising a school concert, she seemed to see him less and less as time went by.

She was settling herself for her afternoon rest when Polly arrived with her new baby.

"Hi, babes!" Polly swung her tiny son onto her shoulder and stepped in to Jess's hallway. "Oh, what a day. Little man here decided to reject any idea of sleep last night and, my god, am I exhausted! At his lordship's beck and call all morning. Can't even think straight!" She kissed Jess on the cheek. "And how are you, sweetie?"

"Just going to flop with my feet up if you don't mind. I'm at the stage where you can't get comfortable at night and anything you do means you have to snatch a nap."

"Oh, tell me about it!"

"But I'm beginning to wonder if it never ends?"

"Oh, babes. It's just today. Normally he's good as gold. And Matt is fantastic. So involved with little Thomas. He can't wait to get home from work and play with him. Loves his bath-time. Honestly, they're like two kids, not one! I hear them chuckling away upstairs, splashing and playing shipwreck!"

Jess wriggled to settle herself more comfortably in the armchair and giggled. "Could we ever have

foreseen what we'd be like, when all we had to bother about at uni was getting the next assignment done
and staggering with a hang-over to the lecture hall on
time?"

"And crying over break-ups," added Polly, laughing
and tickling Thomas so that he chuckled.

"Oh, I didn't have that!"

"No, you didn't – you had Simon." Polly lifted
Thomas up in front of her face which made him chor-
tle so hard it made him choke and gasp for breath. But
it covered her face from Jess. "And how is the lord and
master?"

"Simon? Oh, he's fine. Very busy at work. Looking
forward to the hols."

"Matt was able to take some time off around Tom's
birth. It really helped. But I guess you've timed this
well, with the school holidays coming up. I assume that
Simon will be around?"

"Oh gosh, yes," said Jess. "I'm sure he will."

But he wasn't. Jess found herself still taking charge
of the chores. At eight months pregnant, mowing the
steep lawn was not a good move. But Jess didn't want to
leave it, knowing that she'd still have to do it after the
baby was born. Simon resisted any gardening.

That was, the doctor believed, the reason for her
collapse. He ordered her to bed with high blood pressure. She was only allowed up to attend the hospital
clinic. Jess had told him that Simon would drive her,

but in the event he wanted to go sailing that day; the weather was too good to miss and he hadn't been for a couple of weeks.

"Your blood pressure is far too high. Borderline dangerous," the hospital consultant told her severely. "You must rest. Otherwise you could lose this baby. You're suffering from toxaemia, related to preeclampsia."

Jess felt shaky. "So what exactly does that mean?"

"It can affect the kidneys and cause birthing problems, possibly premature birth. At worst it can, and I'll be frank with you because you must know the dangers, it can cause the death of mother and child."

Jess gasped. She wished Simon was with her. He was out on his boat with a friend. She'd come alone on the bus. "Oh my god."

"Do you have a husband or partner?"

"Yes."

"Is he here in the waiting room?"

"No."

"I would prefer that you are admitted into hospital for the last month where you will have complete rest. We can then monitor you and the baby. I must warn you that it's likely that we will induce the baby early or at term date, depending on the condition you and it are in."

"Oh, please, no," protested Jess, feeling herself sweat. "I would rather be at home, in comfort and quiet." The thought of being in hospital for a whole month was too much to bear.

The consultant sucked the end of his pen for a few moments, and considered the notes in front of him. "Well, I know your GP, Dr Jones, and can be assured that he will keep a strict eye on you. I'll send him a report. I need to be certain that you will not move out of bed except to go to the bathroom." Jess smiled. "I mean it. We will monitor you and if there is any worsening you will have to be admitted."

"Right. I understand. But I know I'll be better at home, even confined to bed for the duration. Please, let me do that."

"Then we need to arrange an ambulance to take you home. You're in no condition to travel home alone." He bustled out of the consulting room and she could hear him talking urgently to a nurse.

Oh, god, why did these things keep happening to her? If only she could convince Simon that he needed to behave like an adult with responsibilities. That she needed him sometimes; it couldn't always be the other way round. Why didn't he listen? She didn't want to 'mother' him; he was a grown man, for goodness sake.

"You are an angel," smiled Jess, as Polly helped to prop her up on her pillows, and set the tray of lunch on her lap.

"I wanted to bring you a glass of wine but I gather that's not allowed, babes!" Polly placed the tumbler of water carefully on the bedside table.

"Where's little Tom?"

"Down in the hall in his baby seat. He's fine."

"Oh, Polly, you shouldn't have to do all this!" tears came to Jess's eyes. Oh why was she feeling so emotional at the moment? When someone was being *kind* to her?

Polly shrugged. "I couldn't leave you alone with no company and no lunch while Simon was out sailing ... *playing with his new toy*," she added under her breath, but Jess heard it and was not inclined to argue or deny. After the capsize, his parents had been persuaded to buy him another, bigger, better, boat. "I'll just pop down and bring Tom up in his chair. He's probably asleep by now. The motion of the car was already making him drowsy!"

They chatted while the baby slept contentedly. Polly was concerned about being away on holiday for a week soon. "I don't like to leave you. What will you do? How will you manage?"

"I'll be fine. I'll think of something Simon can leave for me for lunch before he goes out in the mornings ..."

"Oh, Jess, you can't be all day without anyone here with you. What if something happened?"

"Nothing will happen, Poll, I'm sure. I'll just stay in bed and read. Frankly the drugs I'm having to take are making me so sleepy that most of the time I just doze off."

"And he'll be here to take you to your hospital checks?"

"Yes, yes, I'm sure he will."

Polly gave Jess a doubtful look and grimaced. "Matt says he doesn't appreciate you as he should."

Jess shrugged as she finished her hot shepherd's pie that Polly had brought and reheated in Jess's oven. "In his own way, I'm sure he does. It's just that he is different from other people. Emotionally … psychologically… Sometimes bells ring. It reminds me of someone I knew in Ghana. She had difficulties relating to other people."

"Is it like Asperger's?"

"No, it's more inconsistent; there are extreme ups and downs. And of course he's charming to other people so most don't have any idea. It's only really when he's just with me that something triggers it off. Nobody else can see it."

"Well, we do, Matt and I. We've been on the receiving end."

"I know."

"He's impossible, Jess!"

"Yes, I know, but … I love him. And he's my husband, impossible or not. In sickness and in health, and all that!"

"Well," Polly sighed. "Let's talk about good things. You need comfort and serenity!"

"I certainly do!"

"So have you got the nursery ready? Let me go and take a look!" Polly returned in a moment and shook her head. "Jess, there's a cot in the middle of the spare room, with the twin beds pushed up against the walls?"

"Yes, I know. Well, Simon won't have the spare room taken over for a baby's room. He wants to keep everything the same … in case of visitors." She raised her hand towards Polly. "I know, I know, we've had our arguments about it, but he won't budge."

"Jess," Polly sat down hard on the end of the bed. "He has to accommodate the baby; things won't go on as before. He wants a child but not for anything to change his life. It can't be done!"

"I know." Jess grimaced. "I'm in a bit of a pickle. But please let's drop it. Let's talk about something else!"

Polly sighed.

They chatted and laughed about silly things they shared until Jess was clearly flagging. Polly tidied up and kissed Jess goodbye. "Are you sure you'll be OK?"

"Yes, I'm fine. Simon will be back in an hour or two. I'll have a nap … goodness, I'm so sleepy …"

Jess was taken back into hospital just before term date. Dr Jones had told her that they simply could not leave her any longer; it was becoming dangerous for her and for her baby. The birth would have to be induced.

She let herself go into the hands of the specialists and felt a great relief overcoming her fear of the birth. She knew that she was drugged up almost to capacity, that she was in an induced coma-like state. But she felt euphoric, dreamlike. It was as though she was drift-ing on the breeze. At one point she was aware that she was somehow on a hospital trolley being pushed, very speedily it seemed (*were they running?*), down a long, endless corridor, ceiling lights flashing by as she travelled helter skelter. *Flash, flash, flash* … Someone navigating the drip at her side, keeping close to the catheter in her wrist.

Lifted onto another operating table. Legs pulled up. Simon dabbing her head with a wet flannel. Or was it a nurse? Two surgeons in masks. Nurses fussing around her. Tubes attached to her. A machine at her side emitting strange bleeps. Red lights pinging from it. An excruciatingly bright glaring light over her. She wanted to say switch it off, but no words came. People talking over her, telling her when to push.

Voices agitated. She felt the anxiety. People dis-cussing her over her prone body. Probing, weird sensa-tions. Drifting in and out. Sleep, I need to sleep. But the pain kept rising to a crescendo and then sinking again, like the drumbeats that were echoing through her mind, rising and falling in the still African night air.

Voices becoming urgent. "We're losing her!"

"Baby?"

"Also!"

"Roger!"

A face leaning over hers.

"Jess, can you hear me?"

"Mmm."

"We're going to have to use forceps. We have to get this baby out as quickly as we can. OK?"

"Mmm." *No, I don't want that* ... Push. A last desperate attempt. *It's not going to defeat me!*

Then suddenly a rush. Catching her breath. Pushing. The air around her changing. Busy-ness, but lighter.

"Here we go! Baby's crowning."

"Jess, baby's on his way!"

Jess registered the nurse gently wiping her brow with a cool cloth, and her heart filled with love for that nurse, *thank you, thank you.* "Pant, blow ..." A wail of discomfort, anger.

"It's a girl!"

"Oh she's beautiful! Pink and healthy! Here look."

Jess raised her head a little off the pillow. What she saw took her breath away. A perfect amazing baby girl. Hers. Hers ... and Simon's. Held out to her on a blanket, unwrapped. "Oh," she gasped. "Oh, she's so beautiful. I can't believe it!"

"I need to wrap her and weigh her. You'll have her back to cuddle in a moment. Nurse will clean you up and make you more comfortable."

"Work on Mother, please, nurse!"

"Temperature? Blood pressure?" Bustling around her again. Normal activity.

A deep voice from the end of the bed. "OK, job done. And well done, Jess. A few hairy moments there.

But all fine now. You've got a lovely little girl. Looks very healthy. Your body functions OK. Everything's stabilising. Good work, Jess."

"Thank you, doctor."

Her head felt a little clearer and she glanced around the room. Simon was leaning against the far wall, then on catching her eye he approached the bed. She felt his hot damp hand stroking her forehead. "We made it!" he breathed, bending down and kissing her cheek. "We've got a beautiful daughter! She's lovely."

The nurse brought the baby across and gently laid her on Jess's chest. Jess loosened the white hospital blanket to look at her daughter's perfection. She was indeed the most beautiful thing Jess had ever seen: smooth peachy skin, not chubby or thin, just right. Whispy dark hair covering the top of her head. Jess couldn't take her eyes off her. She stroked the little body, transmitting the overwhelming love she felt, through her fingertips to the little person she cuddled, as if telling her of the powerful unconditional love she would always hold in her heart for her daughter, her first child. She gazed and gazed at her in wonder. Now she knew what Polly knew, what her own mother knew.

"I'm making roast lamb for dinner," announced her mother. "I hope that's OK for you, Jessamy?"

"That's great, Mother. Roast – and on a weekday, too! I do appreciate all you're doing." Jess smiled up at her mother as she nursed little Katherine. She delighted in watching the tiny hands resting contentedly on the breast as she suckled, her eyes fixed on the face above her.

Her mother nodded approvingly, folding her arms over her pinafored bosom. "I'm very glad you decided to feed her yourself. Just like me. I don't like all this nonsense with bottles. It's a lot easier not to have to sterilise all the equipment. And you know baby's getting all the nourishment nature intended."

Jess recognised that her mother had become much more relaxed and somewhat less strict and stiff these days. Even though she was determined to make her beliefs known. And she was enormously grateful to her for coming up to stay with them for a few days to help out while Simon was at work confronting the new term at his school. She clearly wanted to be needed, and she adored the baby. While she was playing with Katherine she wasn't criticising Jess.

"I'll get some roast potatoes and vegetables done."

"Oh, that's lovely. I love your roasties."

"Par-boiled, tossed in the colander to rough up the edges, and in a roasting tray with goose fat. That's what you need to do, Jessamy." Her mother turned at the door and added, "I've made an apple pie. You need to keep your strength up, my dear."

"Thank you." Jess caressed her baby gently and sighed contentedly. She resumed her soft singing of *Morningtown Ride*.

She felt more and more that she lived in an enchanted world, a bubble of happiness with her baby. Just little Katy and her. Even the BBC news reports of the IRA bombings in Manchester and London barely registered with her. She had discussed it with Simon who had, for a while, spoken heatedly about the Bloody Sunday massacre back in January and the recent inquests. She had said, "It's ridiculous; this will never end. They've got to find a compromise" but Simon had shaken his head at her despairingly as though her words were naïve and stupid, so she had fallen silent as she had learned to do, and focused on the baby who didn't offer her conflict and argument.

But she couldn't stop Simon's agitation about Katy's night-time feeding. He hated being disturbed in the night, although it was hardly a disturbance since Jess got up as soon as she heard the baby crying for her feed, and breast-fed her in the other bedroom. Usually Simon barely woke up and was always snoring when she returned to their bed.

One night, though, Jess was feeling utterly exhausted. Katy had awoken three times already and Jess could hardly move. The thought of slipping out of bed and actually moving to the other room was more than she could bear.

"For god's sake, get up!" shouted Simon, pushing her. "I've woken up now, damn it!"

"OK, OK, I'm going," mumbled Jess as she willed her heavy body to move. Little Katy was still yelling her urgent demands as Jess stumbled on to the landing. She felt Simon behind her, pushing her out of the way. "What are you doing?"

"I have to do everything!" he snapped.

"*What*? Getting up in the night several times? Feeding the baby? I don't think so, Simon."

"I've got to go to bloody work in a few hours!"

She turned to him in the doorway of Katy's room. Suddenly he lashed out and punched her in her engorged milk-full breast. She doubled up in pain.

"What on earth …?"

Simon's face went pale. "Oh god, I didn't mean to do that. I don't know what came over me."

"Please, Simon, just go back to bed, for goodness sake."

Jess hobbled into Katy's room and shut the door behind her. She didn't even bother to be quiet now. How dare he? What was the matter with him?

In the morning, he let her sleep as Katy was quiet after her disturbed night. He came in to say goodbye when he was ready for work. He kissed her quickly on the cheek. "Sorry about last night," he said as he fled the room. She heard the front door slam. It seemed to shake the whole house.

As Katy grew more sturdy and settled, the power cuts started. Union disputes and a three-day week meant that many evenings were spent in candle-light, and with Jess cooking on a little camping gas device. She could manage stews with canned meat and vegetables all in one pot.

Her ingenuity became renowned.

"Well," she commented to Polly. "I had much worse in Ghana, so I can manage."

"I get take-aways from the pub. They've got their own generator. I wouldn't even know how to start doing what you're doing, rustling up a proper meal with no cooker."

"Oh, it's quite romantic, actually," smiled Jess. "Isn't it, little Katy-girl?" Katy gurgled and kicked her legs out in her baby seat set on the table where she could watch her mother's activities and engage in her commentaries. "We were reading *Frog and Toad are Friends* by candle-light last night, weren't we? And we're on to *Bread and Jam for Francis* tonight, aren't we, poppet?"

Polly laughed. "I love the way you talk to Katy and read to her, as though she understands. Matt does the same with Tom."

"Oh, she understands every word!"

It was barely eleven months after Katy's difficult birth that Jess was pregnant again. She woke one morning in late July with agonising stomach cramps and bleeding, and she knew this time with certainty that she was threatening to miscarry again.

"I'm glad your husband called me straight away," said Dr Jones. "I know how much you want this baby, and how desperate you are not to lose it, remembering that previous time. You must stay in bed for at least a couple of weeks and hopefully you'll stand a chance of keeping it."

He turned to Simon. "I'm sure I don't need to impress upon you how vital it is for Jess to stay as rested as she can. Could you take time off work or get someone to come to help? And Jess will need to be cared for." He peered over his specs at Simon, who nodded.

"Of course."

When he had shown the doctor out, Simon came back upstairs and Jess heard him go into the other bedroom and lift Katherine from her cot, chatting to her, in the same tone he had heard Jess use. He brought her in to Jess and lowered her on to the bed beside her. It warmed Jess's heart; he so rarely picked her up or cuddled her; he said that he didn't like holding babies.

"Hello, Katy-girl. How are you today, poppet?"

Katy clambered into her mother's arms and said, "Yes. Mama poorly," with a sad look in her eye. She reached up and sucked Jess's cheek in a baby kiss.

"I'm fine, sweetheart, but I've got to rest a bit for a very special reason. We're growing a little brother or sister for you in mummy's tummy. Won't that be great?" Katy nodded enthusiastically.

Under Jess's instructions, Simon brought Katy's clothes and skin wipes to the bed and then went to make baby porridge while Jess managed to wash and dress her.

"I've never done this before. I don't know what to do," he complained.

"Well, it's about time you did, isn't it?" said Jess more briskly than she intended. "I keep saying to you that you really need to know these things, just in case anything happened to me. Now we have that time." While Jess fed her daughter Simon telephoned Jess's mother to see if she could come up to help out.

"Yes, that's fine," he said as he hovered in the doorway. "They'll be here around lunchtime." He frowned at his watch. "I've rung school and told them I can't get in this morning but I'll be there for afternoon school. I'll have to go as soon as your mother gets here. I've got a meeting about next Easter's play after school so I'll be late. OK?" He turned and bounded downstairs before Jess had chance to reply.

Her mother proved a god-send when Jess's second baby was born. She came to stay with them a few days before due date and was there when Jess woke up one morning at eight o' clock and rushed to the bathroom.

"The waters have broken!" she called. Simon panicked while Jess's mother calmly bathed and dressed Katy and gave her breakfast, telling her funny stories about her new brother or sister.

Simon, under Jess's instructions, phoned the hospital for the ambulance, telling them that contractions were already four minutes apart, but when it hadn't arrived half an hour later, Jess said, "I think you'd better drive me to the hospital, Simon. I know we should wait for a sterile ambulance now the waters have broken, but I don't think I can wait. Ouch … Three minutes apart now. Better hurry." She grabbed her bag that was packed and ready and waddled down the stairs.

She waved Katy and her mother goodbye through the car window and Simon drove even faster than usual until Jess had to gasp, "Please slow down! It won't help to have an accident. And you're bumping me about terribly."

She reached out and patted his arm in a calming gesture but his hand was drumming the steering wheel agitatedly and he began shouting at any motorist who might potentially slow them down. Jess clutched her abdomen, pain searing through her body. She tried to practice the midwife's teaching, deep breathing and calming yoga breaths. The contractions were now a minute apart and Jess rehearsed what to do if the baby started to come at the roadside.

Simon wheeled the car into the main entrance of the maternity department and shouted for help. "Hey, hey, so what's the panic here?" asked a plump West African nurse appearing from behind the receptionist at the desk.

"I think the baby's about to arrive," explained Jess apologetically. The nurse patiently walked her to the ward. Far too slowly. Jess clenched her teeth. She was glad that she knew Simon was right there behind her.

"Baby won't come that quickly, honey," smiled the nurse. "Your first?"

"No, second, so I do know what I'm talking about. Waters broke an hour ago. This one's almost here. You need to get me to the delivery room … aagh! …right now!"

The nurse helped her on to the bed and patted her arm indulgently. "Ah'm sure you got time, Mother!" She bent to examine Jess but straightened up immediately. She turned and shouted, "This one to delivery! Fully dilated. Baby coming!"

She was barely on the delivery bed when the midwife said calmly, "Baby's crowning. Puff, puff, puff. Well done! No time for consultant." She chatted reassuringly normally as she worked at the business end. They might as well have been having a coffee together at the kitchen table. "Back in Ghana, we don't make any fuss with childbirth, y'know? All natural, honey-bun!"

"Oh," said Jess between breath-taking contractions. "I was in Ghana."

"Oh really?" The midwife stood up and back from the end of the bed. "Well, blow me down the stairs! When? Where?"

"Cape Coast. Oh, back in 1965, 1966."

"No, no! Really, really? I come from Accra. But I was at school in Cape Coast. Methodist boarding school called …"

"Oh, goodness. I taught there!" In between the ever increasing birth pains that each time threatened to consume Jess, they shared memories. But although Jess's mind flicked back, she was only too aware of the white sheeted room, the huge theatre lights above the bed, the shuffling of other nurses around her. At least she was compos mentis, which she hadn't been with Katy. Then she had been in the other-world nightmare of the vital life-saving drugs, thankfully barely aware of what was happening. This time her mind was clear and alert.

"OK, honey. One last push! Now stop."

Jess breathed in deeply. Soon she would have another little life to love.

"Here we go …wooh, you have a lovely little girl!"

Jess was aware that Simon was hovering somewhere in the room. Nobody had any time to ask him whether he wanted to stay; all focus was on the precipitous birth. Then she . focused back to reality and was aware that he was beside her. She smiled up at him. He kissed her on her head and said, "That's great. Another daughter! Just two more and we have our family complete!"

"Two more little girls?" the midwife looked up from her tasks at the bottom of the bed and smiled broadly. "Well, now, that's a proper family, honey."

Simon straightened himself up and squared his shoulders proudly. "Yes, that's what we want!" Jess felt less sure about that. But it had all been so quick this time that she had no earthquake after-shocks as she had with Katy and she could re-arrange herself with ease, push herself up, leaning back comfortably on the pillow to receive the blanket-wrapped bundle from the nurse. "Let me see her."

"One second, honey," sing-songed the nurse, "Just gotta check …"

Something in the way she spoke made Jess feel chills down her spine. There had been no baby cry. "What's wrong?"

She glanced up at Simon. He looked startled.

"Nuttin', nuttin', honeybun," sang the nurse. Two others had joined her and they muttered together. One hurried out of the delivery room and returned quickly with a doctor.

There was some activity at the sink and scales, and Jess heard the doctor whistling tunelessly through his teeth.

Oh god, her baby! Hers. And Simon's, she must remember.

Then at last a cry. At first a tentative whimper and then a full blown angry wail. Jess exhaled with relief. More murmurings at the examining table. Jess bit her lip. Simon started striding up and down the delivery room.

Then the tense atmosphere in the room changed and Jess dared to hope.

Finally the nurse brought the bundle over to Jess's waiting arms. "She's a li'l mite, only just over premature weight, but long – oh so long, like a thin sausage!" Then she bellowed with laughter at her own joke, large soft breasts shaking and bouncing. "Oh my, she's a cute one! She'll be so so tall!"

Jess looked down tenderly at her new daughter. To her she was perfect. Beautiful. She unwrapped her carefully and saw that all the limbs and fingers and toes were in place. The baby was red and thin and her skin had the look of uncooked chicken, wrinkled and as though the body had not filled it out quite enough. Her hair was dark and curly, her eyes were pale blue and bright, and she looked right up at Jess, stopping the crying and cocking her head to one side as if in curiosity to see what her mother was like. Jess knew that there was no focus in the eyes yet, but she smiled and whispered softly, "Yes, it's me, your mummy. You gave us a bit of a fright." The baby looked quizzically and then made a popping noise that Jess decided was a giggle. "My beautiful little girl."

"You wanna cuppa tea?" asked the nurse as she tidied the bedclothes back in the ward. Jess was still holding her baby close to her, letting the warmth of her body and her love envelop her daughter. She smiled at her baby's sleepy relaxed body, her beautiful little face.

"That sounds the most glorious suggestion I've ever had! I'm so parched dry like an arid desert."

The nurse chuckled. "Ah'm not surprised. Missed y' breakfast, I guess?"

"Yes, this little one came at a very inconvenient time, didn't she? Couldn't even wait for me to eat or get a drink."

"You wanna cuppa tea, too?" the nurse asked Simon as she plumped up the pillows behind Jess and tickled the baby under her chin. "Have a cuppa with y' lovely wife now you gotta new fam'ly, huh? Sit down a minute wid her?"

"Oh, no," Simon shook his head, taking a step backwards. "No, thank you. I've got to get to work." He turned to Jess and kissed her on the top of her head. "I'll be late tonight, so I'll probably miss visiting time. Got a rehearsal for the play. But see you later." Noticing Jess's startled expression, he added, "Your mother's with Katy and she said she'd try to get in for visiting."

"Oh." Jess watched him as he swept away and hurried off down the corridor.

"Here you go!" said the orderly brightly as she handed Jess a cup of tea and the nurse took the baby and settled her in the cot beside the bed. She straightened up and looked at Jess, gesturing with her head the disappearing figure of Simon.

"He always like that?"

WALKING IN THE RAIN

"No, no!" Jess protested a little too forcefully. "He's very busy at work at the moment, that's all." But in her heart she felt angry and abandoned and somehow ashamed.

"'Lo, mummy! I's here with mama!" Jess could hear muttering at the other end of the phone and knew that her mother was helping Katy. She could picture her mother sitting Katy on her knee in the hall, holding the receiver to her ear and mouth.

"Hello, sweetheart! And are you looking after granny?"

"Yes," came the little voice, very serious. "You in hop-it-all?"

"Yes, poppet, I'm in hospital. And do you know who is here with me?"

"Daddy?" the voice very grave.

Jess's heart lurched. "No, sweetie. But I have your little sister, Abigail. She's lying in her cot beside my bed and she is sleeping, but I think she's dreaming of being at home playing with you, her big sister!"

"Yes."

"Mother?" Jess called.

"Yes, Jessamy? Are you all right/"

"Fine. But Simon said you'd be coming over at visiting time because he couldn't and I'm just wondering how you will manage to do that when you're looking after Katy?"

"Don't worry. That friend of yours, Polly, came round and she said that she would sit with Katy while we come over to the hospital. I'll have put her to bed by then anyway. I don't know when Simon will be back."

"Oh, that's great. Please thank Polly very much from me."

"Of course. I'm dying to see little Abigail. It is a shame that Simon is working so hard."

Jess glanced down at baby Abigail as she handed the phone back to the nurse. Hmmm, working so hard? He was rehearsing a school play that he *knew* would be around the time the baby was due. Why had he agreed to it so readily? She gritted her teeth. Why was she so defensive of him? Protecting him? Making excuses.

But she loved him. Even with all his faults. That was what love meant. And commitment. And loyalty. And covering for him. And of course he had his own life, it couldn't all revolve around her and the children all the time, could it? He was the father of the family, for goodness sake. She would no sooner criticise him to other people as be unfaithful to him. No way. Of course she had to support him in all things. Even though at times he was difficult.

Jess was so tired she could hardly think straight. She mopped up baby Abi's projectile vomiting yet again.

Her beautiful little girl was clearly not getting the nourishment she should. She was breast feeding her every three hours but she had no idea how much was actually supporting her tiny body because most was ejected across the room. She just didn't seem to be able to keep anything down.

She had to time her visits to the shops for the groceries in the hour she had between the end of Abi's vomiting and the start of her next feed, and inevitably the next bout. It wasn't easy. She knew that her mother was worried; she was ringing her as often as she could, and came up at weekends to help. Jess managed her time so that she could not only give Katy the attention she needed, painting with her on the kitchen table, and reading her latest favourite story, and dancing together to their Play School record, but also somehow deal with the chores. Something had to give and she was just down to the essentials. But she was still worn out.

The health visitor and the village midwife continued to call in and they were on a regime of weekly visits to the clinic to check Abi's weight and measurements. Neither were following the normal curve. At the hospital the doctors had seemed puzzled.

"We can't find anything clearly wrong," explained the consultant. "Vital signs are more or less within the normal range. It's her lack of growth and physical development that we are investigating. Mental development seems fine; in fact, she appears to be, even at this stage, particularly bright intellectually."

"But the projectile vomiting is at almost every feed."

"I know how distressing this must be for you. But basically this has to come down to a case of pyloric stenosis. This is when the muscles of the upper stomach … here …" He indicated by gently touching Abi's tummy as she lay gurgling on the hospital bed, "… contract to prevent food reaching the stomach itself. It's almost like an automatic reaction."

"Like Pavlovian response?"

"Yes, in a way. A spontaneous rejection of 'hostile matter' within the body."

"So can anything be done?" Jess turned to check on Katy who was pretending to read *The Very Hungry Caterpillar* to her doll on the floor across the consulting room. She knew it off by heart by now. Jess wished she didn't have to bring her to this hospital environment but she had no choice. There was nobody to look after her at home. Simon wouldn't take the time off work (she didn't understand why, since he seemed hate it so much) and she could hardly ask her mother to drop everything to come a hundred and fifty miles to look after Katy for a couple of hours. It wouldn't be fair; she had already helped so much. And Simon's parents had made it clear that they didn't like to be around illness.

"What we normally advise," said the consultant, "is surgery but not until three or four months. We need to keep an eye on her growth on a weekly basis. Your health visitor can do that. But I will need to see you in four weeks. We'll review the situation each month. If surgery is not needed, we will still need to keep a check on development for at least a couple of years until it's settled." He glanced at Jess and smiled sympathetically at her frowns. "I know it's hard for you, and very worrying that we can't provide a label for this. I know it seems inconclusive but I'm afraid that's all I can say. It's a case of wait and see … however difficult that may seem for you."

"Right. I see."

"My advice just now, would be to try, if you can, to keep things as normal as possible." He looked kindly at Jess's anxious face. "After all, it may be that no intervention is needed."

As Jess gathered up Abi and Katy and all their belongings, with the attendant nurse's help, the surgeon watched her.

"You're a brave and capable mother," he said. He waved his hand at the scenario of Jess with her hands full. "May I ask if there is a husband?"

Jess left the hospital with a heavy heart.

"Of course we don't need a new car, Jess." Simon looked up from his newspaper. Jess was sprawled on the floor playing with her daughters. He leaned forward in his armchair. "That's just being materialistic. Keeping up with other people. Wanting a bigger car because other people have big cars. And you know how I hate that. It's small-minded. Bourgeois. Very *bourgeois*."

Jess hopped the toy rabbit across the mat and jumped it on to Abi's lap. She could sit up well now and had a straight back. But she was still very thin and her skin appeared almost transparent. Abi chuckled and flapped her arms up and down in delight. Katy pushed herself up and flung her arms around her little sister's neck. "Love you, lil Abi!" Jess smiled at Katy's sweet nature. Her heart filled with a love for her children that she could never measure or describe.

"It's not about anybody else, Simon. And it's not about a "new" car; it could be second-hand. It's about needing the space for the children's things. You know the amount of stuff we have to take when we go to visit your parents. Or anywhere, for that matter."

"Well that's not often enough to warrant a big car!"

"But on an everyday basis we have to lug around the collapsible pram, the baby seat, the …"

"For god's sake, Jess! We manage perfectly OK now!"

"No, Simon, *we* don't. You do, because you don't come with us when we have to get about with all the stuff."

"Oh, come on! How many times do you have to struggle?"

"Every time I take Abi to the clinic or the hospital for her check ups. You know that!"

"That's only … what?"

Jess sighed. "Twice a week at the moment to the clinic and once a month to the hospital."

"Why twice a week? I thought they'd decided she didn't need an operation!"

"They decided that the pyloric stenosis had settled and there's no longer projectile vomiting. But there's still the issue of growth patterns. I have told you. Several times. She'll be going for check-ups for a couple of years at least."

"I'm sure you can manage that. The person who copes so well!"

Jess glanced at Simon, but she wasn't sure whether he was being sarcastic there. "And then there's the supermarket shopping and …"

"You're saying I don't help you?"

"Please, Simon, I don't want an argument. Certainly not in front of the children. But, yes, I'm saying you don't help as much as you think you do."

"God, he's so difficult. I wouldn't stand it if I were you. I'd tell him where to get off …"

"No, you wouldn't," said Jess, turning back to her hand-smocking she was adding to the little dresses she had made for the girls. There was no family budget for clothes for the girls or herself, so she either remade them from Simon's discarded shirts, where only the edges of the collar and cuffs had worn, or else saved up the family allowance and bought lengths of material from the market and made up the clothes herself. She bent to bite the thread off the end of the row. "And anyway, what would be the point of that? I don't want confrontation and anger. I never did. And certainly not with young children around. That means if he's confrontational, I don't meet like with like. Where does that get anyone?"

"But he's getting away with it."

"Well, not exactly. It generally works out in the end. Frankly, I just get on with it; there's no point in doing anything else. I don't want to get in a state. I don't want to make myself ill. My children are better off with a mother who can cope."

"But you cope and he relies on you. What you need … what every woman needs … is a real man."

"Well, he leans on me, yes. But, you know, the thing is … I married him, and I love him to bits … that's it. In the end, that's all there is."

Polly humphed but added. "I think you're a saint to put up with him."

"I love him," said Jess simply and shrugged.

It was drawing near to Christmas. Jess loved Christmas. Every passing year she thanked god for her little family, her lovely home, her loving, if unstable husband who had not had a real break-down for a long time now. For Katy's caring love of her sister; for Abi's growing stronger. She had been discharged from hospital some years ago, to Jess's great relief. Nothing concrete had ever been found. But Abi was doing well and that's all Jess needed to focus on. Live in the present.

Jess was kneeling on the floor in the living room, wrapping presents and sorting out the greetings cards. She had a part-time teaching job now so she could buy a few things, and part-time working meant that she could still juggle looking after the children, the home, and of course, Simon in his bouts of illness and depression. The Christmas carols LP was on the stereo and she was singing along with *Oh Holy Night*. The carol reminded her of some years before. Her mind drifted back to Ghana and the choir she belonged to; the carol concert that Christmas. *The feeling of wonder that Christmas Eve sleeping out in the moonlight on the edge of the nature reserve, hearing the calls of the ibis on the night air, the drumbeats of the nearby bush villages. Finding the beautiful gold pendant with the tiny kpanlogo drum hanging from it that Jim had bought for her.*

She loved buying presents, considering what surprises Simon and the children might enjoy. She would pay attention to what they were saying and she would somehow know what they would really love. Imagining their faces on Christmas morning. She smiled; they were always so delighted with her thoughtful choices. Simon didn't like buying Christmas – or any – presents. Or cards. He left all that to her. Even for his own parents and his paternal aunt. It always fell to her to include them in her Christmas list and to remember their birthdays and choose, and pay for, their gifts and cards. She didn't mind; it was something she enjoyed. But nevertheless, she was glad that he had no interest in his wider family, his cousins, aunts and uncles on his mother's side, as she didn't have to consider them too. And as he was an only child there was no other immediate family, apart from his father's sister, Simon's aunt, who always spent Christmas with them, as she was on her own.

Simon's parents had asked her what she would like for Christmas and she had said what was on her mind, without thinking, "Oh, earrings would be great! I've just had my ears pierced." Simon's mother had looked askance and recoiled from her. "Ugh, how disgusting. That's dirty. Tarty. Ugh. I can't stand pierced ears. How *could* you?" Nose in the air. Looking at her as though she were a distasteful smell. "With two daughters, as well!" Jess had swivelled round to see Katy and Abi with startled expressions. She was furious, but managed to say in a calm low voice, "Don't ever say that kind of thing in front of my children again. Don't ever disparage me like that!" And her mother-in-law had turned and left the room, without an apology.

She carefully wrapped the box that contained the computer for Katy and Abi. It was the new Sinclair Spectrum, only quite basic but it was all she could afford. Simon had argued with her about buying it for the girls.

"They don't need a computer, for heaven's sake, Jess!"

"They are starting to use them at school and it'll be good to practise at home. There are games so they can play on it too. I think they need to get started with this."

"Why? It's only a flash in the pan!"

"I personally don't think so, Simon. I think this is the next big thing of the future. They made them in the war, the enigma machine and all that, huge machines for code breaking that we're now hearing a bit about. But now they're developing these small home computers and I really think they are the future. I want the girls to be a part of that."

"They're girls! They won't want maths stuff. Neither of us did maths."

"Well, I could have done, actually, but I chose not to, as I enjoyed language and literature more. But being a girl is nothing to do with it. Why shouldn't they be into science and maths and computing if they want to?"

"I think it's ridiculous!" he huffed. "OK, if you want to buy them a computer you can, but don't think I'm paying for it!"

No, thought Jess, why should I think that? It would be a first, for heaven's sake!

So she had chosen the best she could afford. And additionally she had bought the girls something special for each of them so that they had something personal to unwrap too. A little pony set for Katy and some more scalextric for Abi to add to the set she had

bought her for her birthday. For Simon, she had se-
lected the CD player and radio to add to the Technics
stereo tower she had bought them both last year. It already had an LP player, cassette player, amplifier and
synthesiser, but the joy of the system, new to the UK
from Germany, was that you could add to it as you
could afford it. He had been talking about wanting the
CD player and radio for a while, maybe dropping hints
for Christmas.

Simon was in London again for the weekend and
the girls were out playing with their friends, so the
house was quiet. They would be home again soon for
lunch, probably along with several friends. She liked
the peace and quiet, but she also loved knowing that
the house would be filled with happy noises soon too.

Simon wouldn't be back until Sunday evening. He
had offered to serve on a national Quaker committee,
a post which had been difficult to fill as it involved a
weekend in London every month and sometimes more
frequently, so most young people with families were
unwilling to make that commitment, preferring to
spend their non-working time with their spouses and
children. Simon didn't think that way. She remembered how startled she had been when he told her that
was what he was going to do. It had started when she
was pregnant with Katy and, with a short break, had
continued ever since. He seemed to be the committee
Chair now, but frankly she knew little about what they

did; he rarely updated her when he returned or even seemed willing to discuss it at all.

Singing along with the *Coventry Carol*, Jess carefully tied the gold ribbon round the box for Simon's father, and wound the ends round in a rosette. She hoped that he would like his cashmere sweater that she'd saved up for. She had noted that he commented on it when they were shopping a few weeks ago. Her mother's present was easy to wrap; it was a season ticket for a series of plays at the theatre they enjoyed. She popped them into a gold envelope and attached a gold bow to the front.

Her mind drifted again:

Simon out one Saturday on his current toy, his motorbike, bought by his parents for his birthday. Jess beginning to worry as he had been out for hours and it would soon be dark. The telephone ringing. Oh god! Jess, heart thumping, running to answer it, closing the living room door on the girls, giggling, playing Barbie on treasure island, because if it was an accident she didn't want them to overhear before she composed herself. He often had accidents or breakdowns on his wretched motorbike and she was summoned to go to help him out, pick him up, transport the bike back home … Simon's voice … OK, not an accident, thank god … Jess, I've come across these people on the road, car broken down, no AA or RAC, need to wait for some friend to come and help … told them they should come to our house … you'll make them refreshments, look after them … OK?... for god's sake, Jess, it's about being a good Quaker … don't be silly, of course there's no problem with

*you and the girls being on your own … sighing … look, I'll be
back soon, just finishing my ride for today … Putting down
the receiver on the cradle, hand trembling. Very odd. What on
earth had come over him. Doorbell ringing … strangers on
the doorstep …*

The song on the LP changed to *The First Noel.* Jess
heard the front door open and the sound of happy
children's voices in the hall; it sounded like four of five
of them.

"Mum! Can Sarah, Jack and Cass stay for lunch,
please?"

"Of course, sweetie." Jess gathered up the presents
and hid them in a large sack, shoving them behind the
sofa. "I'll make some chicken sandwiches and I've defrosted the quiche I baked last weekend, so we'll have
that. There's a bowl of salad and some fresh fruit and …"

"Yogurts! Ice cream!" Katy and Abi choroused as
they opened the living room door.

"Sorry," Jess nodded to Sarah, Jack and Cass who
all tumbled in and landed on the bean bags. "Family
joke. The staples for dessert in this house!"

"I like coming here," said Jack seriously but with
a cheeky grin then spreading across his plump pink
cheeks. "Much better than home. You always have nice
things to eat!"

"Oh, thank you, Jack, but I happen to know that
your mum makes wonderful meals."

"Hmmm," said Jack bouncing on his bean bag.
"But it's all mushrooms and beansprouts and tofu …"

Jess had forgotten that they were going through a vegetarian, natural, yogi phase.

"I'm taking a year off work," announced Simon. "I've decided to do an MA fulltime for a year."

"Oh!" Jess, confused, mulled over this current news. "But they aren't allowing sabbaticals any more."

"No, but the parents have offered to pay the equivalent of my salary for the year while I do it."

Jess shook her head to try to absorb the new situation. Why hadn't he discussed it with her? Was he afraid that she'd argue? Say that it couldn't be done? That it was not right to expect that of his parents?

"And what about the fees?" was all she managed to splutter.

"And the fees and expenses." Simon enfolded her in his arms and kissed her head. After a moment in which Jess was computing the information, he added, "Jess, it'll be really good for my career. I need an MA. To get promotions."

"But you said you didn't want a promotion," Jess frowned into Simon's jacket.

I'm OK where I am, doing what I'm doing now, he had said, only a few months ago. *I don't want management responsibilities. All the issues of leadership. Sorting other people out, having staff under me, to have to train and look after. I'm happy where I am.* Jess hadn't thought he was, with all his grumbles every night. *And that's the most important thing. That's the only thing that matters, really. My happiness.* Shocked Jess had stuttered, *And the children's happiness? Isn't that the most important thing to you? Because it is to me. And yours too of course.* Simon had stared at her quizzically, *Well, there you are, then, my happiness is the most important thing to you too.*

That's not quite what I meant, thought Jess.

He let her go and sat down again at the dining table where he was working on the Sinclair Spectrum. "This damned thing!" he rattled it, picking at the brown sticky tape he had fixed to it where he had "adjusted it" for his purposes. The girls had given up on it, having asked him several times if they could have it back; *it's ours; mum bought it for us for Christmas...* "I'm going to get a new computer, for my MA work. The parents have offered to buy me a new one as this one's useless now." He looked up at Jess.

"So what about the children's computer?" Jess closed her eyes.

"I'll give them this one back. It'll be OK enough for their purposes." He lowered his head back to the Spectrum, cutting her out.

"Our song," smiled Simon as he brought in two glasses of wine and handed one to her across her marking that she needed to finish that night for her part-time teaching job. She smiled. Queen's *Te O Torriatte* from *A Day at the Races* was playing on the Technics system. Simon had dubbed it "our song" because it was about clinging together as the years went by and candles ever burning. That's us, he often said to her, when his mood was high: "let us never lose the lessons we have learned …" How lovely, she always thought when he said that to her; it made her feel safe and secure. Yes, they had had their difficulties, their rough rides, like everyone else. But through it all they were, after all, best friends, and they took their marriage vows seriously; they were inviolable.

She listened for a moment to the beautiful Japanese words she knew so well by now, with Simon playing it over and over as if it reinforced his feeling of security in their marriage: *te o torriatte kono mama iko, aisuru hito yo* …" It reminded her of her Japanese penfriend who had sent her a delicately detailed costume doll that she still kept. She loved having penfriends as a teenager: Genevieve her French friend with whom she spent holidays in Pontarlier, Sherrie her friend in Michigan, Anna in Russia … she'd certainly learned many lessons from them, about other countries, other cultures. That had influenced her decision to go off to Ghana for a gap year, a yearning to find out about how other people lived, what made them tick.

"Jess," said Simon, sitting down at the table opposite her. "I've been thinking …"

"Oh." The last time he had made an announcement that made her heart tremble, was when he told her that he was going to take a year off his job to do an MA. That had not been an easy year for her. She had found herself with all of the chores, not just most of them, because he had to write essays and assignments and study on campus at the university so much. And of course that was the priority.

She also had her hands full looking after the children and keeping them entertained as there were no provisions in the area for children. There was just one private playgroup in the area where pre-school children could go one half-day a week before they started school at age five. Of course she loved activities with her young daughters, but at the same time, she did wish that they did them together as a family. And while they were at playgroup she was able to do paid work a few hours.

She did all she could to enable Simon to do the MA. She had ended up helping him with his study, with his research and writing his essays. He found it very hard, even though he seemed desperate to do it. Thankfully the essays passed and he received his award and went back to his teaching job, albeit somewhat reluctantly. He seemed to have spent a good deal of his time at university with a female fellow student, writing articles for the college newspaper criticising Mrs Thatcher.

"I've been thinking that we need to move house," he said to her now, breaking in to her thoughts.

"Oh?"

"Yes. This house is not really big enough for us now. Not with two growing daughters. And I need a study of my own. I can't go on working on the dining table."

"Well, OK, that's a turn up for the books, but … fine …"

"I happened to see a house for sale on the way home the other day. It's a four bed detached house and it's also got a granny flat and a large garden."

Jess laughed despite herself. "Oh, Simon, it wasn't so long ago that you declared you didn't ever want a garden and we had an argument about the need for the children to have a safe place to play. You said if we had a garden you wouldn't tend it because it wasn't your choice. You got pretty stroppy about it, if I remember correctly!"

Simon had the grace to look sheepish. "Well, yes, OK. But I still don't want to do the gardening. You've managed OK here, haven't you?"

"Simon, you're not hearing me!"

He shrugged and gulped his wine. "Do you want me to tell you about it, or not?"

"Yes, of course. Where is this house? Do you have a picture? A brochure?"

"Yes, I picked it up at the estate agents. Look at the photo!"

The house certainly did look lovely. It was modern, about five or six years old. On a new but small development, just a few houses on one road. Simon thrust a map in front of her and pointed with his finger, "Here …"

"But that's in …!"

"Yes. I'm applying for a new job over there. It's Head of House and I'll have a deputy and much less classroom teaching."

8

THE THINGS WE DO FOR LOVE

She was baking bread in her new kitchen. The kneading had made her hands feel soft and clean. The deep warm comforting smell of the bread as it baked enfolded her senses as she shaped two more loaves and attempted to focus on the book which was propped up in front of her on the window sill. It was a copy of Robert Cormier's *I am the Cheese* which she was teaching to her Year Tens.

She had returned to work full-time when Abi was settled at primary school. A great advantage of their moving house was that now she was actually much nearer to where Polly and Matt had moved a few years ago, in fact they had ended up in the same small market town. Of course, Simon hadn't realised that when he found the house.

It had been an abrupt searching for a fulltime teaching job in the area, within a couple of years at their new house, sparked by Simon's continuingly coming home from work declaring that he was going to "jack it all in!" and become a truck driver. At first when it started, Jess just shrugged and treated it as one of Simon's outbursts, but she realised that he was still having real difficulties teaching the few classes he now had, and his instability was becoming scary. He seemed to attract disrespect from his pupils and much as he apparently attempted "matey-ness", the whistling and humming in his classes continued. Secretly, Jess thought his approach was certainly not the one she would have taken in his place. But when she tried to discuss it, he simply told her she hadn't got any idea what it was like to teach in a "proper job".

So she decided that if she herself had a salary from a full-time teaching job she wouldn't feel so insecure and frightened. It was not easy for her to know that she and her children were so dependent on his salary. What if he did walk out on his job? He always said that his parents would see them OK but of course she couldn't countenance that. She knew in her heart that the only person she could depend upon with total confidence was herself.

And they were better off with two salaries, although hers was only a fraction of his, since she'd had to go back to the lowest scale on her return to full-time in the classroom.

She was only half consciously waiting for the sound of Simon's door key in the lock. Katy and Abi were in the lounge sprawled on the rug watching Grange Hill before their homework. A pile of exercise books for her to mark sat on the kitchen table; she was trying to ignore them. She wasn't looking forward to marking thirty Year Nine stories which she knew would be, as always, whatever she said, generic or a rehash of a film or television programme.

She sighed as she brushed the top of the loaves with milk and slipped the baking trays into the oven. She wasn't so keen on the school which had appointed her full-time but there was little choice. There seemed to be fewer and fewer jobs available, so she had taken a basic level post again, back at the bottom of the pile. But that was how it worked. Even in 1982.

Polly was teaching a little part-time at the school they had both worked in together before their babies, but she too had found herself without a leadership role, just, as she complained "all the lousy classes." And it was a long car drive away from home. Both of them were now so busy that it was difficult to get time to see each other for any length of time more than a couple of times a month. Matt had a senior position in his law firm and was heading for a partnership and they now had three delightful boys, Tom, the eldest, just a few months older than Katy, Zack, the same age as Abi, and Jake, three years younger. But they did try to pop in to say hello when they could. She'd made new friends of neighbours and at work, but it was good for Jess to feel that there was someone from her past history who lived near.

She drained the vegetables into the left hand of the twin circular stainless steel sinks. She had designed the new kitchen herself. It was practical for her love of baking and cooking for family and friends but it was also stylish and, certainly in her eyes, beautiful, with its parchment coloured cupboard doors and craftsman-made thick wooden round-edged counter tops. In her mind she saw again the cheerful workmen fitting her kitchen, sharing jokes and even serious discussions about the nuclear disaster at Chernobyl and their views of Margaret Thatcher. Her constant excited forays to see how they were getting on with the building project, thrilled at the expectation of a wonderful fitted and sleek family kitchen. Taking them mug after mug of hot strong tea that she was making fresh in the little kitchen of the granny flat upstairs, so that they could have a change from their stewed drinks in their vacuum flasks. Providing them with her home-made sticky ginger flapjacks. Hearing them singing at the top of their voices to the pop radio station, Papa Don't Preach, Bohemian Rhapsody, and, more often than not, The Things We Do For Love, which seemed to be played constantly – and then she'd join in with the chorus, singing along with them, *like walking in the rain* … Dissolving into laughter. Red faced. Shaking her head self-deprecatingly ... Then leaving them to return to her marking or lesson preparation.

Jess smiled at the scenes in her head. She checked the beef casserole in the slow cooker that she had organised before she went to work that morning and slid the defrosted home-made apple pie into the oven. She heard her daughters giggling in the other room and that made her smile. The comfort and peace and love of her home and family assailed her senses. How could she ever want anything else?

Yes, of course, if only Simon could be more contented and stable, if he was *well*, she would be happier. But when he was OK, he was charming and loving. It was just on occasions that he seemed to explode into anger or dissolve into despair. So up and down, flinging himself into extremes. She had come to regard it as some kind of illness. Clearly it was an imbalance of hormones or cerebral chemicals. After much persuasion from Jess, he had started to consult the GP and take medication. She was glad that she herself was so calm and resilient. "Capable" everyone said, she was so "capable"; it made her sound boring. But with Simon around, someone needed to be, and it was down to her. Polly always said she was the "rock".

She remembered how feisty and adventurous she used to be. When she was in Ghana. Now, she reflected, it seemed to be about the strength to keep things together, to look after Simon as she looked after the children, because, regrettably she knew that emotionally he was rather more childlike than she had ever expected. Everything seemed to have turned around.

These days, she dared not think about Ghana too much and what had happened there and after she returned to England. It hurt her to feel any sadness. She loved Simon, despite his problems. Or maybe because of them. He was vulnerable. He needed her. And other people didn't see what she saw every day of their lives.

Jess slid the plates into the oven to heat up as she heard Simon's key in the door. Timed efficiently, as always. She was good at time management and organisation. That was one thing she was good at, anyway. Thankfully. She ought to try for a management role, Polly kept telling her. She did think she might be reasonable at it. Juggling everything in the air at once.

She wasn't like that years ago. And she recalled how it had become a necessity to organise like clockwork right back when she first brought Katy home from the hospital as a baby. *Simon insisted on having his dinner on the table as soon as he came home, whatever time that happened to be, whether or not Katy was ready for a feed or a bath. To avoid argument (although she had tried to explain the difficulties to Simon) she had taken to timing feeds and baths to allow her to have finished by the time he arrived home from work. He was happy to take Katy up to bed while Jess served out their dinner, although of course she was usually already asleep by the time she had played with her in the bubble bath and read her a story. Jess always read to her, even though her mother-in-law made no secret of her bewilderment: "she's only a baby, Jess, she doesn't understand, you know!"*

Jess smiled now to herself; of course she did, and hadn't their early stories together helped both the girls to love reading and books? And anyway it was a lovely cuddle-up time together. Over the years, the girls had thrived; they were clever, lively, affectionate.

"Mmmm, lovely smell!" said Simon as he strode into the kitchen, making her jump from her reverie. He kissed her lightly on the cheek, then lifted the lids on the dishes and sniffed. "Beef! Have you added some red wine?"

"Not any extra. I used some fresh beef stock I froze last week. It's quite rich and there's some burgundy in that, so I didn't think …"

"Oh, I'll just add some of this." Simon opened a bottle of claret and sloshed some into the dish. "Mmmm, that's better." He left the bottle to breathe on the counter top to drink with dinner. "Oooh, do I smell apple pie?"

"Yes, I froze it last weekend. I batch-baked four, then put them all in the freezer."

"Can we have home-made custard with it?"

"Oh. Well, I was planning on cream. I haven't had time to make custard too."

"But you've been home for a couple of hours."

"Yes, and in that time, I've sorted the children, made the dinner, and juggled with my work for my

Year Tens, Simon. I've still got all that marking for the Year Nines! Sorry to snap, Simon, but …"

"Blah, blah, blah. Moaning about all you have to do! Well, if you don't have high expectations of yourself, Jess!"

He was smiling but she felt annoyed, the moments of calm, harmony and peace dissolved. "I have realistic expectations." She turned away and set about laying the plates and cutlery on the table. "Would you call the children, please? Remind them to wash hands."

"Of course I know *that*!" retorted Simon and stomped out of the room.

It was a Wednesday in the middle of term when Simon suffered his worst breakdown to date. He returned home from work unusually early and slumped on the kitchen stool. The children were upstairs with playing with friends in the playroom cum guest room.

Jess, busy sorting out the girls' school bags and checking what was needed for the next day, jumped when she heard the barely suppressed sob. She swung round, expecting to see one of the girls crying over a fall-out with one of their friends. But instead she saw Simon leaning against the door lintel, tears coursing unchecked down his cheeks. He looked crumpled.

"Oh my god, what on earth's happened?" she said, dropping the bags and rushing over to enfold him in her arms. Her breath sank to her stomach and she struggled to regain her respiration as her heart began to pound. Simon said nothing but continued to sob heart-rendingly. For a while he seemed to have no strength in him and he leaned heavily on Jess's shoulders. It flashed into her mind that their stance was something of a metaphor for their lives.

Then a guttural sob that racked his body shook Jess too and he pulled slightly away from her. "Oh god, I can't go on. I can't go back to that school. I can't."

"OK," said Jess, leading him into the living room and setting him down in his chair. He seemed to have no will, no effort left in him. "What happened? Have you got a migraine? How did you drive home?"

He shook his head. "No, no. I just can't ..." He seemed lost for words yet his body seemed to be shaking violently. Jess stroked his head and his back. Put her arms around him. Tried to sooth the shaking and the fear and the desperation she could feel crying out from him. They sat like that for a while, until his shaking calmed.

"OK. Tell me what happened."

"I don't know, really. The Year Elevens were awful, as they often are. But then they started laughing at me ..."

"Oh, I'm sure they weren't ..."

"You don't know!" he shouted, pushing her away from him. He jumped up and started pacing heavily around the room. Stomp. Stomp. Stomp.

Jess quickly slid out of the room and shut the door quietly behind her. She called up to Katy in as low a voice as she could. Her daughter appeared at the top of the stairs. "Yes, mummy. We're just playing pirates …"

"Darling, I need you to be very grown up and kind and tell your friends, and Abi's too, that they will have to go home now, I'm afraid, because Daddy isn't very well. Would you do that for me, sweetie, please?"

Jess could hear items being thrown about the living room. "Just stay upstairs for a bit, will you, poppet?"

"What's the matter with Daddy?" Katy's face crumpled.

"It's OK. He'll be all right soon. He's just had a bad day at work and he's not at all well."

"OK."

Jess found Simon curled up like a foetus in his chair. "I'm going to call the doctor."

"No, no!" Simon wailed. "Please. I'll be OK in a minute. I don't want anything damning on my record."

"But surely we need to get to the bottom of all this?"

"No." Simon sat up and took a deep breath. Jess could see him struggling to regain his composure, fighting against his trembling until he calmed. "I'll go up to bed. I'll be OK in the morning. I'll just take a few days off." He stood up, a little shakily, and puffed out a violent breath. "Would you bring me up a mug of hot sweet tea and I'll take some pills."

He had been persuaded to consult the GP some time before and been prescribed benzodiazepines to help him sleep. But he'd also had a cocktail of mild temazepam and lithium but he still found it difficult to get to sleep, staying up to watch late night television, coming to bed in the early hours even when he had work the next day. Jess worried about the way he took the pills like a kid with a tube of Smarties. She wished he would listen carefully to the doctor and make a proper plan for his medication instead of swallowing tablets as and when he suddenly felt he needed them.

Lately, she had become increasingly concerned about his health and his strategy for dealing with it. She had tried to discuss it all with him, assuring him that they needed to plan the treatment together, that she needed to help him manage his condition, whatever it was. But he wouldn't listen to her. He wouldn't let her speak with his parents about it or seek support from her own. He was totally against anyone else knowing what was going on. He said it had to be just between themselves. On no account must anyone else be involved. So she had to try to control the outbursts, the highs and lows herself, somehow. She felt that she really needed to be able to act in a more pro-active way, not just reacting to whatever was thrown at her.

The next day, Simon was clearly unwell, so Jess called the doctor out, and rang the absence number for his work to tell them he was ill and wouldn't be in that day. No, she didn't know when he would be back; they were waiting for the doctor, she'd ring with further information later and an estimate of the prospective length of his absence. She phoned her own school and let them know the situation. The deputy Head was kind and told her not to worry about work; they would cope without her, and he hoped that her husband would be better soon. Her heart warmed towards him. She then rang her Head of Department and provided work for the cover teacher to do with her classes that day.

She took his breakfast up to him in bed and then drove the children to school as usual, trying to maintain an even keel for them, whatever was happening with their father. By the time she returned to the house, the doctor was just pulling up in the drive.

"Hmmm," said Dr Jones, rubbing his chin, as he finished examining Simon and stood away from the bed. "He needs rest. So you're doing the right thing, Jess. I'm going to sign you off for three weeks, Simon. No, don't protest!" He consulted his papers in his medical bag. "You need to keep on with the medications. But strictly as prescribed. They are designed to stabilise the highs and lows."

"But what is it?" asked Jess, smoothing the covers over Simon and picking up the empty mug to fill it with fresh tea.

"We don't know a lot about these sorts of nervous or mental conditions yet, I'm afraid. There is research ongoing. I don't want to put a label on it as yet. Sometimes it doesn't help. But keep quiet and rest for the moment."

But of course, he didn't. He couldn't stay in bed and after one day he was grouching around the house in his dressing gown. He seemed to have an overload of nervous energy one day, then debilitating fatigue, pain and headaches, even migraines, the next.

Jess went back to work as soon as she felt he was safe to be left, although she always snatched time to ring him over lunch to check that he was all right, and left on the bell at the end of the day to get back to him. To be frank with herself, she was aware that she couldn't cope at home all day with his bouts of deep sorrow, hopelessness and self-dislike, alternating with mood swings to highly self-engrossed, confidence and domineering euphoria.

Jess peered at the bottles of pills in the bathroom cabinet with a frown. She sighed as she replaced them on the shelf and hoped to god that they were to be only temporary. She hated any chemical intervention herself. You really didn't know what they were doing to your system, after all. You could only put your faith and trust in the doctor. Simon had now been prescribed Prozac and eventually Dr Jones managed to balance the uppers and downers to try to level out the severest mood swings.

On the other hand, she knew only too well that his moods had to be controlled somehow if he couldn't get well by himself. She knew a little about it from her psychology at university, but not about the clinical side. She went to the library and read as much as she could to try to understand what was happening to him. But in some ways she found that knowing about what could happen, made her more anxious and frightened. She read that sufferers could turn against the very people closest to them. That bouts of anger, rage even, could be misdirected to loved ones. Her mind drifted back to a couple of incidents a while ago:

She was in the kitchen sorting out the washing when she heard a scream. Running to the hall, heart trembling. Breath struggling. Halting, totally fixed to the spot. A few moments before she registered what was happening. Seeing Simon dragging little Abi up the stairs by her hair, shouting, swearing at her violently. What the hell are you doing? Stop it! Stop it! Simon, for god's sake! Him letting go, looking puzzled. Oh god, oh god, what have I done? Crumpling down onto the stairs, hugging Abi to him. Sorry, oh god, sorry, I don't know what happened then. Loosening his grip on Abi. Looking down at Jess's horrified face. Well, she was being rude. Don't you ever, EVER, do that again!

The memory made her shudder. Then again, another scene crept stealthily in to her mind.

Children quarrelling upstairs. Jess running up the staircase to reprimand them. Simon in young Katy's room, hitting her, yelling: don't you dare be so cruel to your sister! I'll kill you! Jess grabbing him from behind, pulling him off. Stop it, for god's sake! Simon, leave her alone, you'll hurt her. What on earth do you think you're doing? His crumpling on to Katy's bedroom floor, crying. I don't know, I don't know, I just snapped! GET OUT, SIMON. Don't you ever lay a finger on the children again! Such abject apology then. So appalled. Both of them. Should she tell anyone? Should she get help? But from whom? The doctor would only prescribe pills. And they didn't seem to be working all the time. Lawyers? She didn't want a court case, a restraining order. All this was something totally out of her experience. What would any actions mean? That their family was broken, some irrevocable intervention? But she'd promised at their wedding to be faithful and loving as long as they both lived on earth – they both had – she couldn't break that promise. She was thirty six and she needed to find a way of coping herself. What was the right thing to do?

He had never repeated that behaviour but yet it still haunted her dreams. He was extra careful after that. Extra caring and loving towards them. But the maggots of memory were still there in Jess's mind. And so she watched and listened, tiptoed on eggshells around him. Tried to be proactive in avoiding any situation that could trigger a repetition with the children.

And now she hoped that, much as she hated it, the medication would resolve the situation. But there, in the distant hazy haunted parts of her mind she saw again the mango trees of the bush and the thick wild scrubland and she heard again the rhythmic pounding of the drums that met the thrumming of her heart.

"We've decided we're going to move up here, nearer to you all," announced Simon's parents. They were staying with them for the weekend, in the granny flat which Jess had cleaned and prepared for them with the Edwardian Diary bed linen that she knew they liked.

"Oh?" Jess looked up from the potatoes she was peeling to roast along with the chicken. She quickly mentally checked off her tasks: vegetables, gravy, trimmings ready. She could hear the girls happily dancing in the sitting room to their new favourite band A-ha and Morten Harket. She could hear them wailing "*Take on me!*" at the top of their breathless voices.

"We'd like you to start looking for a suitable house for us, somewhere near, in a village hopefully. Something big enough. Something that maybe you'd like to live in because we will probably move to a smaller cottage as we get older, but in the same village. What do you think?"

"That'd be wonderful, wouldn't it, Jess?" said Simon as he uncorked a bottle and poured out drinks for them all. He was getting much better now, thank goodness, Jess thought. The medications were clearly working their magic. He hadn't had a repeat of that awful time. He seemed much more stable. He'd returned to work quite happily after a few weeks off and in fact now even more of his time was being spent as a pastoral leader in the school, which he said suited him much better, as he was dealing with individual pupils and issues rather than teaching big classes. His class teaching had become minimal. Life had become so much easier and he was becoming more attentive and loving to her and the girls. Jess hoped that would last.

"Wouldn't it, Jess?" repeated Simon, insistently, staring up at her.

"Well, yes," she said slightly hesitantly. She had a good relationship with her parents-in-law, in many ways better than with her own parents, although it had to be said that they clearly disapproved of her working full-time. She had only ever said that she had to, never criticising Simon or telling them the truth which was that she had been so concerned about Simon's instability as a bread-winner. They had never found out about his break-downs either. She thought it must be good to be so ignorant of harsh realities. Their lives seemed to have always been so safe and privileged, buffered from any lack of money or status. They'd never had to struggle, as far as she was aware. Never had to live the hard way. Maybe that also precluded you from character-building life events. But Jess knew in her heart that she would have given anything to have things that easy.

But, on the other hand, they had always been affectionate to her. Simon's mother, Hilary, had said several times over the years that she was so glad that her son had married Jess, that she was just like a daughter to them, the daughter they had never had.

"Good!" exclaimed Hilary, smoothing her top over her ample bosom and smiled contentedly. "It'll be so wonderful to be able to see the children more. Maybe to collect them from school and take them home for tea? You could all come over for Sunday lunch after Meeting. We could all go to Meeting together." Jess didn't confess that although Simon went to Meeting faithfully, she tended to stay at home with the children whenever possible. It had become hypocritical to her. "Oh," Hilary carried on gleefully, "and there is a small Meeting in the village to the east of here, up in the hills, you know where I mean? Maybe you could look over there for us?"

Simon's father, John, grinned and swung his arm around Jess's back, hugging her. "Oh yes, that would be lovely, Jessamy, wouldn't it, my dear?" She noticed that his hand trembled a little and wondered if he was ill and whether that was why they wanted to move nearer to them. But he had always been rather nervy even though he had held a high-powered job before he retired.

"Yes, of course," she smiled. "Lovely." It would, indeed, be good to have some help and support on hand. Maybe they could help out with taking the girls to their various classes after school: swimming and dancing, piano and clarinet, orchestra and band. It was all such a hectic rush for Jess after a day's teaching, often trying to be in two places at once. Simon sometimes did one of the runs but it always depended on his availability. Jess was determined that the girls would have every possible opportunity that they wanted, and of course that Jess could afford. She didn't want them to regret not having had the chance to learn something or be involved in something, as had happened to her in her own childhood. She recalled so vividly her yearning for ballet lessons, and piano and riding. But it couldn't be afforded, so she was only allowed a few ballet lessons, then they were stopped through lack of funds. She understood; her parents didn't have the money, and that was that. But for her own children, she saved up and budgeted for their lessons, even if it meant going without for herself.

So, having her parents-in-law around for practical help would be a relief. Of course it would.

In the end they didn't need to spend much time house-hunting for Simon's parents because by a stroke of fortune there was an ideal property exactly where they wanted it, in the village on the hill. If only it was always that easy, thought Jess. But Simon's parents had plenty of funds to buy just what they wanted. And this was a wonderful house. Large and set high on the hill with a commanding view of the valley and woods below. Jess peered out of the huge plate-glass window of the sitting room. She screwed up her eyes. If you looked hard you could actually see their own house. The girls were running around the large garden, marvelling at the fish pond and fountain. Excited screams at the terraces and steps, the dry-stone walls they could hide behind. Jess smiled.

"You think they'll like it?" Simon came up behind her and kissed the nape of her neck, winding his arms round to the front.

"Oh yes, I'm sure they will. It's delightful! The position is incredible."

"And," he added, squeezing her slim body, "Do you think you could see us living here when they decide to move out? I think they're really just wanting to prepare it for us and buy a smaller cottage in the village for themselves."

Jess looked around at the big fireplace, the sun room at the end of the house, the long window seat where she could imagine herself reading. "Yes, actually, yes, I could!"

"Well, I'll ring them when we get home and they can come up next weekend and make an offer."

Wow, thought Jess … just like that! She thought of her own parents in their small rented house in the suburb of the city. She felt guilty that she and Simon should have so much.

It was amazing how money could ease the way so much for some people, thought Jess, as Simon came away from the telephone, thumbs up to her, after speaking to his parents on the day they moved in, just a couple of months later.

"We should go over and help," called Jess, as she tidied up her books.

"Oh, really?" said Simon as he sauntered in to the kitchen. He leaned nonchalantly against the door lintel, head to one side as he appraised her, smiling. She flushed. He still looked so good, so delicious, even approaching the big four O. He seemed so much more confident these days, his features had softened again and his eyes weren't holding the pain she had feared, not so long ago. She didn't know whether he was permanently stable from the medication he was still taking every day, or whether he would slide back into those awful mood swings again. But she knew that she could only grasp the moment. And right now he was good.

"Maybe in a while. Come here," he said gently to her, voice low and sexily husky. He pulled her to him and held her face in his hands, his thumbs stroking the sides of her mouth. They had been married for nearly seventeen years and yet she still trembled thrillingly at his touch. When he was well, he could be so charming. He drew her closer towards him and, as his hands slid down her back and pressed her hips into him, she could feel his need. He kissed the side of her neck, nuzzling her nape.

"Mmmm," murmured Jess. "You smell gorgeous." She snuggled in to him and reached up, running her hands through his fair hair, pressing the pads of her fingers up from the back of his neck where his hair was short and as she knew he loved. He shuddered.

"Aaah, my sexy teacher wife," he whispered.

"Mummy! Daddy! *Really*!"

They swung around to see Katy in the doorway behind them. Jess laughed, and let go of Simon, her hands held out to hug her young daughter. She heard Simon exhale an annoyed sigh as he turned away.

"What? What?" called Abi, behind her, jumping up and down to try to see better what was going on.

"Come on, both of you!" laughed Jess, embracing both her daughters in a big bear hug. "Come on, Simon, you too!" He grunted but encircled them all in his arms.

"Right, come on," he broke away from the group hug. "Get your shoes on, girls. We've got to go to granny and grandpa's to help them move in to their new home."

Simon's parents spent the year doing up their new house. Hilary kept showing Jess the new projects every time she went over there and asking her opinion about the work: "it'll all be for you, of course, so I want you to have a say in it." They had been invited over for Sunday lunch and as she checked that the girls had their coats and gloves, in case it turned cold, even in early May, she thought that her own mother would have loved to be able to buy a house so near to them and see the grandchildren so often.

As they clambered into the car, Simon turned to Jess and said, as if he had only just remembered, "Oh, by the way, I'm going to a conference up in Yorkshire in half term week. Monday to Friday. OK?"

Jess knew that the question was rhetorical but anyway she rarely stopped him from anything he wanted to do or made anything difficult for him. She wasn't prepared to breed resentment or be a clinging wife who kept a tight hold on her husband. She'd never been like that. It just wasn't in her nature. She had no desire to control another person.

"OK. So what is this?"

"Oh, it's just a pastoral care thing. I ought to go, with this role I have."

"Yes, of course."

"The theme is family relationships and sex education," he added. "The new PSHE, personal, social and health education. A load of pastoral leaders and social workers, NSPCC and all that ..."

She wondered briefly why he seemed to be defending this conference group which she had very little interest in. Some of the local people involved had come for meetings with Simon at their house on a number of occasions and she wasn't too keen on them. As far as she could see, most of them seemed to have become suspiciously engaged in pastoral roles in schools which took them as far as possible away from the classroom. And his friends in this group struck her as being, ironically, rather rude, with very few personal or social graces. When they came to the house they almost pushed her aside as she opened the door to them. They treated her like a servant when she simply behaved as any sociable host would, offering coffee and biscuits. She'd rarely come across such a demanding group of people: the coffee was only OK if it was decaffeinated or Columbian medium roast, and the nibbles couldn't have been made with animal fat or sugar. In the end, she'd just plonked a tray down on the coffee table and left them to it, retreating to the sanity and courtesy of the kitchen.

"Do you know, I think I'll probably redecorate your study in half term, while you're away and not working in there," Jess pondered out loud. Simon had commandeered the granny flat now for his study and "away from it all" area. Or at least the living room area of the flat. And the little kitchenette where he had removed the doors to the wall cupboards for some reason. He said it was so that he could have open shelves, but, to Jess, it just looked untidy. The bathroom and bedroom in the flat had not been touched as they held no purpose for him. But he liked the fact that the living room had a big patio door opening out on to a small balcony where he could sit and read on his own.

"Why? It's OK as it is!"

"Well, we haven't touched in there since we moved in and I think it needs freshening up. It's quite grubby and also I don't care much for the magnolia walls. I'll do it while you're away and then it won't disturb your work."

Simon shrugged and fixed his focus on the road ahead.

9

AND I THINK IT'S GONNA RAIN TODAY

It was the day before their wedding anniversary. Eighteen years. But despite her best efforts, booking them a treat and spoiling him, Simon had been oddly quiet since he returned from the conference in Yorkshire. And he had scarcely touched her. Or even met her eyes. Her heart sank as she worried that he was falling headlong into another black depression. Yet in other ways he seemed to be high, leaping upstairs to his study; singing loudly up there to his Queen album. Despite the drugs he still wasn't stabilised on an even keel as she'd hoped.

While he was away, Jess had managed to emulsion the walls of his study and white gloss the woodwork. But when she tried to show him, he seemed distracted. He was clearly in a low grumpy mood. It made her feel tired. She had tried for so many years to keep everything calm and stable at home, but having to walk on eggshells around Simon was frustrating. She tried to keep life gentle and secure for the girls, tried to keep his violent moods away from them, to protect them from the worst of his tempers and ever since those dreadful incidents a few years before, there had been little that was disastrous in front of the children. She hoped that her stability and constancy over-rode Simon's swerving. He said himself that she was the rock for him and for the family.

She had booked tickets for them all to go to the theatre to see the touring production of *Jesus Christ Superstar* which she knew the children were excited to see on stage. They were also thrilled to be allowed to stay up late; they wouldn't be home from the theatre until at least 11.30. Jess had bought the LP record and, along with the girls, had learned the words to many of the songs. Together they had belted out the theme song and bawled over *I Don't Know How To Love Him,* along with suitably exaggerated dramatic gestures.

The evening was wonderful, the production had Jess and the girls totally engrossed. But she was aware that Simon was somewhat disengaged and his attention seemed directed elsewhere. He seemed impatient and agitated, and he did his usual "gimme, gimme" gesture for the tickets and for money from Jess to pay for the programme and sweets to take in with them. It would be nice if he ever suggested, booked and paid for any family outings, but he just always relied on Jess to arrange family treats. She knew also that from time to time he would take one of his colleagues, often his female deputy, to the pub, to discuss school issues, and she always assumed that he paid. Maybe she was wrong.

Jess waited for the disintegration that she was sure would follow in the next few days. But she wasn't going to let his mood cloud the evening, and she and the girls enjoyed themselves, abandoning themselves to the production and the music.

It had rained heavily while they were in the theatre and the streets back home from the city were slick black and shining in the car headlights. Jess and the girls chattered about the production and which parts they thought were the best. Simon drove silently, clutching the steering wheel. Jess noticed that his knuckles were white.

Jess struggled with her key in the front door and was disconcerted to see that the kitchen light was on, which she was sure she had switched off before they left earlier that evening.

As she walked into the kitchen, she realised the reason. On the table sat a large chocolate sponge cake with the wobbly words Happy Anniversary piped in white icing on the top, and a tiny wedding couple holding hands in the middle. A card was propped up beside it: "Have a wonderful anniversary, with loads of love from Hilary and John" and three kisses beneath.

"Ah, look!" Jess called to Simon. "Your parents have been over and left us an anniversary cake. Your mother obviously baked it for us. How kind and thoughtful!"

Simon peered round the doorway and glanced peremptorily at the cake. "Oh, yes," he said and then disappeared upstairs.

Oh dear, thought Jess, when will the storm break again?

She slept badly that night, constantly waking with uneasy thoughts pounding in her brain. The rain was heavy that night, lashing on the window panes. In the early hours she tossed and turned, and for the first time for a long while, she felt her head reverberating with the sounds of drumbeats. She held her hands up over her face trying to blank out the rhythmic rising and falling of sounds in the heavy darkness. It reminded her so vividly of Ghana and the whispering souls and spirits calling to her across the bush; the surging and dying of the wind on the night air, the insistent beat of the kpanlogo donde. Once more, her dreams were garish and crowded as they had been there. And she remembered that haunting.

Eventually, exhausted, she slept, but it was fitful and in the morning she struggled out of bed feeling as though she had the worst hangover ever. Simon was already up and she could hear him downstairs as she went for her shower.

"Katy! Abi! Are you both up?" she called.

"Yes, I'm getting dressed and Katy's gone down."

After her shower she sank onto the stool at the dressing table and peered at her drawn features. Her eyes looked puffy and sore. Right. Makeup out, let's get respectable. Paint a decent face on …

As she swept brown eyeliner across her eyes, she became aware that he was standing in the bedroom doorway, a sense of agitation emanating from him. She could almost smell the sweat. She looked up and saw that he was leaning against the lintel staring at her. It was not a loving stare but a troubled one and she knew that he needed to tell her something that she wasn't going to like. Some money problem? Work? He wanted to resign from his job and let her to be the breadwinner? Oh dear. She didn't have the years of promotions behind her to stand keeping the family on her income. But he had threatened that so many times.

She raised her eyebrows enquiringly. He shifted from foot to foot in the doorway and Jess began to feel very uneasy. Her hand trembled and she dripped the liquid eyeliner onto the dressing table.

"I have to tell you," he said with a slow intake of breath. "I'm leaving you."

"*What?*" She hadn't expected that. Her heart fell, tumbling to inexorable death.

"You heard me," Simon snapped. "I've decided that I don't want to be a husband and father any more."

"*Decided…?* What on earth do you mean?"

"I've found someone else."

217

"*Found someone else?*" She could hear her own voice echoing his as if she were an imbecile.

Jess stared at him with total incomprehension. Her husband. The man she loved. Had nursed through his breakdowns. Had done all she could to keep his head above water when he had become depressed. Had loved and cherished, cared for, would have died for... *What?* He'd "*found someone else?* Like he'd found another job. Or found them another house.

Her mind whirled. Had he been *looking* for someone else? All this time that she had been a good wife, a good mother to the children? Had she not been enough?

He had been having an affair behind her back? Oh god, he'd slept with someone else. Had sex with someone else. Tenderly touched and been touched by someone else. Some other woman that wasn't her, his wife, mother to the children. He'd been loving and intimate with someone else. He'd done the things that were theirs alone, that were just between them ... or that she'd thought were theirs.

"You've slept with someone else?" But ... she couldn't understand ... he was hers. Her husband.

She felt like another person. Someone who was living another, strange life, in some other weird mystifying world totally alien to her. She was trembling. Everything was shaking.

"Oh yes." And he grinned. He actually grinned. As though this was something to be proud of, to relish.

He was pleased with himself. With what he'd done. To her. To their children. It sounded to her as though he was suddenly released from constraints. She saw his mind reliving the intimacies with some other woman. In some other bedroom. "Oh yes, Jess. I've been having sex with someone else. And she was great."

Oh god, how could he? Just like that? As if it was nothing? Yet it was everything to her. It was their closeness, their trust, their marriage, their family, their intimacy, their sharing something only between themselves ...

Jess crumpled. "My god, Simon. What have you done? What the hell have you gone and done?" She felt nauseated and faint. "Who ... who is she, this woman?" She was terrified it was someone she knew. Yet also terrified that it was some stranger, nothing to do with their life, her life; somehow that made it feel even more of a dismissal, rejection. Either way ... there was no good way of looking at this.

"That's none of your business. It's my private life."

Private life? Did either of them *have* a private life? How could you when you were a unit? Yes, they had some different interests and activities, they weren't in each other's pockets all the time (she never wanted that) but surely fundamentally they were a close unit. *Were* ...

This was all surreal. She touched the dressing table, tried to ground herself. She forced her pointed manicured nails deeply in to her cold palms. She shivered. He just stared at her from the doorway, not leaning any more but standing, silhouetted, gesticulating angrily. He hadn't even come in to the room and shut the door to keep this private. Had the girls heard? God, this was appalling. Was he so full of himself, of what he'd done that he didn't even care if the children heard? What was he doing to them all?

"Why, Simon? Why?"

He stared down at her. "Because you aren't enough for me. *You just aren't enough.* I want a woman that all the other men want, someone sexy, fun and desirable but is all mine – but you … you're so squeaky-clean …" She recalled him saying the same thing when she returned from Ghana all those years ago. *God, why had she forgotten that?* And when he rejected her their first night together?

She struggled to speak. To make some kind of shape of her thoughts.

"Don't you understand what this means? Don't you get the fact that leaving us means the family is broken? Our children, our beautiful little girls will be living in a broken home, a single parent family … oh my god …"

He shrugged. "Not my problem," he sneered.

"*What?*" she knew she was raising her voice now, but couldn't lower it. She seemed to have no control over her voice, her body. She was shaking violently.

"The fucking kids are *your* problem," he spat at her. "I don't want to be a fucking father any more. I just told you, for fuck's sake!"

She gasped at the violence of his language and his tone. He *never* swore. Well, only the odd "bloody". Hated it. Said it was unacceptable in a household with children. What was happening here? Was she still in the nightmares of the darkness?

She stared at this man whom she no longer knew. His face was no longer familiar to her. It held hatred in its darkened eyes and mouth. She struggled to remember that she had held him, kissed him, enfolded him. That she had nursed him, touched him tenderly. That they had shared so much: joys and disasters. That he had been her best friend, for god's sake. Yet now she could see only hatred and scorn in his narrowed eyes.

She had no breath. No words. All was gone. In an instant her world had shattered. Stamped underfoot. And yet … and yet … was this some kind of sick joke, a temporary aberration. Was he going through another of his breakdowns?

Why would he do this; why would he go off with someone else, break up his family and abandon his children? There had to be some explanation. While she fought to make sense of it, she thought she heard a noise from Abi's bedroom.

"Simon. Please. Don't you know what the effect of a broken home has on children?" He shrugged. "Don't you even care?" She could not believe that suddenly he could abdicate all responsibility as a husband and father, that he had no conception of the basic truth that he would be a father for ever, whatever he claimed.

You can't just *decide* not to be a father. Even if he did leave them he would still surely be involved with her as far as the children were concerned; wouldn't they still be discussing the girls and making decisions together? Didn't he care about their welfare?

And with horror she realised that she was thinking as though it was inevitable now that he would go.

Because she knew that he'd made up his mind, that nothing would deter him, that he would do whatever he wanted now.

"Oh, 'don't you even *care?*' Huh!" he mocked her with a silly simpering voice that she knew she hadn't used. "No, *Jessamy,* I *don't* fucking care. It's not my problem any more. It's your job to raise them. I simply don't wish to be fucking married any more."

He stared down at her, a sneer making his face ugly. Then he turned and walked lightly down the corridor to the stairs.

Jess just sat there, frozen. This *had* to be another breakdown, surely? Should she treat it as that, and try to look after him, nurse him, support him? Yet he said that he was having an affair, that he had someone else. He'd never done that before. As far as she knew – well, he'd never said that to her before. All the previous occasions had been focused on his problems at work, with teaching, with difficult classes he couldn't seem to manage.

This was different.

This felt like an attack on her, on their life together, on their family.

It didn't feel like a time to respond by enfolding him in her arms, hugging him, loving him better as she had done so many times before.

This was about aggression towards her and the children. Violent dismissal. Rejection. This was not about need, and love, and despair. He had only ever had a breakdown when he was low before, depressed. This time he was high. She couldn't understand it. He seemed to be revelling in his power to hurt them. Why? For goodness sake, why should he want to do that?

She gathered herself and went downstairs with low aching dread in her heart.

She heard his voice in the living room and crept in. He was sitting on the sofa, a child each side of him, his arm around Katy. He was trying to touch Abi, but she was pushing his arm away.

"So I'm leaving. I'm going to another home. I shan't be living here with you any more. But … well, be good for your mother …"

Abi, white-faced, turned to look up at Jess. Her eyes were pleading. Jess opened her mouth but no sound came out. As Jess walked in to the room, the doorbell rang.

"Get that, Jess," ordered Simon, without looking round.

JULIA IBBOTSON

His parents were standing on the doorstep. They looked frightened, quite distraught. Jess realised that she was still shaking.

"Simon rang us and asked us to come round. What's going on, Jessamy?"

Jess shook her head. "I think you ought to ask your son that." She heard Simon coming up behind her and suddenly felt the need to state a fact that she feared he might try to obscure for them. "He says he's leaving us. He's got someone else," she blurted out wildly, and she was aware of the terror in her voice.

"Don't leave them waiting on the doorstep!" Simon pushed her roughly aside and politely gestured his parents to come inside. They stood, fidgeting, in the hall, looking from one to the other of them. "Yes, I'm leaving," he announced calmly as though it was an obvious fact. "Because I've started a relationship with someone else."

The words made Jess feel sick. It sounded much more final than 'having sex with someone else,' or even 'having an affair.' It sounded like permanence. Starting to build a new life. A new relationship. Discarding the old.

Hilary and John stared at him for a moment. The Hilary said, shakily, "It's … it *is* another woman?"

Simon shook his head for a moment in puzzlement, "What did you think she was?"

"Oh," exhaled Hilary, looking as if she would crumble. Jess did not hold her arm out to her.

"Oh, thank god," breathed John, turning to Hilary and putting his arm around her broad tweed-covered back.

"We had an awful feeling," sighed Hilary, "that you were going to say you were gay. Oh, thank goodness for that!"

Jess stared, barely able to take in what she had heard. This was *relief* she saw in front of her. "You mean … it's OK that he's having an affair and is leaving us, but it wouldn't have been OK if it was a man, if he was having a gay relationship?"

"You must realise, Jessamy, this … at least this is *normal.*" Hilary's voice was severe and reprimanding, almost pious and patronising.

Normal? None of it was *normal.* What on earth were they talking about? He was walking away from his family! Deserting his wife and beautiful children.

And she realised that they had been terrified of the thought that he might be gay, that maybe there had been some kind of suspicion there, and that they were more relieved about that than appalled at what he had actually done.

She felt like Alice in Wonderland. In a world of madness and reversals and topsy-turvy ideas. She felt she was falling down the rabbit hole with no idea of where the bottom was, where she might land, whether there *was* any landing. She'd at least imagined that his parents would be horrified, be in support of her and the children. But it hit her like the impact of a car crash, head on, that they were not on their side; they were firmly with Simon, whatever he had done. And that he knew it and that's why he had sent for them. Reinforcements for his rectitude.

And that, she realised, was how it would be.

Polly lowered her glass onto the coffee table in front of her, spilling a pool of red wine on the teak. She pulled out her handkerchief and started dabbing at it viciously. "I just don't believe it!" She covered her face with her hands and bent forward. "It's just so incredibly cruel! Oh, babes!"

"It was Sunday." All Jess could do was to explain the facts, stick to that. Nothing more, nothing less. She felt numb. Feint like a ghost. Insubstantial. As though she had been drawn with a soft kohl pencil that barely sketched an outline. Nothing was filled in. Nothing solid any more.

"Two days ago!" said Polly. "Why didn't you ring me before?"

"Because I felt I couldn't speak. I didn't know what to say any more."

"And has he discussed it with you? Tried to work it out? Whatever his problem might be?"

"No, no discussion. He refuses to discuss it. Says he's going to do what he's going to do. Nothing to do with me. Apparently."

"*What?* Your marriage, your family, the children's future is nothing to do with you?"

"The marriage is, but he's already decided its fate. End of. The rest ... well, that's apparently my problem to figure out, not his."

Polly sat shaking her head. "Unbelievable. Is he mad? Do your parents know?"

"Yes. They're coming up at the weekend."

"God! He *is* mad! I've always had my doubts." She suddenly looked at Jess, appalled, hand covering her mouth. "Oh dear, I shouldn't have said that, I know. He *is* still your husband, after all. What about if you got back together again and I'd said that. You'd never forgive me."

Jess smiled weakly. "I honestly don't think there's any danger of that."

Polly sighed. "Hmmm. OK." She shook her head, trying to shake in some sense. "And ... oh ... and work? The school. Do you want me to ring them?"

"No. Thank you. I rang on Monday morning. I just said I was detained. I'd be late. It's activity week this week anyway, so no teaching. It's the last week of term before the summer holidays, of course. I took the girls to school and then went over. Dan, my head of department, came out to meet me in the staff carpark."

"He knew Simon at university, didn't he?"

"Yes."

"But they weren't ever friends, were they? Wasn't Dan the rugby player? Simon wasn't interested. I re-member him sneering at the rugby chaps."

Jess wondered why they were talking about rugby. Her brain was so fogged. She had barely managed to grill frozen fish fingers for the children since Sunday. Just couldn't concentrate.

Polly reached for the wine bottle and filled both of their glasses although neither of them had drunk any.

"He was so kind. Dan. So very kind. He said not to come back again before the holidays. He hugged me. There in the middle of the staff carpark. In front of the school. In front of all the classroom windows. He said … you don't deserve this, Jess …" He hadn't cared who saw. He had just felt her need and responded with kindness.

It was then that Jess broke down, sobs racking her body. In the midst of all this bomb damage that was her life, someone had spoken kindly to her. Someone unexpected. Who had walked out of the rubble and hugged her to him. She would never forget that moment.

Polly pulled Jess into a hug and stroked her back. "I can't believe he could be so cruel. Why? I mean, you're so lovely, kind, thoughtful, attractive, intelligent, the kids are wonderful, well brought up, no problem to you both … So why?"

"Apparently I wasn't enough for him."

"He said that a long time ago. When you got back from Ghana. And he had a strop. What the hell's wrong with the man?"

"He says he doesn't love me any more. If he ever did. He's apparently been looking around for ages for someone else. And he found someone willing at that conference he went to a few weeks ago."

"Willing? To sleep with him? Huh …! And who on earth is she, this tart who's so much better than you?" Polly sneered angrily.

"Oh, some pastoral deputy headteacher he met. Married with two little ones, a toddler and a baby …"

"Oh good god!"

"Husband's very jealous."

"I bet! Sounds like she spreads it around."

Jess shrugged. She didn't know whether she wanted to know, or didn't want to have any involvement at all. She had no idea where her mind was going at the moment.

Polly just sat there beside her, hugging her, realising that Jess was exhausted and hardly able to talk. Eventually she said, "Look, babes, I'm going to have to go and fetch the kids from school. Let me pick up your two as well and bring them home to you. OK? I won't be able to stay, I'll just drop them off because I've got the swimming run and the football run tonight. But I'll organise things tomorrow so that I can come over. Maybe we can get babysitters and Matt can come over too in the evening …"

"Oh Polly, what would I do without you? But please, you've got your own family to look after. I can manage. I'll have to manage. This is not going to be a flash in the pan. The signs are that it's permanent. That's it. Marriage over. In one moment. One sentence … So I'll have to pull myself up and get on with it, somehow."

She knew that logically, life had to continue. Somehow. The children had to be fed although Jess herself couldn't seem to swallow anything. She had to try to keep things at home on an even a keel as she could. Her own grief had to be put aside. She had to be mother and father now. And give her children all the love they should have from both mother and father. He was gone. She had tried to reason with him. But he had walked out of the door on Sunday and hadn't contacted them since.

She stood in the newly refurbished kitchen of their large house, leaning on the counter and staring blindly out of the window. Her knuckles white as she gripped the edges of the stylish circular twin stainless steel sinks she had chosen so happily just a few months before, not knowing what was to come.

The gentle resonances of 10cc's '*The Things we do for Love*' echoed in her ears and she recalled the way the builders had played it over and over as they refitted the kitchen, only a few weeks ago, and how she had sung along with them as she brought in countless mugs of tea. By the time she heard the refrain "*like walking in the rain* …" she knew that her tears were coursing silently down her cheeks and soaking her hands like raindrops in a storm.

10

EVERYTHING I OWN

Simon's father was standing in the doorway. He pushed his way into the hall and Jess was caught off balance, stumbling. She followed him into the kitchen. *Her* kitchen. But he seemed to have commandeered it and was sitting, uninvited, at her table.

John looked agitated. Maybe he had come to apologise for his son's behaviour. She felt sorry for him. She offered him a coffee, but he refused curtly.

"I've just come to tell you," he began and Jess heard the formal, cold tone, "on behalf of Hilary and myself, that we have had a good talk with Simon and we are convinced that he is still the good, honest, honourable, wonderful son we always knew we had."

What? She was beginning to feel the anger kicking aside the pain and misery and incomprehension. Her mouth set hard.

"She seduced him. Not his fault." John stared at the table. "To be as brief as I can, because I have other places I would rather be than here with you. I have an announcement, Jessamy. We've decided to cut you and the girls out of our wills. We're leaving everything to Simon."

What?

"The girls? Your granddaughters?" was all Jess could utter.

"Oh, he'll give them whatever he thinks is right. We can trust him. But it's entirely up to him whether he gives the girls or you anything. Although I doubt he would want to give *you* anything, after what's happened." He curled his lip.

"So what *has* happened? Please tell me because *I* don't know. I don't know what I'm supposed to have done. All I know is that he says he doesn't love me any more, if he ever did, and that he has decided he doesn't want to be a husband and father any more." John snorted. "Well, if you know anything else, I would be grateful to be put in the picture. Because Simon, my husband, won't discuss anything with me."

"You went to the solicitor's, didn't you?"

"You mean, Simon virtually dragged me there the day after he announced he was going off with another woman, while I was still in shock, as I still am now, frankly, and told the solicitor that he needed to be free to go with this new woman. That's all. There were no actual reasons given. Just that. I have no idea what it's all about."

"Oh, don't you? Then that's your problem." He brushed her away as though she was a dirty fly on his plate.

"Why are you being so horrid to me?"

"You obviously didn't make our son happy, did you, and that's all we're interested in."

Jess thought of all the times she had nursed Simon through his breakdowns, tried to take the burden of – well, everything – off his shoulders. Did his marking and prep for him, if he seemed miserable and tired, or had had a bad day – which most of them were when he was working – showed him how she cared and loved him all the time.

"I tried my very best. I really don't know what more I could ever have done."

"Well it clearly wasn't enough. If you had done more, he wouldn't have been swayed by anyone else, would he?"

"*I beg your pardon?*"

"It wasn't his fault. He was seduced by someone who offered him more than you."

"Oh yes, a life without children and responsibility, he's already virtually said that! Except that this woman has children. Is she going to leave them too?

"Anyway, he wasn't unfaithful. He didn't do anything wrong."

"Wasn't unfaithful? How do you make that out?"

"He no longer felt he was married, so in his heart and mind he wasn't, so he couldn't have been unfaithful."

"But he *was* married!" Was she going mad? Did this make any sense at all?

"Only legally, not in his heart. He was living a lie. So that's not wrong, morally."

"You mean it's not wrong to walk out on your children, to tell your devoted wife she's nothing, to say you've decided you don't want to be a husband and father any more so none of it has anything to do with him any more – he's just not interested any more?" She gasped for breath, suppressing the tears and sobs that were threatening to choke her. But John glared at her and Jess saw the hatred in his eyes. She knew in that moment all was totally lost. There was no support, no sympathy, no understanding. Husband, gone. People she had considered as family, gone. Her life as she knew it, gone.

"No, that is not what happened here. He would never hurt anyone or turn his back on his responsibilities. He just couldn't live with you any more." John rose. "You needed to be a good Quaker wife to him, obey and put his needs first. Consider Simon more. Stop putting yourself and the children first." He fiddled with something in his pocket. "Oh, and Hilary sent you this." He proffered an envelope. Frowning, Jess tore it open. It contained £25 and a note saying: "Get yourself a dress and negligee. It may be your last chance to attract Simon back. Love, Hilary x"

Jess couldn't speak. She pushed the money back in the envelope and thrust it into John's hand. It was all she could do was to shake her head and push past him to open the front door to usher him out.

"Sanctimonious, pompous old git!" scoffed Polly when Jess recounted everything to her – and she remembered every word, every nuance; she would never ever forget, it was branded on her heart. Polly poured more red wine into her glass, topped up Jess's, and leaned back in the armchair. The wine was going to Jess's head and she couldn't help giggling: 'git!' They seemed to be getting through an awful lot of bottles these days. "God! What's wrong with these people?"

"I don't know." She felt hysterical, but didn't know whether she was laughing or crying. "They seem to want to make me feel small, that it's all my fault somehow."

Polly snorted in disgust. "They don't want to think it's their son that's in the wrong. How they can justify that, god only knows! It's obvious to everyone else."

"Hmmm, I don't know that it is. They have a way of making their inventions seem reality. They're very believable, I'm afraid. They certainly seem to have the credibility to make other people believe their version. Nobody will doubt them. After all, they appear to be upright Quakers, honest and honourable, influential and high status, charming. Why should anyone doubt them? Whereas I'm … well, I'm nothing. A nobody. Who would believe me?"

"You're certainly not 'nothing' or a 'nobody', Jess. You're clever and funny. You're stable and reliable and … and lovely! You're the loveliest person I've ever known … well, apart from Matt, of course!"

"Oh, honey, you're very sweet. But I'm being realistic. That's how people are. They go along with the ones who sound most convincing because they're important. Because of who they are in society. Because they can shout loudest. Because they can be heard."

"That's depressing."

"Yes, I guess it is. But it's the reality I'm up against. I'm not a bigwig. I have no status, no money. I have no clout. They have. And they'll probably begin to really believe it themselves soon."

"What? Believe their own lies?" Polly looked Jess in the eye and stroked her arm. She grimaced. "You must feel as though you're going mad. As though you're caught up in someone else's dream world."

Yes, thought Jess, that's exactly how I feel. Trying to hang on to reality while all about her was going insane. Simon and his parents had created a reality that suited them and they were holding on to that, and even convincing others that was what had really happened. Who else would they convince? They knew people at the county council, maybe at the school she taught at. Would it affect her job, would she every day be anxious that she might lose her job? And where would she and the children be then?

Would they try to convince the children? Would they somehow manage to turn the children against her? Her own beloved children?

Would they try to convince her own parents and family? The Quakers they all knew, their mutual friends, their world? The people at the Meeting they had been going to over the last few years? OK, she was not as committed as Simon; somehow she always felt a little uneasy at the strictures, the piety, the puritanism, the judgements. But she had gone faithfully with Simon and the children from time to time, as a family, so that at least the children would be brought up with some idea of religion and Christian values.

But if she was eliminated, rejected from all this, kicked out … if there was a body of people, however much in the background, who thought she was a horrible person … she would feel that darkness shadowing behind her …

Jess leaned back on the sofa and sighed. "You know, I just don't feel comfortable going out anywhere now. I only feel safe here in my own home. And even here, I panic when the phone rings or the doorbell sounds."

"That's only to be expected, Jess. I mean, That Woman – Simon's mother – well! Phoning you like that late at night, knowing you were on your own, yelling and swearing down the phone. No wonder it made you come out in hot flushes and trembling. It would anyone."

"But I felt weak. I felt that I should be being strong and telling her what I really thought. But I couldn't. Somehow I was reduced to a jelly. I never knew she could swear and shout like that! Such a genteel lady-like person! I was completely thrown. And nobody would believe me! Oh, Polly, it was absolutely dreadful!" She still trembled at the memory of that night.

"Well, I believe you. I wonder if she has the same condition as him. What did you say you thought it was? Manic depression?" Jess nodded. "Does it run in his family? Is that what's wrong with his mother too?"

"But … I don't know, maybe if it *is* some mental illness then we should think of it *as* an illness, a disease, and that he can't help it. Maybe we should just think of it as an aberration and sympathise and be understanding …"

"But even if it is a mental illness it doesn't excuse him treating you that way – and his father and mother too." She shook her head firmly. "No, I'm sorry but people cannot go around being like that. There's no excuse. Illness or no. And it may not be that; it may just be that they are nasty people! Society has boundaries to stop people causing harm to others. Surely …?"

Jess shrugged in despair at the situation she now found herself thrust into. She had never liked confrontation and now she felt as though she was getting driven in to it. It was just not the way she was.

But, on the other hand, equally, she refused to be trampled underfoot.

Someone had asked her the other day how she was feeling and she had thought: I feel as though Nazi or fascist jackboots are trampling all over me. That's how it feels to be treated like this by people you trusted, people you thought were your family. But she had just murmured some platitude, as was expected and accepted with a superficial understanding.

And she remembered that after Hilary's nasty phone call, after she had shakily managed to put down the phone, she had collapsed helplessly on the hall floor, sobbing until she was utterly drained. Finally, all spent, she had slept, there on the cold floor, unable to climb the stairs, until she saw the sky lightening and realised it was dawn and she must crawl up to bed somehow and continue the next day as if nothing had happened. To protect her children.

Jess knew that she could only cope with one small thing at a time. Thankfully it was the school holidays, and so at least she didn't have to think about work. There was no way she could manage that at the moment. She felt so shocked and battered. She had no money. The family income had been reduced to a third of the amount it used to be. And she had spent her savings on the new kitchen, never thinking for one moment that she might need that money for herself and the children to live on. Her income was always regarded as an extra, for holidays, clothes for the children and herself, household equipment and improvements, treats, presents. She would at least get her next pay check going in to her own bank account in a couple of weeks' time. But she would have the mortgage and utilities to pay for entirely on her own which she hadn't accounted for. She needed every penny she could find.

She remembered the family holiday that she had booked and paid for herself, as usual, and knew that there was no way she could go on a holiday: the girls were stunned and upset and she was devastated. They all needed the familiarity of home. And she needed the money to live on, to buy food, not for a holiday.

The holiday company from whom she had booked a cottage in Cornwall said that as it was within two weeks of the holiday neither they nor the insurance company could refund her money unless she could send them a doctor's note.

Dr Jones looked on in distress as Jess explained to him what had happened, and he patted her hand in empathy. "Well now, Jess, I can't even begin to guess what made him behave like that. The drugs for the manic depression and the sleeplessness would have regularised his behaviour. Frankly, although the self-absorption is something we do see with this condition, and I think that Simon was particularly within the narcissistic spectrum, the cruelty I'm surprised at."

Jess hadn't even begun to recount the behaviour of his parents.

"The main reason I'm telling you all this," explained Jess, "is that I wonder if you can help. If you can't, I do understand. I know that I'm not ill but a doctor's note is the only way I can get a refund from the insurers for the holiday that we can clearly no longer go on …"

"No problem, Jess. From my perspective, you are suffering from post- traumatic stress, which would be perfectly understandable, and I'm more than happy to write you a note." He began scribbling in his notepad, then tore out the page and handed it to Jess. "And if there is anything else I can do for you, just ask, anything at all … I am so very sorry you've had to suffer this. I know how hard it's been for you to deal with his condition." He shook his head. "Sometimes I can't believe how cruel people can be."

Jess was touched by his empathy, and his support, as she was by so many other people's too. But she knew that, in the end, she was facing it all alone.

She sent off the doctor's note straight away and within only a few days received a cheque for £500. She breathed a sigh of relief. She could buy food until the end of the month and pay some bills that were due. When she had gone up to Simon's study she had found several bills that he hadn't paid and two red final demands. She guessed that his mind had been elsewhere and he wasn't interested anyway, since he was about to leave them. She was desperate to pay debts, and get her finances on an even keel again. To take back control. After all, there was nobody else to help her; her parents couldn't afford to help her financially and it was clear that she couldn't expect any support from either Simon or his parents. So, it was just her now. Well, that was all to the good. She could now make her own decisions.

"Where's Daddy gone, Mummy?" asked Katy as she hugged the girls to her. Children's BBC was burbling away in the background but Jess was unable to focus on anything. She didn't seem able to watch television or a film, or even read any more. Listening to music was the only thing she could cope with although she wasn't concentrating, but it helped to soothe her thoughts as she listened to her favourite Mozart or the choral pieces she used to sing.

"Yes, Mummy. Why has Daddy gone?" Abi chimed in, snuggling further into Jess's side. "Has he gone to be in another family?"

"Doesn't he like us any more in our family?" Katy asked with a seriousness that broke Jess's heart.

"Oh, sweetheart, no. I'm sure that's not the case at all. Daddy loves you both very much. He's just … he's just not very well at the moment. So he needs a break to get better."

"And will he come back when he's better?"

Jess had no idea how to respond to her daughters' confusion and distress. What was the right thing to do? To say? She didn't want to lie and she didn't want to raise false hopes that were never going to be realised, but at the same time she didn't want to tell the truth as she somehow knew in her heart it would be.

"Well, we all hope so."

"Will we see him again?" Katy's mouth was trembling and her eyes were filling up.

"I'm sure you will, darling. As soon as he's feeling better." She hugged her daughters closer to her.

"But if he's ill - and he's not gone to hospital, has he? - so why can't he be ill here at home?" said Abi, shaking her head.

"Maybe he just needs some peace and quiet," said Katy with a serious frown.

What could Jess say? That decent fathers don't go off to get peace and quiet away from their kids? That anyway their particular family and household was not frenetic or noisy or stressful or difficult at all? It couldn't go on like this, Jess knew; that was the only certainty in her life at the moment. Whatever Simon was doing, whoever he was with, whatever he saw his life as now, he must accept that he had a responsibility to his children. He couldn't abdicate that. If needs be, she would have to cope alone. But the children shouldn't be rejected.

She had no idea how to persuade him of this. When she had tried he had simply scoffed at her and reminded her brutally that he had left them and no longer had any interest in 'responsibilities' or 'fatherhood'. He had his own life now: a single life, and one that didn't include them.

When he rang her to demand that she gave him the money she would have transferred to the joint account for the household bills, if they still had a joint account, she resisted the impulse to slam down the phone. Instead she took a deep breath and made a suggestion.

"Simon, we really need to talk about the children, about how to work together for them …"

"*Your* problem. *Your* job," he shouted down the phone. "I've already made this clear, *Jessamy*!" He spat her name out as though he hated its very sound. "I'm not coming back, *Jessamy*! It's over!"

"Simon, please …please, just listen to me … maybe we can come to some agreement …" she heard him grunt. "Maybe if we just say you're having a break … you can go and do your own thing, whatever … and then in, say, a year's time, after everything has calmed down, we agree to meet up and discuss what we want to do …?"

"Why the hell would I want to do that? I've made my decisions! It's you that can't accept it! And anyway, I wouldn't feel free to sleep with other women if I was still married to *you*. I'm not prepared for you to make me feel guilty."

She drew in her breath slowly to try to regain her balance and calm. "I just don't know if maybe you are in some kind of crisis right now, and that maybe in a while when you've done what you want to do, when you've considered it all a bit more, you may change your perspective …?"

"Are you saying that I don't know my own mind?"

"No, Simon, I simply think that we need to consider and discuss before we do anything irreversible."

"I'm not going to change my mind. Why can't you accept that? What's wrong with you?"

"I'm trying to do the best thing for the children, Simon. They miss you. They want to know what's going on. They're very distressed …"!

"Don't try to blackmail me!"

"I'm not trying to blackmail you. I simply want to work out what's best all round, for everyone – but especially the children. I'm so afraid that they will be damaged if …"

Jess heard Simon slam down the phone and for a few moments she stood with the receiver to her ear, unable to move, trying to still her breathing, trying to gather herself.

However awful it was for her, Jess knew that she needed to try her best for her children. Her nights were now filled with terrifying nightmares, of being thumped to the ground and trampled on, but she would wake immediately when she heard the girls crying and she would jump out of bed to go in to their rooms to comfort them. Katy heart-rendingly, slept with one of her daddy's old jumpers. "It smells of him," she told Jess, "so it makes me think he's still here with us, mummy." *How could he have done this? How could he be carrying on doing this? How could his parents think all this was OK?* Jess felt as though her heart was bursting with grief.

She knew that, however appalling for her personally, she would give everything she had if only she could go back to how it was before, even with the difficulties that followed Simon around, the moodiness and the obstructiveness. And the cruelty, yes, even that. Because the only thing that mattered to Jess was the girls' happiness, comfort and security. The only thing.

Well, not the only thing. She knew that she still cared that Simon was OK. She had loved him for too long to just switch off.

Yet in all the impenetrable quest for understanding, for an answer to the "*why?*" that stopped up her throat and choked her, she began to imagine that, without any other answers, it must be *her*; she must be to blame, something she did, something she had said? And so she had to build bridges, somehow, she had to fight to get back what they had before. She could only remember the good times: Simon holding her tenderly, Simon saying that he loved her, so much, Simon smiling and gently brushing her hair out of her eyes, Simon playing his jazz loudly filling the house with happy noise, Simon confiding in her about his troubles at work, trusting her, Simon grinning as she wore a new clinging dress, Simon discussing plans with her, even Simon occasionally lifting one of the girls high and swinging then round with joyous whoops ...

What had she done to destroy all that? How could they go back and try it again …. This time she would be a better wife, a better lover, a better ... whatever he wanted ... just to be together properly again as a united family. If only he would let her care for him again, like she used to, get him over this terrible time, as she had done before, The strength of her love for him, for their family, surely should be enough to bring him through this, bring their family and them both through this?

On the radio the Boy George number drifted into the room: *I would give everything I own, give up my life, my heart, my home ... just to have you ... back again ... just to hold you ... once again ...* So plaintive, so right. Her heart felt as though it was being strangled in her chest.

The telephone rang. Jess's heart thrummed. As always now when the phone rang or the doorbell chimed, her heart raced with dread and she could feel herself trembling. She picked it up slowly, hand shaking, gathering her slow wits to confront whatever it may be.

"Jessamy," came her mother-in-law's strained voice. Jess's heart plummeted. "I want to have the girls this weekend."

"Oh, well, I'm not sure what exactly we're doing but they have dancing and music on Saturday ..."

"Jessamy," Hilary interrupted briskly, "I'm not negotiating. We have a right to see our grandchildren."

"I'm not stopping you seeing them; I'm simply saying that we have other commitments on Saturday …"

"I'm sure it won't hurt them to miss classes one time." Jess could almost hear the pursed lips. She really hated this feeling of having to parcel up her children and send them to these people who were being so horrid to her as if it was their right to demand them whenever they wanted, regardless of their own lives.

"You know that I don't like them missing. Perhaps they could come on Sunday – if they want to, that is?"

Jess could hear an aggravated impatient intake of breath. "It isn't a question of what they would *like*. Simon is here and he should see them. For goodness sake, Jessamy, we all wish you would stop being so obstructive!"

Obstructive? Jess felt a headache pound in her skull.

"You don't understand what it's like for us!" Hilary screamed. Oh god, was she going to start that again?

"Hilary, it's pretty awful for me, too, actually."

"Jessamy, I can tell you it's worse for us!"

Jess refused to join in with this sort of competition. But Hilary wasn't finished. "Simon's girlfriend rang today." Jess flinched. Girlfriend? That sounded so wrong. He was married. He couldn't have a 'girlfriend'. "She seems very nice." Hilary paused as if reflecting on how nice the 'girlfriend' was. "Well … off with the old and on with the new. That's how it is. She has my blessing."

Jess was still feeling bruised when she heard Simon unlock the front door (*she must retrieve the door key from him; he shouldn't be doing this*). She went out into the hall intending to ask for the key back, but she saw his face, dark and furious. He waved a photo in front of her face, but she couldn't see what it was. "For god's sake, how dare you! How dare you tell my mother she can't have the fucking children when she wants. How dare you cross her. How dare you play fucking god with her life!"

"*What?*" Jess felt her body trembling uncontrollably. "For goodness sake, Simon! Why are you behaving like this? What am I supposed to have done to you? You're behaving as though you're punishing me. Why?"

"Because you were my *wife!*" he spat at her. She struggled to grasp what he meant. Why would you punish someone simply because they were married to you? It didn't make any sense.

She was aware that the girls were upstairs in their bedrooms, playing and listening to music. She hoped to goodness that they couldn't hear. She glanced upwards.

"The girls are upstairs, for goodness sake, Simon!"

He snorted with derision and held the photo right in front of her eyes. It was of their little family: Simon on the left, then the children and Jess. Glaring at her, thrusting his face to hers, he began to tear the picture.

"W – What are you doing?" and she knew that her voice shook. She didn't want it to, she didn't want him to see that she was so afraid. He slowly tore the photograph between the image of himself and those of Jess and the children, separating himself from them. Then he screwed up the half with their image on it and threw it down on the floor.

His face was red and angry. He shouted, even right into her face. "I dreamed last night of coming round here and setting fire to the house!" Jess drew in her breath, horrified. "And I burned it to the ground. And I got rid of *all* of you! Out of my life! As if you never existed! I *killed* you all. *Me*! I did it – what I have wanted to do for fucking years! And, you know … *you know, Jess* … I woke up happy, as though a burden had been lifted from my shoulders."

Jess held her breath as she felt his fury and the threat beating into her. His eyes were wild. Cold.

She didn't see it coming.

The blow of his fist to her left eye. It knocked the wind out of her and sent her staggering across the hall. Her back felt the sharp blow of the handle of the understairs cupboard door. She cried out in pain and slid down the doorjamb, crumpling on the floor. She could see him looming over her as she lay prostrate. She couldn't move to defend herself from his blows. He kicked her chest and she felt her ribs crack. She rolled away from his feet, and looked up at him, horrified, gasping for breath. He just stood there, unmoving, glaring.

Then almost as suddenly, she saw through her one blurred eye, that he had stepped away from her. His face was white and horrified.

"Oh god! What have I done? I'm sorry, Jess. I didn't mean to do that!"

She made no move. Her ribs hurt badly, her cheek stung harshly and her eye, she knew, was swelling up and she couldn't see a thing with her left eye and little from her right which was blinded with tears. She just looked up from the floor and stared at him. The husband she had loved dearly, cared for and nursed in his illnesses, his breakdowns, made love with in his good times, her lover … come to *this*? She stared unable to move she hurt so much, the pain in her ribs rasping her breath.

She heard him let himself out of the front door, and only then could she move, shifting her weight as far as she could until she yelped with pain and fear. She heard the music in the girls' bedrooms upstairs. She prayed that they hadn't heard what had happened.

She stayed on the floor for some time, hardly daring to move her muscles too much. Eventually she could push herself up and sink heavily on to the telephone seat. She stared at the phone. She needed help. Who could she call? She knew that Polly and Matt were out. Her own mother would be horrified, and probably be panicked. Biting her lip, she slowly dialled the number.

"Yes?" demanded Hilary.

"It's Jess. I don't know what to do. Simon has just been round and … and beaten me up. I can hardly move. And the girls are here, upstairs. I need help. I think I have cracked ribs and a black eye. Please …?"

Jess heard a sharp intake of annoyed breath. "Nothing to do with us, Jessamy. He's our son, and he can do whatever he likes. I'm sure he had good reason to punish you. Now get off this line and behave like an adult. We've been patient enough with you!"

Jess staggered in to the living room and lay down on the sofa for a while. She shut her eyes. Why on earth had she imagined that they would help her and the children? The world juddered around her.

"Mummy, what's the matter? What's happened?" Jess forced her eyes open and made out the silhouettes of Katy and Abi standing over her. Their faces were pale and anxious.

She pushed herself up and tried to suppress the pain. "It's OK, sweethearts. It's just … silly clumsy mummy fell into the hall door. Banged into the door handle … hurt my eye and my ribs. Not to worry. Be OK in a minute."

Katy stroked her arm and Abi clambered up on the sofa beside her. "Don't worry, mummy. We'll help to get the tea."

The following day, when the girls were out playing with their friends, Jess telephoned the police. Polly had come rushing round last night and told her, in no uncertain terms, that she must report the assault. "I can't," Jess had said. "He's still my husband."

"If you don't want it to happen again, than you must!"

A uniformed policeman called round within the hour but seeing her conscious and sitting up on the sofa, he shook his head.

"To be frank with you, this is what we designate 'a domestic' It's a domestic dispute which doesn't come into the police's remit. It's between the husband and wife. We can't do anything."

"What? You mean that a husband is allowed to do whatever he likes to his wife?"

"Well, as bad as that sounds, that's about the gist of it. A wife is still really the property of the husband …"

"Even in 1986?"

"Yes, I'm afraid that's the law for you!"

"That's positively Victorian."

"Afraid so. And frankly if you took it to court, it'd probably get thrown out anyway. A domestic, you see." He shook his head, as if explaining a simple fact to a backward child.

That was it, then.

There was no help. No support. She felt so alone.

And there was no going back now.

Jess made a doctor's appointment to see what she should do about the cracked ribs and black eye. There was little to be done about the ribs; they had to heal on their own. Dr Jones gave her arnica cream for around the eye, and instructions for rest and a cooling eye patch. Of course, he asked her how it had happened and she told him the truth.

He frowned at her and shook his head. "Look, Jess, if ever that happened again, any assault, any break-in, any violence at all, just ring me while he's there and I can get right over there and section him. I can't do it after the event, but if I see it happening, I can. It's the only way. He won't do it himself and it has to be voluntary unless someone else like me witnesses it. Really you, and your children, need to be protected from him."

"Oh my god, I hadn't been thinking of it in those terms, doctor." And it crossed her mind that it wouldn't be possible, pragmatically, to distract him long enough to make a phone call.

"Well, Jess, you need to now, I'm afraid. You need to start thinking of the seriousness of it. This is domestic violence, abuse."

"But he's still my husband."

"He came in to school yesterday doing his advisory teacher stuff, stalking about, throwing his weight around, god of all, god's gift to women," said Polly. Simon had decided to take a new role with the county council and leave his teaching job. The school had, Jess heard, been relieved. "Did a presentation on sex education and parental responsibilities. Oh, and child abuse. The awful things that divorce does to kids. Couldn't believe it. To be honest, Jess, I had to walk out in the end."

"You know, that's not even anything I can laugh about."

"The Head 'arrested' me afterwards and asked me why I had walked out. I told him. I said, this is a man who walked out on his lovely wife and kids, went off with someone else, and said he'd decided he didn't want to be a husband and father any more. Just like that. And as far as his precious sex education goes, he went off to an STD clinic to be tested, and said how *interesting* it was, how it would help give *credence and authenticity* to his PSHE teaching!"

"Oh god! So what did the Head say?"

"He said, well, you can't trust rumours. So I said, his wife is my best friend, I *know* what happened."

"And?"

Polly screwed up her face. "He stared straight at me, shrugged his weedy shoulders, and said, oh well, boys will be boys."

"Oh, that's appalling."

"Yes, I said, 'bollocks! And I don't care if you sack me.' And I walked away from him. They stick together."

Jess sighed. "Oh, goodness, this is getting dire all round. I do hope you don't suffer for that."

"No. He didn't apologise. But he sent me a note about a conference he wanted me to go to next term to represent the school. So, no, I don't think he'll sack me."

"Oh thank goodness."

"He's still a bastard! I'll never see the Head in the same way again. Not that I ever thought he was great, rather a 'yes man' for the county education department. But now … urgh!"

She was in the midst of the heart-breaking task of completing a form for the solicitor about the grounds for divorce. She hated it. There was no way she wanted to divorce her husband but she couldn't risk a repetition of the behaviours he'd been displaying. He had been aggressive about it, although she had no idea why since he had insisted on dragging her to the solicitor's soon after he walked out. He had told the solicitor that he wanted to be free of the family and responsibilities. The solicitor, an efficient young woman called Sarah, who appeared puzzled and disconcerted at Simon's diatribes, had told him that he couldn't be 'free' of a legal marriage and children, but he had scoffed at her. Eventually it was agreed that he should engage a different solicitor as she couldn't act for both of them in the circumstances. Jess had then had a private meeting with her solicitor in which she had been able to detail exactly what had happened, without Simon's self-promoting interruptions.

Jess felt heart-weary and low as she circled the 'adultery', 'abandonment', 'unreasonable behaviour' and 'cruelty' grounds as instructed by her solicitor and according to the guidance notes with the form. God, this was dreadful.

The door bell rang and she began to shake. Simon had said he might come over that day to collect some of his things from the house. He was currently living with his parents; they had converted a large room up-stairs into a bed-sitting room for him, rather like you would do for a teenage son. But much of the time he was apparently up in the north with the "girlfriend". She felt sick to the core. How could she see him again? How should she comport herself?

Thankfully the girls were out with friends; she didn't want them to see this.

She opened the door cautiously and stepped back holding up her hand in warning. "I'm sorry but you get what you want and then you go. I can't risk any vio-lence again. Nobody could be here with me today but a friend is on stand-by at the end of the phone if you try anything on, Simon." That wasn't strictly true but she felt the need for reinforcements and a deterrent. Why on earth hadn't she said she'd take them over to him and dump them on his doorstep?

His face darkened. "As you will."

"I have to tell you that the doctor and the police know what you did and they are also on standby. I'm getting a restraining order."

He looked frightened then and strode quickly to the living room. He began to sort roughly through the LP records, his Queen albums, his Cream, his jazz … "Is this yours or mine?" he asked gruffly.

Jess shrugged. "Mine, but you take it. I'm not about to argue." The sooner he was done and out of the house, the better. Never mind what the cost of replacements. He piled up records, books, bits and pieces. Then he started on the furniture.

"Wait a minute. You can't take the furniture. You were told by the solicitors that you couldn't take any furniture or equipment that would make it difficult for us."

Simon swung on her angrily. "Well, I'm taking these chairs. They were bought for me, by my parents."

"OK, OK!" Should she just let him take anything he wanted and at least come out of this without any more broken bones? But something inside her railed against the unfairness of what was happening. She bit her lip until she felt the saltiness of blood.

For an hour she looked on as he decimated the house, helpless, shaking in grief.

Finally he was finished. "Look I've hired a van but I can't take my motorbike and boat, and I'm getting new replacements anyway, so you'll have to sell them and give me the money." Numbed, she nodded. She couldn't even think straight any more.

He left. The door closed behind him and she put the chain across. Tomorrow she would employ a workman to change the locks.

11

SWEET LITTLE LIES

J ess put an advertisement in the local paper, free for items under £10, and sold Simon's boat and motorbike for £9.99 each. They were snapped up very quickly, although several people came to view and were clearly suspicious. They tried the motorbike and found that it worked fine; they inspected the boat for holes in the hull and found it all perfect.

She sent the £19.98 to Simon at his parents' home and refused to take his irate phone calls.

She checked her purse and counted out the five pounds she had left. She needed that for the girls' school dinners next week when they were back for the new term. So she couldn't go and buy anything. She scrabbled in the chest freezer for something to make for herself and the girls for dinner. She was able now to make proper fresh meals again for the children, meat and vegetables, and remember to time the potatoes and broccoli, and watch the lamb under the grill. She had emerged from her 'fish finger phase' as she called it to the girls, trying to make light of her grief.

But she still couldn't eat much herself; she felt no interest in food as she used to. And somehow she was unable to swallow it down; her throat felt constricted all the time. Food was just something she pushed around her plate at mealtimes as she encouraged the girls to eat. She looked down at her skinny arms delving into the freezer. She had lost nearly two stone: weight that she could scarcely afford to lose. At six and a half stone she felt thin and frail. It just dripped off her these days. Little food, little sleep, stressed out. Her throat was able to swallow milk, porridge and yogurt, so at least her nails were still strong and pretty and her curly hair, that she'd had permed a while ago into the "big" style that was all the mid-80s rage, was still a glossy chestnut.

She found a meat pie that she could defrost and re-heat, and she pulled out some chicken breasts that she could put in the fridge for tomorrow. She was actually able to plan ahead again, from one day to the next. She found herself able to visualise the next day, again, instead of being swamped by the absolute present. She put the pie on a baking tray on the counter top. Suddenly she felt a sob rising up through her chest as she realised that she had baked the meat pie when Simon was still with them. He loved home-made pies, meat and fruit ones, home-baked bread and cakes, quiche and cheesecake, apple and blackberry crumbles ….

🐚

"Why have you still got this double bed?" demanded her mother. *Did she really think Jess would prioritise buying a new bed just because she'd slept there with Simon?*

"Because I'm used to it and I can't afford to buy a new one."

"No, I mean that it looks slutty – as though you might be expecting to have some other man over here for … well … you know … *sex* …" *Good god. As if she was possibly thinking of that right now! Anyway, chance would be a fine thing – two kids, exhausted from a full-time demanding job, plus a moonlighting job to make ends meet.*

Jess had taken on an examiner's role and also started tutoring at the local evening classes, thanks to Polly and Matt's offer to babysit, and she needed to prepare for both of the jobs, as well as her 'proper' full-time job teaching school. It was the only way she could see that they could possibly manage with the sudden huge reduction in family income.

She knew that there were many people a lot worse off than her, but at present, until she could get her act together, and until the divorce went through, she had to continue to pay the mortgage and utilities for a large house which Simon had wanted to buy and which they had managed fine when the family income was three times larger than now.

"Mother, I don't have the strength for anything other than necessities." Jess sighed wearily.

"You don't still love him, do you?" Her mother peered closely at her, over her spectacles, making Jess squirm.

Jess paused. Did she? He had hurt all of them, emotionally and physically. She supposed she should think of him as a monster. But she kept remembered the loving, charming Simon, the father of her children, her lover. And she felt her heart breaking again.

"Yes," she whispered, "I suppose, despite everything, I do."

"Oh Jessamy! How can you still love someone who treated you and the girls like that?"

Jess shook her head slowly. "I just can't switch it all off. He was everything to me, my best friend, everything. I know it's all changed. *He's* changed. But you know, *I* haven't. And I can't turn it off."

Her mother grimaced and opened her arms, enfolding Jess. No more words were needed.

It had become a burning issue with Jess to try to get to the bottom of what was wrong with Simon. She'd researched the manic depression issue and violent mood swings, anger and narcissism, and all she had read seemed familiar and echoed what she observed in Simon's behaviour. The problem was, for her, should she see all this as an illness, that maybe he could be treated for, and recover, or whether it was so ingrained as a mental illness, a personality disorder, that it would always be like this – and therefore not something she could live with. And maybe not something she wanted her daughters to be exposed to. Certainly she had, as much as she could, protected them from the excesses of his behaviour, his aggression and obsessive selfishness. Should she 'love him better' or was that ridiculously unrealistic?

She'd hung on to the belief that 'love conquers all', but did it? She'd held tight to the idea that she was 'the rock that he could cling on to' and that everything therefore would work out. But would it? And who would get hurt in the process? In the end, was it all worth it, or should she just give up on him? She hated to think like that; it felt so defeatist. But, for herself and her children – what was best?

"Nobody else can decide that for you," said Jack, the educational psychologist she had met at an education leadership day conference. "I have to say I think you are being amazingly good to him." They were sitting in the coffee bar at the conference venue sipping filter coffee before they set off home. "Very thoughtful, understanding and caring." He patted her hand. "He can't see what's right in front of him! But of course that's what happens in these cases."

Jess flushed. She'd had a few chats during the day with Jack as they seemed to have found themselves in the same groups. He was much older than her but kindly and somehow comforting. He was a professor of educational psychology, so Jess felt quite in awe of him. But he knew about general psychology and psychiatry and Jess had taken the opportunity to pick his brains. He was easy to talk to, very empathetic, and she realised that she had told him more than she normally divulged to other people, apart from her closest family and friends. She had talked to him about Simon's behaviour and his state of mind, what had happened when he left them, and it seemed professional and natural to do so.

"Look, Jess," said Jack as he stood up and picked up his briefcase from the floor under the table. "If you want to keep in touch and maybe come down to the university where I work, I'm happy to try to help you further. If you think I can be of any help. And I have a colleague, a clinical psychiatrist, who may be helpful too. Sometimes just talking it through with an objective, neutral 'other' can help. But … entirely up to you."

He handed her his business card and added, with a smile, "I wouldn't charge you consultation fees!"

Jess peered at the card. "OK, thanks. I may well take you up on that." They shook hands and Jess drove home feeling more peaceful; talking helped. Polly talked with her, and Matt, but of course she was aware that they were involved, that they had a prior view of

Simon and that it wasn't very positive. Maybe someone neutral might be more clear-sighted. Not that she
wasn't grateful and thankful for Polly and Matt's support, of course she was; she'd have collapsed entirely
without it.

The following week, Jess rang Jack and they arranged for her to go down to speak with him and one
of his colleagues. She would have to stay over as it was
too far to drive there and back in one day, and Jack assured her that he had a spare guest room. If she could
get her head around some of this, it would perhaps
help her to understand Simon's behaviour. Not that
anything excused what he had done. But perhaps it
would help her to move on from it.

Hilary grabbed the chance to have the children
for the weekend, and Jess even detected a warmer encouragement for her to do this after she had explained
what she was doing. But she didn't feel happy about
letting Hilary and John look after the girls for a whole
weekend on their own, even though they promised
to take them to their ballet and music classes. Simon
would apparently only be around for part of the time
as he was going up to Liverpool for most of the weekend. Not that he would have been much help anyway.
Jess made it clear that she would not have him taking
her precious daughters up there to see and spend time
with 'the girlfriend', about whom she knew almost
nothing apart from the bed details that Simon had
chosen to regale her with (the love bites, the foreplay,

her amazing body – for god's sake, why did he have to tell her all that – to hurt her even more? Why was that necessary?)

Jack and his colleague proved helpful and reassuring, and Jack was a kindly, gentlemanly host. He advised that Jess try to persuade Simon to go for a series of sessions with Marriage Guidance Counselling and a psycho-therapist. His colleague talked to Jess about some of the symptoms of manic depression, narcissism, OCD and self-obsession, and asked her about Simon's behaviour. It was one of his areas of expertise. He told her that bouts could be triggered by the smallest things that she probably couldn't predict.

"He clearly has a control problem – he tries to control others because he feels he can't control himself," said Jack's colleague. "But yet he does control himself enough to be able to avoid outbursts when there's someone else there, at least most of the time. So when he's with you, alone, the control mechanism is relaxed and he flares up at you."

"I guess that figures."

"It's not a coincidence that people with this condition tend to hurt the ones they're closest to and that they actually love the most – although I'm sure it doesn't feel like that."

"It certainly doesn't."

"And you seem like a strong woman, perceptive and understanding. Clearly he's in denial about his MD. You challenge his behaviour – speak out if what he's doing is dangerous or damaging. So that triggers his denial to fight back, to project his feelings on to you, to turn his anger outwards."

"Well, it seems to figure with what Simon does."

"If he was with a 'doormat' of a woman, he might fare better, possibly. It wouldn't make him any better within himself, mentally and emotionally, but if his partner took it all, took the abuse and was subservient, he wouldn't have the need to lash out … but then, what would it do to her and their relationship? And there's always the chance that he'd erupt anyway. It's not going away."

"I don't know how to think about it all. If it's an illness, albeit a mental illness …?"

"But, Jess, even so, nothing 'excuses' physical and mental harm to someone else. Nobody can or should live with that."

But barely a month later, at a social group of professional women that Jess had joined, she was chatting to a new acquaintance about their children, when her companion suddenly gasped and turned to her, hand flying up to cover her mouth, and said, "Oh, no, not Jessamy Arlington-Smith! I never realised, I only just twigged … Oh my goodness …!"

"What? *What?*" Jess was startled.

"Your husband is Simon Arlington-Smith? *Hilary's* son?"

"Ye-e-es. *Was.*" Jess's palms became sweaty and her heart was thrumming.

"And you have separated …?"

"Ye-e-es."

"I'm sorry. I just never …" Her new friend took a moment or two to smooth her skirt over her knees and compose herself. "I know Hilary from the Rotary Ladies' Inner Wheel. Do you know that she's been telling everyone that …"

Jess felt queezy.

"Oh, I know now, because I've got to know you, that it's all lies … But she's been telling everyone that it wasn't Simon's fault, that he didn't have anyone else, that it was *you,* and that he couldn't live with that any more, that's why he had to leave … Now I know, from talking to you, from the way you speak about your family, that's not true, it'd never be true … But she's telling everyone that you had other men, a lot, and that you had a dirty weekend with someone only a few weeks ago and expected them to have the children for the weekend while you had your evil way with some chap."

Jess knew that her mouth was gaping in horror. How could Hilary tell people such lies? She *knew* that Hilary knew the truth. She had heard Simon tell them he had another woman. She had told Hilary herself that she was going to see someone about his behaviour to her, then and now, to try to understand it and make things calmer for the sake of the children. Why would she do this? Yet John had visited her that time and said some ridiculous things in support of Simon's behaviour, hadn't he? Had they *decided* what they wanted to believe and just … *believed* it – their own lies? And what if they told these lies to the girls?

"She's been telling people all that rubbish?" squeaked Jess, unable to trust her own trembling voice. "My god." And who else had she – they? – lied to? She felt outrage welling up through her body. How dare they?

And how on earth was she supposed to squash those rumours? It was, after all, slander, surely? People couldn't go around telling lies about someone like that, besmirching their good name, surely?

"If ever I hear of anything like that, I'll put them straight," declared Matt, walloping his knee with his fist. Jess had fled in bewilderment and despair to her friends' house after she had dropped the girls off at music lessons on Saturday morning. Polly was out and Matt was looking after the boys, sprawled on the floor with their Scalextric. But at Jess's whispered revelation he had sat up abruptly.

"If I were you, I'd sue them for slander, defamation of character."

"Oh, no, Matt," Jess slumped. "I just haven't got the strength. I couldn't face it; more solicitors, lawyers, court cases. It's bad enough with the long slow awfulness of the divorce proceedings. I can't take any more. I feel exhausted, physically, emotionally. Suing for slander as well … pfft, no I couldn't."

"As a lawyer – OK, not family law, or slander issues, but really, Jess, you need to stop them doing this."

Jess shook her head and sighed. "Matt, I'm trying to be positive about everything. It's the only way I can cope. Please don't suggest court."

Matt pushed himself up and in two strides he was in front of her, leaning in to her, hugging her to him. "God, Jess. I don't know what else to suggest other than the law."

He held her for a moment, and then released her before she could wind her arms gratefully round his neck. "I don't know what I'd do to him if I ever met him again!"

Jess snorted a low laugh. "Well, then you probably wouldn't be allowed to be a lawyer any more!"

He raised his hands to her shoulders and held her away from him, looking in to her eyes. "I'll speak with the mother-in-law. Unofficially. I'll be careful, but I want to make it clear they cannot go around doing that. Would that be acceptable?"

Jess smiled. "Thank you, Matt. I don't know what I'd do without you …" It was almost imperceptible but it didn't escape Jess's notice that Matt raised his eyebrows. "And Polly, of course. You've both been wonderful." Matt sighed.

As he opened the solid oak front door for her, Matt said, "Sorry about the mess."

"Mess? What mess?"

"The cleaner's been as usual yesterday, but the boys and I are a bit … untidy! Boys together … you know!"

Jess glanced around the immaculate, stunning, hallway with its full height plate glass windows and polished wooden floors, and inclined her head, frowning. "What untidiness? Matt, your house always looks amazing."

"I just thought that now …" He shook his head. "Forget it. Stupid."

Nothing dramatic happened over the next few days and Matt rang Jess to tell her that he'd spoken with Hilary. "I told her that it had come to my notice through a mutual acquaintance … blah blah … and that I had to advise her that you would be within your rights to consider suing her for slander and defamation of character. That we all knew it was all lies, and that although you were reluctant to go ahead, that I, as your close friend and a lawyer, was trying, unsuccessfully at present, to persuade you to think about it. She was very defensive, gabbled a bit, but must have realised that she was on a hiding to nothing since she was lying. I think I warned her off."

"Matt, you're a star! Let's just hope nothing else flares up in retaliation."

"Hopefully not. She'll have to be careful now she knows you have a friend who's in the law. Obviously she doesn't know I'm not in *that* kind of law!"

But what did happen was that the following Saturday Simon suddenly and unusually rang Jess to tell her that he wanted to see the girls and that he had been advised that he had the right to do so. *Why would he have suddenly thought of that when he had all along declared that he wasn't interested in them?* He would send his mother and father over to pick up the children and they would spend the day with them all.

Jess was quite aware that she couldn't refuse that request and that at some point she would have to go to court to claim the children as her own and her right to custody. Her solicitor had explained all that. So she made the suggestion to the girls and they pulled unwilling faces. "Don't want to!"

"You don't have to if you don't want to. I'll never force you. It's very difficult in these situations. But I have said that you, individually, will make your choices and that I will respect whatever you want to do." Abi had immediately hugged her and Katy had paused but joined the hug too.

When Hilary and John rang the doorbell, Jess felt the pangs of fear that would haunt her for a long time. She flushed hot and cold. Her palms were slick with nervous sweat. She opened the door cautiously but they pushed through past her.

Jess helped the girls on with their coats and then went in to the kitchen to pick up their bags for the day with their books and toys in. Abi dawdled in after her as if she wanted to delay the time of departure as long as she could.

"Do I have to?" she asked.

Jess hugged her, "It wouldn't be right to not go now, this time, as you've already agreed, would it, sweetheart? I don't think you can let someone down at the last minute. But maybe think about it for next time." Abi nodded. Jess looked up from her daughter and saw that John was blocking the doorway back in to the hall.

"Excuse me!" Jess said firmly as she pushed past him, holding Abi's hand. As they walked in to the hall, she stopped in her tracks and drew in her breath. She could see that Hilary had Katy pressed up against the wall, her arms blocking the child's escape. Trapped. She barely heard Hilary's low voice.

"Any time you want to come and see your daddy, just ring me. Here's the number. Keep it in your pocket. Don't show mummy."

She must have heard Jess because she looked up away from Katy and straight at Jess. Her eyes glared triumph.

Of course she knew that Jess could do nothing about it. She couldn't tell her daughter to ignore her grandmother. That her grandmother was acting wrongly. It would appear that she was trying to keep her away from her daddy. Jess knew that all she could do was to try to ensure that Katy knew that wasn't the agenda. All she could do right then was to mouth to Hilary "enough!" and to glare right back. Hilary tossed her head and led the girls out.

Jess fiddled around the house while the girls were out at Hilary's house, doing and redoing the same chores that didn't need doing in the first place. He fingers were clumsy and her hands shook. What was Hilary – and, she supposed, Simon   saying to the girls, her daughters? It made her tremble to even think of it. She no longer trusted him as a loving, thoughtful, sensitive father. Why the lies and the foul behaviour towards the girls' mother; what was that all about? She would never feel easy about him seeing them now, in these circumstances. It all seemed to just get worse and worse …more frightening … more threatening …

She breathed a sigh of relief when she heard the car door in the drive and heard the girls running up to the door. She checked that they were alone and unchained the door, opened the deadlock and let them in. They both looked pale and drawn. She hugged them as if she would never let them go. Tears flooded her eyes but she wiped them away before the girls could see.

Could it possibly get any worse?

The solicitors' exchange of letters began. Jess opened each one with shaking hands. God, what now? The first letter from his solicitor enclosed a list from Simon about all that, he claimed, he and his parents had provided for Jess. She cried when she read it. It was so misleading, it was absurd. How could someone falsify their life so much?

The second enclosed a list of all his expenses, claiming that he could not possibly afford to pay maintenance for the children, and indeed rejecting the idea that he should be expected to share in providing for them at all. Beside each item was a cost, or an amount set aside in his budget (*budget? When had he ever budgeted for anything?*) At the bottom was a figure total beneath a declaration of his salary and the heading "amount remaining for maintenance: NIL".

Jess read the list with mouth agape. His expenses included 'entertainment', 'dining out', 'presents and gifts', 'the costs of a new car', 'rent'. She was astonished. *Rent?* He was living at his parents' house as far as she knew, and they would never charge him rent. *New car? Entertainment? Dining out? I wish!*

"What on earth is all this?" she asked Sarah, her solicitor on the phone. She was feeling increasingly that her life was now running out of control. "Why 'rent' and can he really claim a new car and entertainment ahead of providing for his children? Is this remotely acceptable?"

"No," said Sarah, "It's not acceptable. But legally, yes he can. And it all depends on the judge when you get this to court as a divorce nisi petition. If the judge believes that it is your husband's right to expect these features of his new life, then we don't have much of a leg to stand on."

"But surely, nobody can accept that, however curmudgeonly the judge might be? It's surely a question of priorities. I haven't claimed any expenses for myself. It's all mortgage and utilities and food and the children's activities. No question of a new car or going out and enjoying myself!"

"You'd be surprised at how misogynistic many of our judges are! We had a case last week where the judge, Justice Jermaine-Hempleton, ruled against the mother because he decided that she was to *blame* for the husband's adultery. I think they live in a different world."

"Oh god, I hope that I don't get one like that!" Jess bit her lip. "Actually I wish you hadn't told me that."

"Oh, I'm sure you'll be OK with yours. It's not just about the adultery, after all; it's the abandonment and cruelty as well."

"Oh I don't know. I'm not at all sure about the cruelty bit. I mean it wasn't *that* bad. I mean, I managed."

"Oh, Jess, come on! No husband should behave as he did. Believe it, for goodness sake. Oh, and as far as the rent business is concerned, I understand from this new address and my enquiries to his solicitor, that he has now moved in with some other woman. I question the 'rent'!"

Jess shook her head in confusion. "Wait a minute. What happened to the woman he apparently left us for? And what happened to the mews house/apartment, or whatever, that his parents bought him?"

"Ah, things have apparently moved on for him. He split up from the original woman named in the divorce proceedings. His parents bought him a house of his own. I don't know whether he sold that, or is renting it out – there's no mention of any financial benefit from a sale or rent – but there seems to have been another woman there with him, co-habiting on a temporary or permanent basis. Now he is living with this third woman whom he claims to be 'renting from'."

"Good god!" Jess felt sick and dizzy. How on earth had all this happened in the space of a few months? Barely a year? How much he had moved on into a different life. She realised her hand was shaking as she held the telephone receiver to her ear. She wondered how much the girls knew of all this. Dread filled her as she thought of her precious daughters being exposed to this unstable life of their father's. It was all so unfair that she could do nothing about it.

"I think the best we can do, quite honestly, Jess," continued Sarah, "is to demand maintenance for the children, even at the lowest level, negotiate from £300 per child per month – although I suspect that the other side will pull this down to half that, and a maintenance order for you which is required legally – although again I suspect they will say, as they are already claiming, that as you work you have a regular salary, and that they will only agree to a nominal sum of a few pence a year."

"Good god!"

Both their solicitors recommended marriage guidance and a therapist for Simon's issues. At first Simon refused, arguing that he didn't need any 'marriage guidance' since he didn't regard himself as married or indeed as ever having had any meaningful relationship with Jess. Both Jess and her solicitor were flummoxed. Jess shivered with a mounting feeling of helplessness.

Eventually Simon agreed to go, but not with Jess. He claimed that it was for him alone, in order to sort out some of his problems that didn't involve Jess. But Jess insisted that she go on the first occasion at least, knowing that in his current frame of mind he would not represent what had happened in anything like a comprehensible fashion. Neither the marriage guidance counsellor nor the psycho-therapist, both of whom Jess insisted on keeping in contact with, in order to monitor what was happening, on the grounds that it affected her daughters, let alone the divorce, were satisfied with their sessions with Simon.

"There seems to be a question of arrested development," the therapist reported hesitantly on behalf of both of them. "I can't give you any details since it's confidential, but I feel that you need to know for the sake of your own and your daughters' safety. He appears to be entrenched in the emotions and mind of a fourteen year old when it comes down to sex, relationships, and adult responsibility. I've never come across anyone so completely self-absorbed, in that he seems incapable of recognising anyone else's feelings. On the other hand, he can often appear to be charming and sociable. This is what we are now calling bipolar, with narcissistic tendencies. Indeed he seems to have an almost recklessly dismissive concept of the women in his life. Has he ever shown this to you?"

"Well, in a way … there have been incidents. And one of my daughters told me … very upset … that he had claimed that 'women like being hurt'. I found that very damaging."

"It must all be very confusing and even nightmarish to you?"

"Yes." Jess swallowed her distress. She felt so glad that someone official had some recognition of what she was going through.

The therapist paused in thought, the steepled his fingers beneath his chin. He took a quick breath. "When he has access, what does he do with your daughters?"

"He has lately been taking them to rehearsals of an am-dram play he's in. It appears to be a bedroom farce, featuring him and someone I understand is his current girlfriend, and quite iffy scenes. I'm not happy about it. My daughters were quite distressed, well, the younger one especially. The older one laughed it off. But I don't think it's appropriate."

"And I understand you haven't been given his addresses?"

"Not since he left his parents' house, no. He refuses to speak to me now. Only through his solicitor. So I have to find out through them but of course I don't necessarily know when he moves, or has a different domestic situation, so …"

"I find this unacceptable for you and your daughters. However, in law, there's little we can do."

"I know. My solicitor has said that she's worried too, but apparently legally there's nothing I can do about it until he actually causes harm."

"I am happy – well, happy clearly isn't the right word! – to write a statement for court about my concerns about your husband's mental state and the safety of the children. The problem is that judges are tricksy beasts and if you get one who is misogynist or curmudgeonly, as many are, he won't take any notice."

"That's what my solicitor said, too," said Jess, heart sinking. "I just don't know what to do."

The therapist paused. "If I were you, I'd move as far away as you can and don't give him your address."

Jess knew that this simply wasn't possible, as she was sure the therapist also knew, but it was clearly a recognition from him of Simon's state of mind.

She mulled over what the therapist had said to her. In a way it confirmed her own assessment, and yet it frightened her. He had stated categorically in a number of cruelly scribbled letters to her that he absolved all responsibility for her and the girls. Why should he give her any maintenance: she had a job, after all; he'd waited until she had a job again before leaving them so that she could support her daughters (*her* daughters?). He had his life to live, without them. It was all her fault anyway. But if he wanted access times they had to go. When Katy or Abi were reluctant (or even downright refused to go) it was again all her fault.

He didn't seem to know who he was, what role he was playing, or what he wanted.

Was he stuck in a fourteen year old boy's world of confusion? Jess had found out that when he lived with his parents after walking out, they had supported him totally and his mother had cooked meals for him as though he is still a teenage son. His parents helped to buy him the bachelor pad; he had told them how much (or how little) he was prepared to pay from his salary and they covered the rest. But of course it was registered in his name. It felt to Jess as though they were aiding and abetting his walking out on his family.

And as she thought about it, she recalled his neurotic obsessive gestures: constantly fiddling with his fly, flushing the loo before he'd even finished weeing. Was he always like that? She had no recollection that he was like that before they were married or before they had the children. What was that about? Had he regressed as their marriage flowed on – and she hadn't noticed? Was all that her fault too?

"Oh god, I don't believe it!" exclaimed Jess as she opened yet another solicitor's letter. She sank on to the kitchen bench and dropped her head into her hands. She'd dealt with the notice of application for divorce proceedings, but as they approached the swearing of the affidavit for the divorce petition towards the de-cree nisi, the details of all aspects of Jess's life had to be stated and confirmed, and the letters from Simon's solicitor were becoming increasingly vicious. Jess was crushed. Apparently Simon had to remain legally joint owner of their family house until such time as it was 'disposed of'. That meant, according to Sarah, the time when she could pay him off. He was insisting on an 80% pay-off, on the grounds that he had contrib-uted most financially, over the time that she had been raising the babies. Jess knew that if she had to do that she would never be able to buy an alternative house for herself and the children. Did he really want them to be homeless, too?

"We'll try to knock them down to 50% at most, on the grounds that you spent that time looking af-ter the children of the marriage and of course him too, and supporting him in his career." Her solicitor sounded confident but Jess felt anything but. She had come to realise that neither Simon nor his family had any desire to support them in any way. Her own family seemed battered by it all, especially as they had previously been friends with these people. And they were all supposed to be 'good Quakers', publically anyway.

"Do you want to hear the good news first – or the bad?" asked her solicitor the following week in which Jess had hardly slept for worry. "We've managed to knock them down. And they will not demand payment immediately. But I'm afraid that Simon is insisting on a clause that states that the arrangement ends on the girls reaching the age of sixteen. In other words, at that time you have to pay him off, whatever your circumstances. And the other requirement negating the delayed pay-off is if you have a 'partner'."

"So he can have partners, but I can't? Not that I've time, but it's the principle!"

"Well, Jess, I'm afraid that it's a question of concession. If you don't pay him off now, he's still joint owner legally, so he can call the tune, as it were."

"But it's not *reasonable*! If only he could be decent and honourable about it all!"

"Oh, the number of times I've heard that, Jess! I'm afraid that as these things drag on it becomes less and less so. Very few are able to behave in a civilised and caring way as you have, in these circumstances."

"I feel as though my life has been torn apart."

"Yes, I can understand that. Oh, and there's another down side …"

"OK, tell me the worst. Get it all over with."

"There will be a clause that he can demand you maintain and decorate the house to his satisfaction."

"*What?* He's never been the slightest bit interested in the maintenance and decoration of the house – why make that a clause now?"

"Again, legally he has the right to protect his investment in the house."

"So he'll be constantly looking over my shoulder, peering at the house, then?" Jess pondered for a moment. "But, wait a minute! He wouldn't dream of paying any of his money to do anything on the house; it's always been me who paid for decorating and so on … so he won't want to point anything out, will he?"

"Ah, sorry, Jess, but he doesn't have to pay towards it."

"He doesn't even have to pay half?"

"No."

"But I'll be having to pay all the mortgage now, not just half as before."

"Makes no difference, Jess, I'm afraid. He'll always be joint owner of the family house, whoever now pays the mortgage. It's about investment."

"But …but his parents bought him a house, a bachelor pad …"

"I expect they would argue that it wasn't worth as much as the family house."

"What do I do, Sarah?"

"If I were you, as the pay-off is the percentage of the equity, I would sell as soon as you can, before house prices rise as they're set to do, pay him off, and get him out of your hair."

The decree nisi hearing took place privately in court and Jess was not required to attend, thank goodness. She couldn't believe that it had come this far into hell barely a year after Simon had walked out on them, and with such venom. It all seemed to have happened so quickly and in a whirlwind of decisions, pleas, legal arguments, and tears. She really truly did not want this enmity and aggression between them; she longed for talking and agreeing, negotiating quietly and with understanding and love, not this increasingly insane animosity.

Jess was informed that her solicitor Sarah could apply for the decree absolute six weeks after the nisi was granted, but that in the meantime she would need to attend a court hearing for the custody and arrangements for her children. It all seemed so *wrong*, that she should have to go to court to plead for her own daughters whom she had carried inside her for nine months, breast fed, nurtured and brought up pretty much herself on her own. They were hers, flesh of her flesh. To what extent were they Simon's?

Jess turned the letter over in her hand. It wasn't the legal letter she had come to know so well. She didn't recognise the handwriting on the envelope: an elaborate cursive copperplate script, very neat and deliberate, very correct.

She tore it open.

> *Dear Jessamy,*
> *We are sorry to hear from your husband and your mother-in-law that your family situation has now changed and we would like to visit with you in due course to discuss your new arrangements. We suggest a visitation on Monday evening 5th at 7.30pm. We hope and trust that this is convenient to you.*
> *Yours in Christ's love,*
> *Samuel Brown and Geraldine Foulds (elders)*

Goodness, she hadn't even attended Quaker Meeting since her world turned upside down. How could she? Her parents-in-law apparently still went and they were hardly nice to her. The woman she used to call her friend at Meeting, Mary, had, she felt, betrayed her, passing on to her a Waitrose bag of worn shoes for the girls, cast offs from her own children, while inviting Simon to a party 'to meet other women'. Thinking she might be glad of some shoes in these new circumstances …! She'd thrown them straight in the bin.

Jess's first impulse was to decline firmly. But part of her was curious to know what they intended. After all it was nothing to do with them. Nobody from Meeting had helped her, provided any support. She felt that she was something of an embarrassment to them.

"You must at least meet with them, Jessamy," begged her mother, "and I am sure that they will provide support and guidance in the love of Christ." Jess was doubtful about that but grudgingly agreed. She didn't want anyone to be able to say that she had spurned help so she deserved all she got.

"So, Jessamy," said Geraldine Foulds as she sat, straight-backed and poker-like, on Jess's sofa on the due day of the 'visitation'. Even as she and Samuel had stepped through the front door, smile-less and unbending, Jess knew that this was going to be a disaster. Her mother had advised and encouraged her to accept the invitation, as a Quaker, she should give them a chance to say what they wanted to say, and they would be helpful and understanding as 'elders'. But she knew as she ushered them into the sitting room that she had made a mistake. A big embarrassing mistake.

"So, Jessamy, you were brought up as a Quaker to be understanding and of course to forgive. So we would like to discuss what you are doing to ameliorate this situation you have found yourself in."

Jess felt her face go hot with barely suppressed annoyance. She felt like a weak fool to take her mother's advice on this and submit to her entreaties. Never again would she do that.

12

THORN IN MY SIDE

The court in the town was an old depressing building which only exacerbated Jess's despair. This was where her marriage, that she worked so hard for, would be ended, and the custody of the children decided. By some judge who knew nothing about them or the children, nothing about the lead-up to this most traumatic moment in her life, but would simply sign a paper.

She had dressed carefully that morning: a simple but elegant dress, curly chestnut hair pinned up, and as she glanced sideways at the mirrored pictures that lined the courthouse walls, she saw her reflection and thought she looked like a stereotype of a romance writer, slim figure, long neck, wisps of hair escaping from her topknot and curling round her cheeks. Somewhat ironic.

She walked along the corridor, aware of the grim grubby people ranged on benches along the wall, some with legs spread out relaxed as if they were familiar with this process, and others huddled into themselves. She looked around for some sign of where to go, some assistance. She wished that Sarah, her solicitor, had been able to come with her but she had rung the day before to say that she had been called unexpectedly to another court. She'd added that she hoped that she didn't get Judge Jermaine-Hempleton, one of the worst misogynists in the circuit; she'd heard that he might be due, and thought she'd better warn her. Jess thanked her, but knew that she'd have no choice but to sit it out.

Eventually a severe-looking female court usher came to her and asked for her name and court papers, then ushered her in silence to the family law court. She sat in the court room, cold and numb. The benches and dark wooden panelling were unwelcoming and somehow threatening. The other people around her, awaiting their fate, were huddled shadows. She smoothed her cream jersey dress over her knees and crossed her slim legs. At least the ubiquitous shoulder pads, draped cowl neckline and high heels helped her to feel a little more confident. Power dressing they called it; she didn't feel very powerful at the moment. She felt like a criminal.

She was not expecting Simon to attend the hearing; there was no obligation for him to do that, but at the last moment he rushed in, very late, making a big noise at the door. Everyone's head turned at the commotion, but she turned away, not wanting him to sit alongside her in this situation. She couldn't bear that. She was aware of his eyes upon her and glanced sideways towards him. He nodded his head in acknowledgement of her presence, but his eyes were cold and his mouth an impatient grimace. He sat across the courtroom, legs splayed wide, arms raised to spread along the back of his bench, as if this was an everyday occurrence to him that held no emotion. Why had he come? Just to sneer at her, mock her? In triumph at his power over her? To gloat over the destruction he had caused?

Her breath was uneven, ragged. She felt the oppressive silence, broken only by the occasional whispers around her from the other benches, nervous, frightened. From time to time the court usher's cold voice called out to summon the next victim into the judge's chambers.

The other people sat there in the courtroom, uncomfortable, shifting on the benches or as still as stone carvings as if they felt that any movement would bring down upon them the wrath of the whole legal system. They were mostly women. One woman had brought her mother and children.

Finally, Jess was called into the judge's chambers, a bleak, cold, empty room with a huge wooden table in the middle. There was a small transom window at the end, that was open. She heard the sounds of car engines outside, the traffic showing that everyone else was going about their everyday business, while she was in this grim building ending her marriage. A solemn policeman stood guarding the door. As if she should be prevented from taking flight.

Simon followed her and she was aware of him smiling at the court usher and thanking her, as though it was some social occasion in which he was casually confident. He sat down beside her.

The judge sat at the far end of the long table, as far away as he could possibly be from her. It seemed deliberate. His assistants sat either side of him. She screwed up her handkerchief in her damp hands beneath the table, her eyes fixed firmly straight ahead at the judge. He appeared late-middle-aged, bulky as though he lived well, greying neatly-cut hair, manicured finger nails, eyes staring at her over half-moon glasses, his robes and his frowning face lending him the authoritarian air of a god about to hand down his unquestionable judgement to the inferior mortal beneath him. Which of course he was, mused Jess. All three of them stared at her intently. She felt as though she were on trial. She was aware of Simon beside her, relaxed yet alert, and she felt rather than saw, the confident smile on his face.

The judge was introduced with daunting reverence. Justice Jermaine-Hempleton. Jess closed her eyes and reigned in her shaking breath. *It had to be, didn't it?*

Finally, when she could almost bear it no longer, his assistants shuffled papers towards him, and murmured. Then the judge looked up at her again and his expression was heavy with disapproval. His assistants either side of him looked up at her likewise. She felt an overwhelming sense of threat in the room, and she gripped her tissue with whitened knuckles. *Oh god, get me through this today, and I will never, NEVER, have to go through this again; I will never again be so humiliated by anyone, or made to feel like this, small and at the mercy of someone else. Because nothing will ever be as bad as this again … Just let me get through this next half hour …*

There was a long formal statement about the court and its purpose by one of the assistants. Then a statement of the issues of the divorce application that had been presented to the court. It sounded like the judgements of the juries and sentencing by the judges Jess had seen on television shows.

"The petitioner will address Justice Jermaine-Hempleton as 'your honour', as will the defendant to the petition if he is so addressed. You may not speak, other than in response to His Honour's questions. You may not …" There followed a list of warnings. Jess felt wobbly and hoped to goodness she didn't faint. The room was already trembling around her.

"So," boomed the judge down the long table. "So *why* have you brought this divorce application before this court?" It felt to Jess, aggressive and demanding as if he couldn't possibly fathom out, even with all the details in the papers of Simon's behaviour, why she should possibly want to do this.

Jess took a deep breath. "Well, your honour, as you will see from the court papers, the divorce application and deposition, that my husband ..." she continued with a summary of what he had surely already read.

The judge stared at her, frowning. "Wives promise to obey ..." Jess did not interrupt him to point out that in her marriage vows she had not actually promised anything of the sort, and didn't believe in that anyway. She was well aware that she dare not antagonise anyone. "In a marriage it is expedite that the wife is engaged in activities that are all focused upon her husband's happiness and contentment. You have, like all wives, promised to ..." and he continued for a full five minutes with a stern lecture to her about the duties of a wife towards her husband, sermonising to her that the fate of her marriage rested in her own hands, that she clearly had acted in a way that made her husband take the actions he had. By the time he had finished Jess felt sorry for his wife, if he had one, and that thought seemed to calm her anger somewhat. She sneaked a glance sideways at Simon and caught him smirking triumphantly. So they had decided it was all her own fault somehow.

She closed her eyes, feeling like a miscreant. What had happened here? This was not right. It was, again, like a Kafka nightmare. Would she find herself, any moment, taken down to the docks and thrown into a cell?

The Judge sighed an exaggerated sigh of exasperation at the stupidity around him. "I accept the defendant's statement of resources and confirm that only the minimum maintenance payments for the children of £170 per child per month be required of him. He will be granted reasonable access to the children of the marriage, as he might demand. Since the petitioner has an income from her salary as a school teacher, I judge that a nominal maintenance order for her of five pence per annum be confirmed by order of this court." He added various other statements which Jess barely heard.

"Does the petitioner have anything to say?"

Jess shook her head dumbly.

"Speak!" boomed the judge crossly.

"No, your honour." If only she could shrink beneath this table.

"Then this hearing is dismissed." He rose and his assistants signalled to Jess to rise also. Then she was ushered out, past the policeman who stood stone-faced.

She stumbled outside into the warm air and the dusty everyday busy-ness of traffic and shoppers. She took a deep breath and prepared to force her legs to walk up the hill towards the car park. She needed to get home quickly away from this madness that her life had become. But outside the courthouse a sharp yell stopped her in her tracks. She swung round to see Simon, red-faced and furious, catching up with her, shouting. She hesitated for a moment too long, and he was upon her. She stepped back away from the glare of hatred in his eyes and she felt the hardness of the iron railings of the courthouse boundary pressing into her back.

"What the hell are you doing, Jessamy? Why are you doing this to me?" he yelled. "What have I ever done to you?" He leaned in to her and she felt the cold spittle on her cheek. As she raised her hand to wipe it away, he grabbed her wrist hard and pushed her further back into the sharp railings. She should have run, yet running away was not something she did. Suddenly his behaviour was no longer frightening; it was ridiculous. And she was jolted out of the dumbness and shock of the courthouse.

She took a deep breath, expanding her chest, pushing out her bosom, and pulled herself up to her full five feet two. "How dare you? Don't you EVER do that to me again. We're no longer married. You have no rights over me. You never did. You wanted out, so now get out of my life!"

Jess needed time to consider how she was going to deal with her future and that of the children.

She had read that divorce was like a bereavement, and that it took the course of emotional stages following a death: shock, disbelief, loss, hurt, anger, acceptance, then finally moving on with hope. She thought that she was probably somewhere in between the anger and acceptance stages. The preceding stages were still there, but without the intensity that had rocked her previously. She now felt that she could be more objective, rational. She could see Simon as he really was and it angered her that he had destroyed her family like this. And she didn't want him back. She knew that what she had wanted was for it to be as it had been. Or as she had thought it was. Clearly he was not the person she thought he was; anyone capable of such cruelty, selfishness and nastiness, was not a person she now had any desire to live with. If only she had had the benefit of such insight back then. And she knew, too, that he was never going to want to come back, would never ask to be forgiven because he clearly had no notion that he had done anything wrong. So she just had to accept the situation, however galling.

As far as he was concerned nothing was going to change; he had somehow morphed into a nightmare. She no longer bothered to read about manic depression, bipolarism, narcissism or self-obsession. It only left her feeling empty. Why try to understand something that was not going to end well. OK, she now had labels to attach to his behaviour and that was in some ways gratifying. But it would not make it any easier for her to deal with him now, to persuade him to talk to her or to discuss the children's future. There was no point in wishing he was capable of something more. Much as she wanted to have as reasonable a post-divorce as possible, much as she longed for them to be able to be 'amicable', to put the girls first and to meet to mutually decide what might be best for them, she knew that this was never going to happen. He did not want the responsibility nor to be accountable, so she knew that her future was to make decisions alone and to be blamed if anything went wrong.

But that was what she must look forward to. When your back was against the wall, what else could you do but push forwards as best you could.

She hated access days. After the initial resistance to bothering to see them again, when Simon was in the throes of his new passions, his mother had persuaded him to take an interest in his children, to 'demand his rights' as she expressed it. Hilary was still, apparently, engaged in portraying him as a wonderful father, and a misunderstood and mistreated husband. He would need to be seen to be doing something other than ignoring his children, if that image was to stick.

She watched now through her kitchen window as the girls lagged behind him, backpacks over their shoulders, taking their toys and books with them, Katy slightly ahead, Abi dragging her feet reluctantly behind him, glancing back at the window where Jess stood trying to smile encouragingly. Simon had turned up at the house in a brand new Range Rover, driver's window down, arm resting on the door frame, sunglasses obscuring any emotion. He had climbed out of the car onto her driveway and sauntered, jacket held over one shoulder nonchalantly. Jess thought, objectively, that he looked quite glamourous. Like the men Polly used to go for. Well, like Matt, in fact. Some woman somewhere would think she had got quite a catch in Simon, one way or another.

Even while she was opening the front door to him, he was demanding, "Where's their pocket money? They might need it today," and gesturing the familiar 'gimme gimme' with his hand.

Jess recalled the previous access day when her mother had been staying with them for the weekend, helping out with the girls as Jess did her marking. Katy looked so miserable as the time approached for Simon to collect them that Jess asked her if she was unwell.

"Yes, mummy, I'm not feeling at all well. Can I stay here with Granny instead?"

"Well, I'm not going either!" chimed in Abi, banging her Meccano on the floor. "I want to stay with Granny!"

For a moment, Jess's heart had sunk as she wondered how she could avoid the inevitable anger from Simon when she told him. Then she thought – no, I've made it quite clear that it has to be their decision, they were not to be forced. Yet she knew that his fury would be trained on her.

JULIA IBBOTSON

In the event she couldn't reach him on his phone and eventually he rang her to say that he couldn't take his 'access rights' that day as he was taking his girl-friend out instead.

Everyone had breathed a sigh of relief. And Katy had suddenly become perfectly chatty and lively, with no sign of the mystery illness again.

Now, Jess watched as Simon guided Katy into his car and began to shout and gesticulate at Abi. At first she assumed he was telling her to hurry up, in the impatient manner that had become increasingly pro-nounced lately. But then, as Abi turned back to the window with her face contorted with fear, she realised that there was something else, more dangerous.

Jess ran to the front door and wrenched it open to hear Simon yelling at Abi, "What have I ever done to you? Why are you being so nasty to me?" Across the road, his shouts had brought neighbours to their win-dows and they were peering out nervously. It wasn't the sort of neighbourhood where people yelled aggressive-ly to each other. Jess felt their eyes on her too.

"What's going on?" she called to Simon. "What are you doing?"

Abi ran to her and clung on to her, crying.

Simon swung round to Jess. "She's being silly, She won't get in the car."

Jess took a deep breath. "But Simon, I have said quite clearly that of course they should come with you on access days if they want to – but if they don't, I am certainly not going to force them to. It's their choice. They're old enough to be able to make their own decisions."

Simon's face was puce with fury. "But why would she not want to come? What have I ever done to her to deserve that?"

Jess tried to slow her breathing. "Please Simon, don't do this." She looked towards the car as Katy peered through the window. Holding Abi's hand tightly, she opened the car door. "Katy, are you OK to go with daddy or would you rather stay home?"

"No, I'll go with daddy," Katy whispered.

"OK, poppet. But tell daddy if you want to come home, won't you?" Katy nodded.

Jess turned to Simon, with Abi still clinging to her arm, and said, low, "I'm trusting you this time, because legally I don't have much choice. But I'm not happy."

She was well aware that her solicitor Sarah had told her that she could not deny his access unless he actually hurt one of the children. As she led Abi back into the house and waved Katy off, her own words rang in her ears: *yes, but then it would be too late!*

Jess was exhausted, emotionally drained, so tired of having to constantly be picking up the pieces of the chaos Simon was still wreaking in their lives. She stared blankly at the copy of the decree absolute that dropped through the letterbox. This was it then. A marriage wrenched apart. A family broken. A horrible feeling of failure swept through her. This was the last thing she had ever wanted.

But …it was what she'd got. There was nothing she could ever do to change it now. He'd got his way. And even with that sinking feeling, she knew that she would make the best of it, as she'd always done. She would be happy, successful, she'd be independent, she'd love and be loved … some day … properly by someone who was committed to her and her family. She'd do all the things she wanted to do but couldn't when she was with Simon.

She walked into the hall and assessed herself in the full-length mirror. Hmm … she breathed in fully, pushing out her boobs, raised her chin defiantly, pulled in her tummy … and forced a smile. What a difference. She kept telling herself she was a strong woman. Then she found a sheet of paper from the bureau in the living room, and a pen, and sat at the kitchen table.

The top item on her list had to be moving to a new, more suitable house that she could afford and manage on her own. She had to 'make a clean break' as her solicitor said, and that meant getting Simon off her back as co-owner of the house, so that those horrible 'conditions' were expunged and she would no longer need to worry about him critically assessing it every time he came for an access visit, and being anxious about what he might say. She didn't want him, in his present negative state of mind, having any influence on her life now. She didn't want him to be able to call the tune, to dictate to her. It was no good for her or the children. And the only way was to create as great a distance as she could. She needed to make a fresh start away from the home that held so many memories, of happier times, but also of what he had done. The vision of him standing in the doorway of their bedroom and saying those fatal destructive words would never leave her while she lived there. And she hoped that the girls would be able to start a new life too.

What next? What did she want to do with her life that she had been denied with Simon? He had mocked her attempts at getting a promotion, so that was the next item. He'd become angry when she suggested that she might apply for a masters degree at the university where she gained her BA. So that was next. Then all of a sudden, the floodgates opened and she started scribbling wildly. Catch up with friends: she hadn't seen Polly and Matt for ages, so absorbed and focussed she had needed to be in the divorce proceedings. Make new friends. Maybe join a group of like-minded people, women and men. She had joined the local women's professional group, which was where she'd discovered Hilary's betrayal, but was that really what she wanted? But, then, how was she going to go to any events in the evening while she needed baby-sitters for the girls? Maybe that was something for later when they were old enough to be left for a couple of hours. That would only be another three or four years. She was not about to ask either Simon or Hilary any favours, and while she had no partner to leave her own children with, how could she build any credit in a ba-by-sitting circle like she used to do? She couldn't rely totally on Polly, it wouldn't be fair.

OK, so going out was going to be difficult, but what about dinner parties or wine and cheese evenings at home? She'd tried to do that with Simon but he was so unpredictable with guests that she'd abandoned that plan. She could still do that – and catch up with friends and colleagues at the same time.

As she thought more about coping, she realised that she was finding alternative ways, being positive as she had promised herself. She remembered the old cliché, sink or swim. And she was not about to sink. As much as anything, she refused to give Simon that satisfaction.

"What about this one, then?" Jess swivelled round in the car and smiled at Katy and Abi, nodding with her head towards a pleasant modern house on a new de-velopment not too far from their current family home. "What do you think?"

Katy considered carefully, frowning, head bent to one side. "I think it looks nice … but …"

"I do too!" said Abi, leaning round her sister to get a better view.

"But I think that an old house, a cottage or a rectory, would be even better," added Katy who was reading '*The Ghost of Thomas Kempe*' at the moment.

Jess laughed gently. "Well, the problem there, Katy, is that I don't think I could manage to look after an old house. Old houses tend to get all sorts of issues like damp and dry rot and leaking pipes. I think that, at the moment, while I'm a single parent, we have to find a small new house that I can maintain and look after on my own."

Abi elbowed her sister out of her frown and said, "yes, we need somewhere that mummy can manage."

"Let's go and see if we can look inside then."

It wasn't really what she would have liked and it was small. She'd got used to much more room in their family house. But there were three bedrooms, albeit small, and a tiny study too! There was a sitting room and a dining room, separate but linked by double glazed doors that you could open to make a larger space. The living room had a large window and a French door to the terrace and lawned garden. The galley kitchen had a built-in double oven and hob. And there was a single garage too, an open-plan front garden and its own driveway. Everything was small compared to their current house, but neat and compact. She'd just have to clear out a whole lot of furniture and belongings, but that was no bad thing to have a clear-out of her life.

That night Jess sat at the table, papers spread around her, working out her finances. She'd hired an estate agent and put the house on the market. She felt heavy and sad; she'd come to love this house, but it was the only thing she could do. It was a great house but it held heart-squeezing memories … and she had to pay off Simon and get her finances straight and live within her new means. It had been very hard this past year, she'd paid off Simon's debts and she didn't want any debts of her own. She'd known hardship but she'd always put the children first. Involuntarily her hand moved to her stomach. She'd had an enforced diet this year, but – silver lining! – she'd lost weight and her figure had improved in consequence!

Her pen underlined the final number on her calculations. Yes, she could pay off Simon, pay the costs of removal and only need a small mortgage to buy the house they'd seen in the village down the road. A new start.

"Hi, Jess, it's Terry from the estate agent," came the low voice as she picked up the receiver. "Good news! A couple from just up your road want to come to view the property this morning. They're very keen. They know the house as they go past it every day, and if there's nothing wrong in the viewing, they're happy to offer the asking price!"

"Wow, it only went publically on the market yesterday!"

"Yes, fantastic!"

"OK, let's do it!" Jess was shaking with a flush of excitement and dread. Things were moving on quickly, much quicker than she'd expected. If they did make an offer she could go ahead with her own offer to the owners of the property they'd seen in the village.

Jess had to call on her parents for help with the move. Everything had happened so quickly. That seemed to be the story of her life at the moment. Furniture was sold or given away and Jess hardened her heart to the inevitable stress of disposing of a life that she had thought was forever. The girls helped to pack away their own belongings into the huge packing cases that the removal firm had left them. She heard laughter from upstairs as her mother jokingly chivvied them up to stop playing with the toys they were supposed to pack up. She had organised her father to simply keep plying them all with mugs of tea and biscuits which she'd arranged on the counter top in the kitchen. He could surely manage that without messing up. But in between he would sink with relief onto a chair and hide in silence behind a book, ignoring everyone as usual.

Jess had decided to pay the extra for the men to help wrap up delicate possessions and equipment, to relieve some of the work from her own shoulders.

But it was still exhausting to empty a whole house and garage, a whole life, into boxes. She suppressed any tears that might be lingering at the back of her eyes, and just got on with the work, trying not to think. The men had asked her if they could play their radio, and she had gladly agreed, happy to sing along mindlessly. It reminded her of the workmen installing her new kitchen – goodness, that seemed such a long time ago now – and she forced away the memory.

"What a shame, though." Jess looked up from piling her books into the packing case in the sitting room, to see her mother in the doorway. "To have to leave your lovely house."

Jess winced. "I don't have any choice, Mother. I can't afford this one any more, not on my own, and I can't look after it properly without help."

"But Simon didn't help you anyway."

"No, but I couldn't afford to buy in any help if I needed it." She sighed. "It's just better this way."

Jess looked round at the huge fireplace that she had designed and had built for them, then out of the patio door to the garden she had so lovingly tended. She glanced through the door into the kitchen and remembered how she had designed that too, only last year, with the assistance of the kitchen planners. A flash of That Song wafted ghostly through her mind: The Things We Do for Love … *What a different meaning it had now*, she thought.

But now she had to leave it all behind. It was only material acquisition after all; she could start again. But she knew that it was more than that: it all represented a life that they had shared as a family – or at least she had thought that it had been shared, with Simon.

Polly's phone rang and rang. Jess listened with growing unease. She had tried to contact her several times recently but with no success. She'd left messages on the voicemail. But nobody had rung her back. Granted, she had lost touch over the awful period through the divorce, when the children and solicitors and courts had absorbed all her waking thoughts, on top of her paid work. Somehow there was no energy left or space in her brain to give to friends. She had felt totally drained. Now she chided herself; she shouldn't have let it go on so long without crossing that other bridge to her old friends. She was completely remiss. Whatever she felt, she shouldn't have let that contact go.

And yet, why hadn't Polly been in touch with her, knowing what she was going through? Or Matt? They had both been such friends, ever since university …

Voicemail clicked on, a remote and standard unknown recorded voice telling her that there was nobody to answer her call, and could she leave a message after the tone and then someone would get back to her as soon as possible. This time she spoke more urgently.

"Please get back to me – one of you! It's Jess. I've moved house, not far, but I need to give you the new address. I'm so sorry it's been so long. I feel awful. I hope you're both OK." Her voice cracked and she quickly finished the call.

Twice, Jess drove past their house, but each time it looked dark and there were no signs of life. What had happened? It wasn't like Polly to have been out of touch for so long.

Finally when she rang, someone picked up.

""Hello?" said Matt, and even with that one word Jess could tell that his voice sounded strained.

"Oh, Matt, thank goodness I've managed to reach you at last!"

"Jess?"

"Yes." Her heart thumped loudly in her chest as she felt suffused with dread. "What's the matter? What's happened?"

"We've been … away for a while," Matt hesitated. "I think, Jess, it'd be better if you came round. Do you mind?"

"No, of course not. Shall I come over now? The girls are at concert rehearsals. I don't have to pick them up for an hour or so."

"Yes, that's fine. The boys are out too."

As Jess drove, she couldn't stop thinking of all the things that could have happened. Something had happened to Polly. Was she seriously ill? In hospital? But then why hadn't they let her know?

Matt opened the door and ushered her inside. His face was pale, very unlike his usual tan, and he looked exhausted. The house was silent, almost eerily so; there was none of the music Polly always had on in the background. Jess thought it must have been like that in her own house the first few weeks after Simon went when she couldn't bear to hear any of the music they used to play. Matt led her into the elegant sitting room and she sat on the stylish cream leather sofa, watching Matt lower his tall frame wearily onto the armchair opposite her. He looked … defeated. He sat, thighs wide apart, elbows resting on his knees, hands falling slackly between them, head bent. She stared at the top of his head, his dark curly hair. He didn't move for a few agonising minutes while Jess's heart thumped louder and she flushed hot and cold. Oh god – what on earth was it? She was scared to ask, scared to know.

Then Matt slowly raised his head and looked intently over at her. "I don't want to tell you. But I have to. You have to know, I think. It's only fair."

Jess's heart skipped several beats. "What? What, for god's sake?"

"It's Polly. She's … she's left us …"

"No, no, she can't have. What do you mean? She adored her family … you, the boys! She'd never do anything … oh god!" She saw the devastated bleakness of Matt's eyes and she knew it to be true.

"I didn't want to tell you. I've been trying to avoid you. You've got enough on your plate at the moment. But I guess it has to be confronted. Oh Jess, I'm so sorry …"

"I can't believe it. I can't take it in." Jess shook her head and her hand pressed her brow as if to try to force the information into her brain with some sense, some rationale. "But …but she always hated the idea of anyone leaving their family … she was scathing about Simon leaving us … she could have lost her job over her views of him … why would she do the same herself?"

Matt looked down for a moment, then raised his head, his dark eyes scouring hers. "Oh Jess," he said sadly, "I know you were great friends over many years, but I guess you already know she could be … well, a little impulsive, especially where men were concerned …"

"Oh, I know at university she had a bit of a reputation, but surely not after you were married?"

He sighed. "People don't really know what goes on in a marriage. They only see what someone wants them to see. You and Simon always seemed so close, despite his … difficulties, so I guess that's what she wanted you to see in her too."

He looked so sad that Jess pushed herself up from the sofa and knelt in front of him. "Oh, Matt, I'm so sorry. I know what it's like. It seems to happen to the best, truest people, doesn't it?" She reached up and hugged him to her, pressing the back of his head into her neck as he bent low towards her. "So you have the boys?" She felt him nod into her shoulder. "Oh god, what a mess these things are." She grimaced. "And where is she? Do you know?"

Matt pulled back a little from Jess and scowled. "Yes, she left me a note. Succinct. But excited, wild, rushed. As always. Typical Polly."

"And …?"

"Jess … she's with Simon."

13

I CAN SEE CLEARLY NOW

Matt brought Jess a brandy and sat beside her with his arm loosely draped around her, patting her shoulder in comfort. She was in a state of shock, mind whirling in a carousel of questions, puzzlement, confusion. She tried to analyse how this could possibly have happened. She went over and over things that Polly had said to her in the past year, desperately trying to find some clue, some explanation.

She swerved from silent numbness to allowing words to tumble unchecked and unconsidered out of her mouth, desperate to make some sense out of all this. Never in her worst nightmares had she ever considered this outcome. Her best friend? Her husband? No, not her husband any more, of course. Her ex-husband. It must have happened since she had heard via her solicitor about Simon's circumstances, because Polly had certainly never been mentioned. It had been … oh, what was her name, the last woman Simon had admitted to … the so-called 'landlady' … and she was the … what? … third, or was it the fourth since the one he left them for? So this new relationship with Polly must have happened since the sworn affidavits for the court papers … so would that have been before she had to undergo the court appearance, when Simon had assaulted her in the street? Had he been with Polly then? Was he laughing at her then? Or after the court when he was claiming access to the children? No, it must be more recently.

Had the girls seen Polly with Simon? No, surely not – they would have told her.

How could she? She never seemed to like him much. Or was that Matt? No, surely Polly had been scathing of Simon too. She seemed to recall her calling him a bastard on several occasions.

Snatches of occasions when they had all been together, not very often, fragments of conversations … suddenly she questioned them all. They had taken on new meaning now. New interpretations. As though everything that Polly had said could be translated into an altogether different language.

What now?

She had lost a husband. And now her best friend. What had she done to make that happen? Simon was so angry and antagonistic towards her; what about if Polly was infected with that too? Then she remembered that she'd already effectively lost Polly.

Jess realised that Matt was saying something to her amidst the fog of her mind. "Sorry?"

"I'm afraid that I've told Polly that I'm not happy for Tom, Zak and Jake to be with Simon. I'm sorry to say this, Jess, but I just don't think he's a good influence – not the sort of influence I want my sons to be exposed to."

"You don't have to be sorry to me, Matt," Jess whispered, swivelling her head towards him. "I worry enough about his access to Katy and Abi, But I can't do anything about that. There's no reason why Polly can't see the boys on her own, though, without Simon being involved at all. People have those sorts of arrangements all the time."

"To be honest, Jess, it may not even last. Polly has her enthusiasms. But she soon moves on to something else."

Jess sighed. "I do remember that at university. But I thought she'd grown out of it. Simon's the same. Impulsive, madly enthusiastic, then quickly bored."

They sat in silence for a while, each lost in their own thoughts. Jess was biting her lip raw. What a tangled mess.

"So what happens if Polly changes her mind and wants to come back?"

"I've thought about that, over and over. If it happened maybe I'd think differently. But, frankly, at the moment, I don't think I could deal with it. How could we go on with that in the background? However much you forgive, you can't forget. There's too much pain. How would we ever be able to have confidence that it wouldn't happen again? How could I ever really trust her again? How could the boys?"

"Yes, I know."

"I think that some people are trustworthy because you know that they would never do anything to harm the family. It simply wouldn't be possible for them. They would never want to. Unthinkable. And then for others, they go with what they want at the time, without much regard for the consequences."

"And it only hits afterwards. When it's too late. But you can never take it back. Like a speeding arrow."

"Did you ever suspect it of Simon?"

"No, I don't think so. It never occurred to me that he could be unfaithful or walk out on the family. Now I feel that was naïve. But I guess it's easy in hindsight, isn't it? But it was all mixed up with his difficult behaviour anyway. When you live with someone with manic depression and narcissistic syndrome, you put it all down to instability and illness. Although I was only vaguely aware of all that at the time. I just tried to look after him."

"No such excuse – or reason, rather – for Polly. She simply lives for the moment … To be honest, Jess, I've always known it in the back of my mind."

"Even before you were married?"

Matt looked at her and she could no longer read his expression. "Mmm, yes, I think so, if I'm really honest with myself."

"So … why?"

Matt moved his arm from her shoulders and fixed his eyes on the far side of the room. "I'd already lost what I really wanted."

Jess was not sure how she managed to collect the girls and drive them all safely back home to the security of their new little house. Matt had all but insisted that he drive her car, but she assured him that she was quite capable now and she had only sipped a little of the brandy, not really liking it. It reminded her of illness, bereavement and shock, and somehow held a bitter taste for her.

She locked the door behind her, shutting out the world and its madness. She wanted to hide away in a burrow with her girls, to hibernate until the world became light again. She thought of Simon and Polly together, and she felt nauseous. God, how could they? She was beginning to get some of her life back in control again after Simon … and now, another shattering blow. In some ways she felt the betrayal more keenly.

That night, after she had tucked the girls up safely in their beds, hugged them especially tightly, and retreated to her own room, she knelt by her bedside and prayed, as she hadn't done for a long time. She buried her head in her hands and prepared to sob out her despair.

But it didn't come.

She felt numb and stunned. But it was not like before, when Simon walked out. When she had sobbed her heart out on the sitting room floor every night, prostrate, crumpled and crumbling, shedding all her strength, weeping it into the carpet. Had she become immune to hurt? Or just stronger.

How was she going to tell the girls? Did she need to? But if she didn't, what if they saw them together on the street?

"Dear God, give me the strength to do the right thing for the girls," she prayed. *"And for Matt. Be there for him too."*

In the morning, she felt a deep sadness fill her. Polly had been with her through so much. They had faced so much together. It was as though she had died.

She got the girls ready for school, checked their school bags as always, and drove them the few miles to the lower school site. On the way she managed to chat and laugh as though nothing had happened. They listened to their choice of cassette and sang along. There was something ultimately soothing and calming to slip into the normal routines.

Then fifteen minutes later, as she retrieved her briefcase from the car boot, adjusted her high heels and her pencil skirt, and strode into her own school reception she thought how thankful she was that she was not teaching in the same school as Polly now. How embarrassing that would have been; everyone knowing. Here nobody need know about the latest blow if she chose not to speak of it. For the first time in her life she could separate the career part of her life from the family part. She had to if she were to survive. She stretched her spine and neck, pushed her chin up and held her head high. She determinedly pulled her facial muscles into a smile. It was amazing how much better it made you feel to smile, whatever you felt like inside, and soon she felt as though she actually was really smiling. Here she was Mrs Arlington-Smith the efficient and admired teacher of English and Drama, not poor Jess with a broken life.

It was some days before she could start to think more clearly without images of Simon and Polly intimately together invading her mind. They popped up as she read, as she did her marking, as she tried to chat and giggle with her daughters, as she cooked dinner. But in time, they began to burrow themselves in the recesses of her mind and heart.

"But I can't seem to forget … not really," she told Matt, as they walked along the river through the park one Saturday morning, all their five children running on ahead, exploring the trees and bushes for hideouts. It was a beautiful day: golden sunshine dappling the grass and the sound of birds in the huge oak trees.

Matt had decided they all needed exercise and fresh air – although to tell the truth the children already actually had plenty, Jess saw to that. But Jess was grateful for time out and to escape the paint fumes of her attempts to redecorate the new house and make it more their own, in their own style. And she was acutely aware of how rarely Simon had taken them all out as a family, ever.

Matt and the boys, Tom, Zak and Jake, had picked them up in Matt's big roomy Mercedes and driven them to Chatsworth Park. The kids all loved the freedom of the parkland and they'd been promised the farmyard too, which they still adored even though they were a little old for it by now.

"Every now and then it all bubbles up from deep underground where I've tried to bury it." Jess bent to pick a stray twig that had fallen beside the path and stroked it reflectively. "Simon sometimes snaps when he comes to collect the girls – 'move on, *Jess!*' he says, apropos of nothing at all. 'Get another bloke.' As if just 'getting a bloke' to replace him was all I wanted. As if he imagines I'm pining for him …"

"Probably hoping that's the case," grunted Matt, burying his hands deeper into his pockets, although it wasn't cold. "It makes him feel in control, powerful."

"Hmm. He still seems to find me a total irritation in the background, as if he really wishes that I didn't exist at all. Well, I guess that would be easier for him. He's got what he wants, materially and financially – his parents have seen to that, without him having to really work hard for it. And he has his freedom from responsibilities of family and marriage …" she hesitated to mention Polly.

"And Polly," Matt echoed her thoughts. "But it won't last. I'm sure of it."

"No," sighed Jess. It was all so stupid. Childish somehow. "And then what?"

They walked on in silence.

"I used to long for him to say he was sorry and to ask to come back, although I never knew for certain what I'd say. It was bad anyway. And now it's too late. It's done."

"You must still feel angry, though, about him doing what he wanted without any consideration for you and the children. Without even discussing it. A unilateral decision. I certainly can't imagine what was going on in Polly's mind."

"Well, sometimes, yes. Because for all his selfishness he's got what he set out to get. And that strikes me as being so wrong." She angled the twig in her hand and flicked it to skim the water of the river. "But I don't want to feel deep resentment, Matt, to let that consume me, to be negative; I just want to get on with life and make the best of it. I can't change the situation; I had no control over what has already happened but I do now have control – well, some control – over my life in the future."

"You must resent what he did to you, in some way?"

"To be completely honest, yes I do, in a way, resent it … him … that he put me in such a situation, that he made me into a single mum, that he hurt and shattered the family life my daughters had, the course of their future, that he destroyed *all* that we had. He left us without any proper explanation or discussion. I get the impression that he's got what he wanted, whatever that might be, as he always has, regardless of anyone else. He refuses to talk to me, except when it suits him. And that's usually just moaning about something that doesn't suit him. He walked out and left me with two children to bring up alone. How can he have done that? Yes, I resent that. Of course I do. Who wouldn't? He *used* me, Matt."

"Polly speaks on the phone sometimes. She wants 'to be friends'. At the moment I'm not sure how to be that. I'm not sure that we ever *were* friends really. Lovers, yes, partners, yes, but friends? I don't know."

"Well, that's better than Simon being so cold and dismissive."

"He's still a mixed-up kid."

"Yes, but a mixed-up kid with a long marriage behind him, an ex-wife who thought she *was* a friend, a best friend, not just someone to be used, and, most importantly, two children."

Matt slipped his arm round Jess and hugged her sympathetically for a moment. "We'll get through it." Then he dropped his arm and scanned the park ahead. "And where have those kids got to?"

"Over there just on the edge of that copse," pointed Jess. "I was keeping my eye on them!"

"And they think they're free of parental restraint!" laughed Matt. Jess giggled. He was such a nice, perceptive man, easy to talk to. How come Polly had left him for the likes of Simon, knowing what he was like beneath the confident, attractive exterior? Even at university so many years ago, Matt had always been WYSIWYG – what you see is what you get; not that there weren't depths to him, but they were clear and apparent, there was nothing secretive, no hidden personality issues – as far as she knew.

She watched the five children playing and shrieking together up ahead. All the same dark hair and clear eyes, similar build, talking the same language. They could be mistaken for brothers and sisters. And in that thought swirled all the disappointments of her marriage to Simon.

"I don't think that I ever want to marry again," said Jess so suddenly that Matt did a double-take as he glanced sideways at her. "I mean, I couldn't trust that a man wasn't hiding some mental disturbance, or difficult insecurity, or personality problem, that would one day rise to the surface again. I used to think I was quite perceptive about people, but how wrong I was!"

"No, you weren't wrong, you knew he was difficult, or needy or whatever, you just thought that the Dr Jekyll side would supercede the Mr Hyde." Matt smiled at her. "And you wanted to look after him, to care for him enough to make that happen. But love just doesn't conquer all in the end."

"No. I didn't see it coming. And yet now, in retrospect, I can see that the signs were there all along. It's true – love *is* blind. And I'm simply not risking it again!"

Matt stopped on the path and turned to look at her. Jess couldn't read his eyes, partly because it was a momentary pause and then he turned away. "OK, enough serious talk. We need to run until the jolly pheromones kick in and the serotonin boosts. I'm going to race you to that oak tree by the bridge. Last one buys lunch!"

"Right!" shrieked Jess as she took off, thankful she was wearing her jeans and trainers and not her boots with heels, however low and chunky they were.

"Hey! Not fair! I didn't get to say 'ready, steady, go!' laughed Matt, following on her heels. "I'm not letting you win, you know, Jess!"

With all the running up and down stairs at school all day, Jess was quite fit, despite her weight loss which she was only recently starting to regain. Matt gained on her and flew past, but Jess was nothing if not competitive and pushed herself forwards, breath beginning to rasp. In front of her, Matt started to fool around, pretending to run in slow motion, humming Vangelis's Chariots of Fire theme. Jess laughed, bringing tears to her eyes.

She didn't see the tree root until it was too late. She tripped and fell helter skelter, the ground rising to meet her with a confused momentary force that winded her. She heard shouts of "Jess!" "mum!" flashing through her consciousness. The earth beneath her was damp and cold, her heart racing instead of her feet. Unfocused dark people were gathering around her, hands on her head, her arm. She blinked rapidly and felt the hard ground. Her vision cleared to identify Matt and all the children bending over her. Katy was stroking her hair.

"Oh god, I'm so sorry," said Matt. "What *was* I thinking?"

"No, just one of those things," gasped Jess. "I just tripped. Chance in a million. Could've been you."

"Phew!" she exhaled as she struggled to sit up. How ungainly, she thought, how clumsy and foolish. "Ouch." She twisted and felt down her leg to her foot. It was the left foot that she had injured in Ghana, damn it. Always the weak part, the vulnerable old injury.

"Jess, let me just examine your foot," said Matt calmly. He untied and carefully wriggled off her trainer and felt around her foot, her ankle. "It's not broken. Just bruised. But I bet it'll be painful."

She allowed him to help her up but it felt very sore to put any weight on the foot. She leaned against Matt and he supported her weight, arm round her back.

"Mum, are you OK?" Katy anxiously peered into her face. Abi was crying. Tom and Zak were picking up the contents of Jess's bag that had burst open and disgorged make-up and pens and keys over the grass. Jake was hopping from one foot to the other in his anxiety.

"Boys, see you get everything," directed Matt. "Tom, there's a notebook ... and a packet of ... er ... lady things just there."

"Got them, dad!"

"Put them all safely back in Jess's bag ... and tidily, please!"

"Mummy, do you want a stick to walk with?" asked Abi through gulping tears, proffering a thin bent branch she had spotted on the ground.

Jess couldn't help giggling. "Oh thank you, sweetheart – all of you sweethearts!" She caught the boys' blush. She took the stick from Abi and pretended to lean on it, although Matt was actually taking her weight.

He shuffled to take more weight to compensate for the wobbly stick. "Just the job, Abi. Thanks."

"Are you going to be alright, mum?" asked Katy, a worried frown on her pretty face.

"I'm OK, darling, just a little sore in the old foot. No bones broken!"

"Do you think you could hobble to the tea rooms if I hold you up?" asked Matt. "I think a cup of good hot sweet tea is required."

"Of course. Honestly I'm fine. I don't want to spoil our day. I can prop my foot up and ask for some ice cubes and I'm sure it'll be good soon." Jess smiled. She hated fussing and she really felt fine now. Her foot was still tender but not as bad as in the first shock.

"I could always carry you, if you like?" Matt grinned. Jess smiled and shook her head, but she was touched at his – and the boys' – solicitousness. It had been a long time since anyone had looked after *her* so automatically and generously.

Matt kept glancing sideways at her as they made their way across to the tea rooms, checking she was alright. "It's your injured foot, isn't it?" he whispered, "From the shooting in Ghana?"

Jess looked up at him quizzically. "Yes, but how did you know?"

He squeezed her arm. "I know it all and I've remembered it all."

She felt the warmth of his arm around her as they walked, the children slightly ahead. This was someone she didn't need to explain things to, someone who was a comfort, someone who knew her history. It was a good feeling. To have a good friend, even though it wasn't Polly, was somehow a wonderful relief, and she felt an ease flow through her body.

At the tea rooms, the waitresses, dressed in their black dresses and white Victorianesque pinafores and caps, ran to help as soon as they entered, with kindly murmurings and orders softly called to minions for cushions and an extra chair for Jess to prop up her foot. Tom helped with her jacket, and the girls took her bag and slid it carefully under the table.

"Really, I'm fine," objected Jess, but the staff fussed around them and ensured that they were all comfortable. Matt gently raised Jess's foot onto the chair, flashing an amused conspiratorial grin at her as he did so.

The children were quickly preoccupied with the menus, and, for the girls, the excitement of ordering baked beans and chips, which they rarely had at home, or anywhere near Jess for that matter. She hated the smell of baked beans.

"The joy of forbidden fruits," murmured Jess, and Matt laughed.

"The boys will order some ghastly muck like burgers and gherkins," added Matt.

"Yet suddenly I feel hungry!" Jess said. "I think it must be the aftermath of shock."

"Anything you like. I'm paying." Matt raised his hand to fend off Jess's objection.

"And I didn't even beat you in the race!" smiled Jess.

"No. True." Matt pretended to ponder. "But I was always going to treat you."

"Oh, so that race was on false pretences?"

"Hmm, guess so."

"Well, in that case I think I'll have the eggs benedict and side salad," said Jess to the waitress as she hovered with her order book. She scribbled it down and scanned the table, smiling.

"Madam, you have a lovely caring family," she said, shaking her head. "Quite rare these days. All the arguments and sniping we see."

Jess spluttered, "Thank you." Matt's head was buried in his menu all of a sudden. There were five red faces round the table, the same expression on them all. When the waitress moved away, they all giggled awkwardly. Matt lowered the menu and smiled at Jess.

"Jess. It's your birthday tomorrow."

"Yes. I know that, Matt." Jess smiled down the telephone receiver. But she was not looking forward to it one bit. A dreadful big zero birthday. Her mother had phoned her a few days ago and asked her if she wanted them to come up for the weekend and go out for dinner. But she'd made her excuses, remembering the last time, when her mother had spent her birthday meal quizzing her coyly, but loudly, on very private matters, in front of waiters and other customers. It had been a horribly embarrassing occasion. So although Jess appreciated her mother trying to help and not wanting her to be alone on her birthday, she had invented another engagement. Birthdays had ceased to be joyous now, her own at any rate. A signpost of getting older without a partner was not something she wished to dwell upon, and it was not an occasion for great merriment any more. And anyway, she was some-what restricted about going out, with her baby-sitting problem.

"Well …" Matt began, and Jess could hear his grin down the phoneline. "I've also got a reason to celebrate. I've been offered a full partnership in the firm. And nobody else handy to celebrate with …"

"Oh, right! So I'm the most handy person available?" she smiled in mock offence.

Matt laughed. "You know that's not the case. But I thought that we're both on our own, so why not get together and have a jolly dinner somewhere smart."

"I'd love to, Matt, and, seriously, many congratulations on the partnership, but I don't have a babysitter and I won't leave the girls alone yet."

"No, of course not. But my boys are away at their grandparents for the weekend." He paused. "Polly's parents. Polly may be there for some of the time. But not Simon, so don't worry about that."

"Okaaay …"

"So the girl who does my babysitting, for a ridiculously huge fee, is therefore available and happy to sit with your two."

"Wow, you've got it all sorted!"

"Yeah, and she's fine, before you ask – trustworthy and capable. Actually it's my secretary."

Jess had visions of a capable middle aged lady, plump and motherly.

"So, how about it? I was thinking of Carlo's? Everything on me, of course, including babysitter. What do you think?"

Jess had never been to Carlo's; it was much too expensive and Simon had always scorned it. But she knew that it had a wonderful reputation for excellent Italian food, which she loved, and attentive personal service. It would be so lovely to be spoiled for once. "Well, I think it's an offer I can't refuse! Thank you so much, Matt."

"Great. Andrea will be with you about seven so that you can all get to know her a little before she sits, and I'll pick you up just before eight. Is that OK with you?"

"That's more than OK with me, Matt. That's wonderful."

"Good."

"But, Matt, will you be able to book a table at Carlo's now? I hear they get booked up very quickly and you normally have to book weeks in advance."

"That's OK, Jess, all done already. I take clients there sometimes. They know me."

Jess was pretty much ready by the time the doorbell rang to signal Andrea's arrival. She had decided, after much consideration, to wear her simple knee length black lace dress. It fitted well over her figure which was filling out in the right places again now. Her hair was scooped into a thick messy up-do. She popped in her simple tiny Venetian glass earrings that trembled just below her lobes.

"You look beautiful, mum," whispered Katy from the doorway.

"Let me look! Let me look!" shouted Abi, pushing he sister out of the way. "Yes, you do, mummy. Like a beautiful film star."

"Thank you, my two gorgeous girls!" laughed Jess, hugging them. They were already in their night clothes and dressing gowns, having promised to be in bed by eight thirty.

She slipped on her black heels and went downstairs to the front door, smile ready to welcome Matt's homely babysitting secretary.

"Hi, I'm Andrea," said the vision of glamour on the doorstep. She was tall, slim, with long thick blonde hair draping over her shoulders. She was wearing well-fitting jeans and a figure-hugging baby-pink top – and that figure was to die for. Her beautifully manicured finger nails were a gorgeous burgundy red to match her lipstick. Jess thought she must be gawping.

"Hi, I'm Jess … well, obviously," she stuttered, standing aside to usher this apparition of sophistication into the hall. "D – do come in."

For all her nice dress and hair, Jess felt uninspiring and not a little daunted beside Matt's secretary. But she smiled and led her into the kitchen. Why did Matt want to take her to dinner and not this gorgeous creature? She looked to be in her early twenties. Men of Matt's age liked younger women, didn't they? And she was around him all the time, every day. Then she shook her head and her thoughts away: *Wait, Jess, why are you thinking this way? Matt's just a good friend.*

She showed Andrea where the coffee and such like were, and pointed out the canapé nibbles she had baked earlier. "So do help yourself while I'm out."

"Wow, they look delicious! I wish I could bake. I'm hopeless in the kitchen. Too busy to learn, really. And I must say, Jess, your kitchen is lovely. Pretty and compact. I'm looking out for these things at the moment."

"Thanks. Well, come in to the sitting room."

The girls jostled in and Jess made the introductions.

"What gorgeous daughters you have, Jess! They're delightful!" said Andrea. "We're going to have a great time! Well," she peered at her watch, "for an hour or so, I think, while we get to know each other. Then I guess it'll be your bedtime, at – what – about eight?"

"Eight thirty!" chorused Katy and Abi indignantly. Andrea glanced at Jess who nodded.

"They're allowed to read in bed after that, though," added Jess.

"Oh good. And what are you reading, Katy?"

"*Adrian Mole* ..."

"… *aged thirteen and three quarters*!" finished Andrea. "Love him! And you, Abi?"

"*The Big Friendly Giant*," said Abi, hopping from foot to foot. "I like Roald Dahl. He's my favourite."

"You said that LM Montgomery was your favourite yesterday!" Katy scowled.

"Yes, but that was because mummy was reading it to me. And also I was in my *Anne of Green Gables* orphan phase. But today I'm in my fantasy giant phase!"

Jess couldn't help laughing. Andrea did too. "Well, I think that's wonderful. I wish I had two daughters who loved reading."

"Don't you have any daughters?" asked Abi sympathetically.

Jess began to object to her daughter's personal questions but Andrea said matter-of-factly, "No, Abi, I'm afraid I don't. I have three lovely nieces, who I love to look after. But I suppose I'm more of a career girl. And I'm saving up like mad to buy my own house."

"My mummy has two daughters *and* she's a career girl as well …" started Abi.

Jess was about to divert the conversation, when the doorbell rang again. She opened the door to Matt.

And held on to the door edge.

He was dressed in an expensive-looking dark grey suit, which fitted well over his strong chest and emphasised his broad shoulders, and a crisp white shirt and russet tie. One hand was resting in his trouser pocket, jacket hem hooked up over his wrist. She seemed to see him for the first time. Tall dark and handsome just didn't adequately describe him. He had a neatly designed unshaven shadow across his jaw and upper lip, just enough to look attractively masculine and strong.

Jess realised that he was really gorgeous. He smiled ruefully at her. "Um … may I come inside?"

Jess realised that she was gawping again. She moved her hand away from the door and gestured him inside. "Gosh, sorry!" *Gosh?* She had come over all school-girl-ish and unnecessary. "Sorry."

Matt smiled and lightly kissed her cheek. "Glad I have that effect on you. And I'm sorry too – for arriving so early. But I wanted to be sure that Andrea was OK with the girls. Or rather that the girls were OK with Andrea." He touched her cheek where he had planted his kiss. "And that you are happy to leave her in charge of them."

Jess felt flustered. "Oh, yes, she seems fine. They're talking about books."

"Ah, that's my Andrea," he grinned and moved into the sitting room. "Hello, Andy."

Andrea looked up at Matt from the sofa where she was ensconced with Katy and Abi and a pile of books on her knee. Jess caught the look in her eye as she nodded to Matt then lowered her eyes beneath long dark eyelashes. She really fancies him, realised Jess. Matt raked his fingers through his hair. She noticed where it curled at the nape of his neck and at his ears. She noticed his wide strong mouth. She felt herself flush. He turned to her and smiled, amused as though he could sense her heat. She noticed that his teeth were even and shiny white.

"Well, I'd better … er ….finish getting ready," she stammered.

Matt sat and talked to Andrea while Jess ran upstairs again to powder her nose and check her hair again.

When she returned downstairs she found Matt in the kitchen. He was leaning against the counter, long legs apart, both hands in his pockets. She looked enquiringly at him.

"Fine," he answered, although she hadn't asked him anything. "She's getting on fine with them. I've checked she knows the rules for bedtime and she's got the phone number of the restaurant and I've told her we'll be back about 11.30 ish. OK?"

"Yes, absolutely. Thank you." Jess reached up on tiptoe and kissed him on his cheek. How sweet he was. Then she realised that she had left a lipstick mark on his face and started to rub it out, but he caught her hand and gently kissed her palm.

"Better be going," he whispered.

Carlo's was busy and Jess's eyes swept the restaurant. It seemed that every table was occupied. The walls were decorated with huge paintings of Italian masters and alcoves framed alabaster statues of Venus, Apollo, and even a small scale replica of the great Michelangelo's David. Puccini was playing softly in the background and Jess recognised an aria from *La Boheme*. From the lavish chandeliers to the off-white columns and the soothing terracotta colours of the walls, the room was just beautiful. Florentine. There were even ivy-clad balustrades and tubs of deep red geraniums.

"Sir! Good to see you again!" a heavily Italian-accented voice jolted Jess from her reverie.

"Carlo!" said Matt, holding out his hand. Carlo shook Matt's hand, placed his left on top of both, shook again enthusiastically and beamed.

"I have your table ready for you as requested, in the nook under the David." Carlo ushered them forward and Jess felt Matt's hand on the small of her back, guiding her through the room. It felt attentive and solicitous. "Not your usual table, of course, Mr Havers. But most appropriate for your beautiful companion tonight." Carlo turned to Jess and beamed again. "Bella, molte bella, signora." Then he spoke in fast Italian to Matt.

Matt smiled, and glanced at Jess. "Si, si. Grazie mille."

"Per favore, signora." Carlo pulled out the chair for Jess. Then he settled Matt and shook out their napkins with a flourish and laid them expertly onto their laps, at the same time gesturing authoritatively to a waiter to bring the menus. Another waiter appeared with the wine list for Matt.

"An aperitif for madam?" Jess looked enquiringly at Matt who said "I think madam might enjoy a glass of champagne?" He raised his eyebrows to Jess.

"Ooh, yes. I love champagne."

"I know you do … I remember." He looked up at the wine waiter. "We'll order the other wines when we've decided on our courses. Thank you."

The menu was delightful. After much indecision, Jess chose tomatoes, mozzarella and basil to start and then fettuccine with a seafood sauce of lobster, prawn and langoustine. Matt ordered antipasti, then bistecca fiorentina with insalata mista and a bottle of Brunello di Montalcino.

Champagne poured and waiters discretely out of sight, Matt raised his glass to Jess. "Happy birthday, Jess."

"And happy new partnership to you, Matt." Jess clinked the rim of her glass against Matt's. "This place is magnificent."

"Glad you like it." He smiled. "You'll have guessed, I'm obviously trying to impress you. Positioned under the David …"

Jess frowned. "Hmm, quite well endowed. But do you feel daunted?"

"God, no." Matt grinned at her mischievously. "But then that's for you to find out …!" He paused as Jess gasped, and gazed up to the David in contemplation. "Actually, that's not awfully impressive. I think you'll find …"

"Hey, hang on!"

"No, no, just kidding! Let's relax and I'll try not to tease you. We deserve a lovely evening, wining and dining, don't you think?"

"Yes, indeed we do. So … do you ever have time for drama any more?"

"Ah, yes, the drama group at university! I don't know. Maybe I grew out of it. But I do still like to go to the theatre when I can. Or, at least I did. Not so easy now, of course."

The evening passed by far too quickly. The food was wonderful; Jess's pudding of amaretto semifreddo was to die for. Matt absorbed her enthusiasm with amused delight. Far too soon it was time for espresso and a small liqueur.

"I feel quite light-headed," laughed Jess. "And relaxed. I'd forgotten what relaxed felt like!"

"Good," Matt grinned. "Me too. And we've put the world to rights over dinner, like we used to do at uni." He gazed at her face. "I'm glad you've been able to relax and do something maybe a bit different." The way he looked at her reminded Jess of a time so very many years ago, in Ghana, in Accra, with Jim … when they had dinner at the Ambassador. Matt reminded her of Jim, strong, dark, and very attractive. She was very aware of his masculinity and how it melted her. And then she remembered what happened after dinner that time. She felt hot and wondered if Matt could sense her feelings.

He reached across the table and touched her hand gently. There was such tenderness in that gesture that Jess shivered. It had been so long since a man had touched her like that.

Matt raised his hand to the waiter for the bill, deftly signed the paper that nestled in a leather gold embossed folder, and passed his card over.

As they approached the gilt rimmed revolving door where a uniformed concierge waited, Carlo appeared from nowhere and bowed. "Grazie, sir, madam. And madam, we hope you will accompany Mr Havers again. We look forward to seeing you both again soon."

"Grazie mille," nodded Jess. Matt shook Carlo's hand, and then they were out in the cool wet darkness of night. It had started raining while they were in the restaurant and the pavements were mirrored black and shiny, lights above the shop windows reflecting gold and red. Jess shivered and Matt put his arm around her and opened his large umbrella to cover them both as they hurried to the car. Walking in the rain. Jess felt the warmth from Matt's arm around her shoulders, and glanced up at him. He smiled down at her and she felt protected, safe. "Your Italian is good, Matt."

"I had to go to Italy, to Rome, rather a lot for business at one time. We had a major client over there. It was supposed to be corporate law, but between you and me, it may have been a mafia cover-up." He laughed and shrugged. "I picked the language up – the polite and maybe a bit of swearing too. The Italians are very broad in their use of language."

"I'm impressed!"

Matt squeezed her shoulder.

Andrea was dozing in front of the television when they arrived back at Jess's house.

"All's quiet," she said. Jess went upstairs to check on the girls. They were snuggled up in their beds, sleeping peacefully. She closed their doors carefully so as not to disturb them and returned downstairs where Matt was helping Andrea on with her jacket and handing her a cheque.

"Great," said Andrea, stuffing the cheque in her bag and looking adoringly up at him. "Another step towards the house!"

"Many thanks, Andrea," said Jess and as Matt closed the door behind her she added, "And thanks, Matt, for a lovely evening … and for everything. It was just wonderful …"

He turned to her, loosened his tie and raked his hand through his dark curly hair, and smiled that fantastic intimate smile. "Well … ?"

Then suddenly she was in his arms, and he was kissing her gently, hesitantly, questioningly. The touch of his lips on hers for the first time filled her body with a breathless mist. He slowly brushed strands of her hair back from her cheeks, her forehead, and kept his hands cupping her face as he leaned slightly back from her.

"It's your call," he whispered.

In answer she lifted her face to his and her arms around his shoulders, the back of his neck, her fingers stroking the nape of his neck and up through his thick hair. He groaned in pleasure. It had been such a long time. She pressed herself against him, feeling his hard body and his need for her. His hands gently pressed her back to lock into him, and travelled up to her neck, the back of her head. His kisses moved from gentleness to a deeper desire. Jess reached up and loosened his tie properly, her hands travelling inside his jacket, over his broad muscular chest.

In her bedroom moments later, she quietly closed the door behind them as he tugged off his tie and shrugged his jacket to the floor. She began to undo the buttons on his shirt then pulled it off his torso. "Mmmm," she murmured, and he smiled and kissed her again deeply before he unzipped her dress and she wriggled it to the carpet.

"Mmmm, yourself," he said, eyes sweeping her body, taking it all in. "You're beautiful, Jess. Even more gorgeous without your dress."

Matt guided her to the bed as he kissed her and when she felt the edge of the mattress behind her knees, he lowered her onto the bed and manoeuvred himself above her. "I've waited for this so long," he murmured low and his eyes never left hers.

"Matt … when I saw Andrea … I thought … well, working with a gorgeous creature like that … why does he want me?"

He lowered himself upon her and nuzzled her neck, then he kissed her forehead and raised himself up slightly from her. "Oh, Jess. Why on earth did you imagine I would want Andrea? She's my secretary. And she's a kid!"

"Not so much a kid, I think!"

"To me. What's the matter, Jess?"

"Oh, you know … stretch marks, birth tummy … and all the rest …"

Matt gently moved from her to the side and stared at her for a moment, then he began to kiss her throat, her breasts, her stomach, her thighs … especially her stomach and thighs. He looked up at her. "You are wonderful. This line," his fingers traced her skin, "is a scar from an appendix operation, and these are the marks of giving birth to two lovely daughters … Why would I not want all those? I may have a vested interest in those marks, after all." He smiled up at her, sharing a secret between them, "I want them to be mine too. They're *you*, Jess, they're your life, your vitality, your strength. I love you, Jess, I have done for years, and that means I love everything and everywhere that's *you*." He shifted his position and stroked her face, then lowered himself upon her again and this time his kiss was so deep it reached her soul. She enfolded him in her arms, pressing him down onto her and into her.

The shrill sound of the phone startled her and she opened her eyes, confused. Matt was holding her close to his warm body and her head was snuggled on his wide muscular chest. For a moment she couldn't think where she was, then her mind cleared and she pushed herself up, reaching out for the phone on the bedside table, glancing at the clock and registering that it was still only seven thirty on a Sunday morning.

"Hello?" she frowned.

"What the hell are you doing?" came Simon's irate voice. She held the receiver slightly away from her ear and turned to Matt who had propped himself up on his elbow beside her. "I know you've got a man in there! There's a fucking great Mercedes in your drive."

"*What*?"

"How can you do that to me? With someone else? How can you? And I know the girls are there. My daughters! How dare you have some man there in front of *my* daughters!"

"*Simon*!" She looked baffled at Matt. He held out his hand for the receiver; she knew that he wanted to protect and defend her, and for that she felt a comforting warmth, but she also knew that it would be red rag to a bull if she let him speak to Simon. "Listen!" she said firmly with more confidence than she felt, as he yelled his diatribe down the phone. "Listen, Simon. We are divorced. That means you have no right to do this. I don't want to slam the phone down on you, but I'm going to put it down now and I don't want you to do this again. If you do, I'll ring the police." With a shaking hand, still hearing the angry yells, she replaced the receiver on the hook, then she thought again and replaced it beside the phone. She couldn't believe the hypocrisy. How on earth could she ever have contemplated having him back in her life again, at any point?

Matt stroked her back. "I'm sorry about that. But you're right. He doesn't have any hold over you any more."

"No," whispered Jess, snuggling up to Matt again, and brushing her fingers through the dark hair on his chest. "He doesn't."

A little later, Matt drew away from her and said, "Jess, I think I should get showered, dressed and respectable again downstairs before the girls see me here." He smiled and kissed the end of her nose. "I think we both should. Come on, woman! Get moving."

Matt was sitting in the kitchen at the breakfast bar, demonstrating to Katy and Abi how his new laptop worked, which he had brought in from the car.

"Hey, look at this, mum. You can play games on it and … and everything!"

"Games? I think you play games on your old computer?"

Katy looked up at Jess with a scornful expression. "Oh, mu-um! This is not like our Sinclair Spectrum that dad pinched and mucked up and stuck together with sellotape! This is The Works!"

"Oh, right," nodded Jess, smiling across at Matt. "Sure thing."

"Oh, mu-um! Don't say that. It's so old hat."

Jess signed zipping her mouth and Matt reached out his hand to her and wound his arm around her lower back, squeezing her hip gently. "Well, look," he said thoughtfully. "The boys won't be back from their grandparents until teatime, so what about if I teach you how it all works?" He grinned at Jess questioningly. "Actually, when I've got it all set up for you, it's really my birthday present to your mum, so maybe she'll let you use it from time to time."

"Oh, goodness, no, Matt," Jess protested. "That's far too generous. You took me for a posh dinner for my birthday!"

Matt gently patted her bottom. "This is the real present, Jess. For your writing."

"My writing? But I haven't written anything much for years."

"No. But you used to write. Poems. Short stories. You did at university. Certainly in the first couple of years. And you were good, so I think you should write again. Maybe a novel?"

"Goodness. Well … yes, maybe you're right. I used to love losing myself in my writing. In fact when I was a little girl I used to tell people I wanted to be a writer when I grew up. It didn't quite work out, but … yes, I'd like to try again."

"You could be a famous author, mummy," shrieked Abi, clapping. "We could be rich!"

"Well, I don't think that happens, poppet, but … hmmm …yes, I'd like to give it a go. If I've got time. And if I've got enough material."

"You've got enough material," smiled Matt, his hand stroking up her spine.

And so, it was a week later, when the girls were in bed, that she sat at her desk, stared at the laptop for a few moments, took a deep breath and started to type …

July 20ᵗʰ 1986

That was the date Jess would remember for ever more. It would be embedded in her brain and her soul.

She stood in the newly refurbished kitchen of their large house, leaning on the counter and staring blindly out of the window. Her knuckles white as she gripped the edges of the stylish circular twin stainless steel sinks she had chosen so happily just a few months before, not knowing what was to come.

How odd it was that dates had such resonances across the years: she had told her students that Shakespeare had entered the world and left it on 23rd April, St George's Day, only 52 years apart. That George Orwell had mulled over what to call his futuristic novel and ended up reversing the last two digits of the year he wrote it: 1948 became the famous novel title 1984.

And now, with Jess, 20ᵗʰ July was the date she refound the love of her life, 20ᵗʰ July 1968 was the day she married him, 20th July 1986 the day she lost him. Reflections and reversals.

The gentle resonances of 10cc's 'The Things we do for Love' echoed in her ears and she recalled the way the builders had played it over and over as they refitted the kitchen, only a few weeks ago, and how she had sung along with them as she brought in countless mugs of tea. By the time she heard the refrain "like walking in the rain …" she knew that her tears were coursing silently down her cheeks and soaking her hands like raindrops in a storm.

Her mind travelled back to twenty years before …

If you enjoyed *Drumbeats* and this book, *Walking in the Rain*, and want to know what happens in the end to Jess, why not try the forthcoming third and final novel in the trilogy, *Before I Die*, to be published Spring 2016?

REVIEWS on any of Julia's books are very welcome on Amazon at http://www.amazon.co.uk/Julia-Ibbotson/e/B0095XG11U/ref=ntt_athr_dp_pel_1

and Goodreads at https://www.goodreads.com/author/show/6017965.Julia_Ibbotson

To find out more about Julia, go to her WEBSITE, and you are welcome to leave a comment, at www.juliaibbotsonauthor.com

ABOUT THE AUTHOR

 **Julia Ibbotson** is an author and academic, and lives in the middle of the English countryside in a renovated Victorian rectory with her husband, an orchard, a kitchen garden and far too many moles. Her four children are now grown up and she has four grandchildren. She was a school teacher for many years before becoming a senior university lecturer, researcher and writer. She loves travelling, choral singing, walking, sailing and swimming, as well as, of course, gardening and cooking for family and friends.

Her books include the Drumbeats trilogy:
Drumbeats,
Walking in the Rain, and the forthcoming
Before I Die

Memoir/recipe book:
The Old Rectory: Escape to a Country Kitchen

For children:
S.C.A.R.S, the children's fantasy story of dragons, knights and a boy who slips through the fabric of the universe into a parallel medieval world threatened by the evil Myrthor, the heart of darkness.

Academic books include (among many academic papers):
Talking the Walk
International Research in Teacher Education: current perspectives

40063068R00205

Made in the USA
Charleston, SC
24 March 2015